HE WILL BE MINE

KIRSTY GREENWOOD

For Lynette. My hugely intelligent, cool, witty and kind-hearted big sister who I look up to so much.

CHAPTER ONE

Nora

There comes a point in the day of every freelancer when they have to consider a single very important question.

Should I bother getting dressed today?

A conclusion can usually be established by considering a small number of follow-up enquiries, i.e.:

1. Do I need to leave the house at all?
2. Am I expecting a delivery person to show up at the door?
3. Are my pyjamas as soft as clouds?
4. Do said pyjamas have a bunch of extra room in the waistband to accommodate that massive cheese toastie I plan on having for lunch?
5. Am I at ease with eschewing typical conventions of how a twenty-seven-year-old adult should behave and willing to just sometimes be a lazy-ass bitch without shame or guilt?

I find myself asking these questions a lot lately and my answers usually lead me to the sofa in a drawstring waist. Being a virtual admin assistant might be one of the dullest jobs known to humankind, but it's super laid-back, and working flexible hours from home means that some days (or lots of days lately) I get to have a long bubbly bath mid-morning, or a 2 p.m. mega-nap, or read delicious romance novels in between emails, or re-watch one of my favourite movies, *Sleepless in Seattle*, starring my favourite actress Meg Ryan, whenever I damn well please. It's a pretty peachy life for your common or garden variety introvert.

I plonk myself onto the living room sofa, peer at the old, slightly tatty *Sleepless in Seattle* DVD case and I sigh.

'Not today, Meg Ryan,' I say to her perfectly adorable face.

Unfortunately I *do* have to get dressed this morning. I have to leave my cosy little flat and go outdoors and I have to do it for the most terrible of reasons: my adored mum and dad died two years ago today and my sister Imogene insists we meet for a walk around their beloved local park to visit the memorial bench we got in their honour. There, we will most likely sit and cry for a while and then Imogene will proceed to nag me about my "worrying lack of a life" or maybe try to set me up with some basic bro she knows because I am in my "prime fertile years and not exactly in a position to be fussy over guys".

Yikes.

I head into the bedroom, gaze at my pale blue soft-as-clouds pyjamas folded on the bed and tenderly pat them. Then I peer over to the stack of romantic comedy films and the *Harcourt Royals* novels I'd much rather be burying myself into today and tomorrow and the rest of the fore-seeable, frankly.

I pull my thick waves of dark hair back into my favourite purple velvet scrunchy, put on a big T-shirt and some jeans and try not to worry about the fact that the shadowy bags under my eyes could carry a week's worth of groceries.

'I already miss you, indoors,' I whisper theatrically, before reluctantly pulling on my raggedy but super comfy trainers and leaving my beloved cocoon.

* * *

'You look really pale, Nora. Are you eating?' is the first thing Imogene says when we meet by the river in Brigglesford Village park. She's dressed in a perfectly clean, dazzlingly white sleeveless blouse and stylish tight black jeans. My one-year-old niece Ariana is in the pram beside her, dressed in an equally clean and dazzling white sundress. I lean into the pram and smother her in kisses.

'Hello, my juicy pudding,' I say, laughing as she blows me a giggly, spit-filled raspberry. I take off my sunglasses and smile at Imogene. 'Hello to you too, dear sister.'

We give each other a brief, slightly awkward arm pat before setting off down the river path side by side.

As we stroll, Imogene looks me up and down, her eyes lingering a little at my belly and thighs, currently a comfortable size 16. 'Well, obviously you're eating,' she says. 'But are you eating *properly*? Not just cheese toasties all the time? Are you getting any sun? You do look pallid. It's July! It's a heatwave. You should be tanned. Look at my tan!' She indicates her gym-honed golden arms proudly. They look suspiciously patchy at the elbow.

'That's fake tan, Imogene,' I point out.

She shakes her head firmly. 'Not all of it. Some of it is natural tan. From actual vitamin D. Most people in this country are deficient in vitamin D, you know? It can cause mood changes if you don't get enough...'

'I can take a supplement.'

'And what's up with your voice? You sound all croaky and raspy. Like Michael Bolton, but not sexy.'

I clear my throat. She's right. I do sound croaky. But then it occurs to me that I haven't actually spoken to another human in four days. My voice box is a little out of practice, that's all. 'Just a, uh, dry throat,' I lie with a shrug. I don't know why I lie. Being holed up in the house on my own a lot isn't something I should feel embarrassed about. If I don't mind, then no one else should, right? I like it there and I'm not doing anyone any harm.

'You look like you haven't slept, either.'

Imogene's right about that one. I haven't been sleeping properly for, ooh, around two years now. Hence those lovely 2 p.m. mega-naps I've grown so fond of.

'A little bit of make-up might make you feel better. A bit more put together, you know?'

I touch my face self-consciously. I actually can't remember the last time I wore make-up. I used to wear it all the time – being on the plainer side of pretty meant I was well versed in the art of a bold lip and a couple of lashings of mascara, but I've definitely gotten out of the habit recently. It doesn't matter though. It's not like I'm seeing anyone or going out much these days.

'I'm fine,' I tell Imogene firmly. 'Stop fretting, you turd. I love you and I know you're trying to look out for me, but I'm all good, honest!'

'Hmmm.' She examines me, her eyes flickering with pity, which I've got to say makes me bristle a bit. Just because I might not have my shit all together and wrapped in a millennial pink satin bow like her doesn't mean I'm someone to feel sorry for.

Rounding the corner, we step into a clearing and approach the black cast-iron bench we had put up after Mum and Dad died. It's clean and shiny from yesterday's summer showers. The flower garden surrounding it is in full, colourful bloom: pinks, yellows and oranges scattered here and there like thick oil-paint splotches. It's a beautiful spot.

My stomach folds as we approach the bench. Hearing Imogene start sniffling beside me, I reach out and grab her hand, giving it a gentle squeeze. Together we look at the golden plaque's engraving.

Emily and Daniel Tucker. True soulmates to each other, beloved parents to Imogene and Nora.

We park our bottoms, Imogene rolling the pram back and forth in front of her, and for a few moments there's nothing but the sound of the occasional passer-by, the chirrupy birds overhead and the crunch of the gravel beneath the wheels of Ariana's pram.

I think about Mum and Dad. At the funeral service, everyone kept saying how they were the perfect couple. They *were* the perfect couple. Theirs was a true love story. The night they met, back in the late 80s, they saw each other across a crowded garden at a New Year's Eve party. As the clock struck midnight, and the fireworks sparkled and fizzed above them, they laid eyes on one another and knew instantly that they were meant to be. *A big thunderbolt*, was how Mum described it: *right through the belly.* Dad told me that when he saw her smiling, mischievous face, he felt giddy, like he'd been missing her his entire life and now here she finally was. He said he knew that everything from there on out was going to be great, even the bad parts because he and Mum would be together for them and that was all that mattered. The whole thing sounded so magical to me. Like something out of one of the *Harcourt Royals* romance novels I'm addicted to. They were so genuinely happy together, right until the very end.

I glimpse sideways at Imogene, who is still crying gently, trying to keep it subtle for the sake of Ariana and, I suppose, me. She only allows herself to get sad on this one day each year. The rest of the time she is all go, never stopping, organising everyone around her, making sure that everything is perfect.

On the surface, it would be so easy to think that Mum and Dad dying didn't affect her as much as it affected me. But I can see that right now her heart is quietly breaking all over again, just like mine is.

'I'm so sorry,' I say in a small voice.

Imogene looks up at me, her eyes red, her mascara slightly smudged at the inner corners. She reaches a hand out and rubs my arm. 'For God's sake, Nora. It wasn't your bloody fault.'

She's lying to make me feel better. Because, the truth is, it was absolutely my fault.

I'm the reason my parents are gone.

CHAPTER TWO

Nora

I was a precocious eleven-year-old when I decided I was going to sing and write songs when I grew up. I'd seen Joni Mitchell performing on the telly and was immediately obsessed. For Christmas that year I was given a little red guitar and started writing songs every chance I got. For a good while, the songs were mostly shit; ditties about the next-door neighbour's aloof cat, or sickly ballads about Jamie Braithwaite at school and how he was totally the best at drawing in the whole year and maybe also would marry me one day. I thankfully improved with time and writing songs became my very favourite thing to do in the world – that magic feeling of pairing words and phrases together with the exact right melody to create something that didn't exist before.

The night of my parent's accident, I was in a showcase gig at a cabaret club in London. I'd been invited there by an indie label A&R rep who'd seen me play at a dive bar in Sheffield city centre. There would be a bunch of record label people in the club and I'd get to show them what I could do, maybe even get signed! After years of trying so hard, of borrowing money from my parents just to survive, working odd jobs and hustling my way through the pub and club scene, I finally had a real shot.

Mum and Dad were encouraging of singing as a hobby, of me doing something that I loved, but as a career option? The lack of security that came with it worried them. When I got the showcase, I insisted they come to watch. Why? Because I wanted to show off. To prove to them that I was going to make a career out of this, show them that people were actually willing to pay money for my skills. Important people who knew what they were talking about.

My parents were the best, so, of course, they said yes, even though it was a four hour drive away and Dad had been feeling under the weather recently. I'd warned them not to be late, to *please please please* not show me up on the biggest night of my life. And that's why they were rushing on the motorway...

The hideous memories are interrupted by Imogene shoving her phone at my face as we tread around the park.

'You know, Nora, Roger Pepper would be a *great* choice for you,' she says in a determined voice. 'He's a catch. And he's got lovely teeth. Here's a picture.'

Imogene is about to hand me the phone when we pass by a tall woman walking a golden-coloured dog. The dog jumps up at my knees excitedly, almost pushing me over into a boggy puddle.

'Oh!' I exclaim, never quite knowing what to do or say when confronted with overeager dogs, or any dogs come to think of it. The pooch's owner gives me a benevolent smile as if I should be thrilled about the fact that her pooch clearly has some sort of beef with me and is currently trying to wrestle me to the ground. 'Um, ha ha. Good dog? Get off me, good dog,' I say gawkily, shaking the dog off my leg and stepping slightly behind Imogene.

'Oh my goodness, so cuuuute!' Imogene gushes to the

woman, ruffling the dog's ears and making up for my lack of appropriate response. 'His little faaaaaace!'

'Aww, thanks,' the woman says with the same pride as if she had given birth to the dog herself. 'Your toddler is gorgeous.'

Imogene and the woman get into a little small talk – my least favourite thing in the world. Imogene tries to bring me into the conversation, but each time I go to say anything, I stutter and mumble and blush stupidly, which has been happening a lot lately. So instead I just let them chat, lean down to the pram and play peekaboo with Ariana, chuckling as she jumps and giggles delightedly whenever I say 'Boo!' and reveal my face from behind my hands. So much more fun than small talk!

Once the woman and her dog have left, Imogene finally passes me her phone, picking up from where we left off. On the screen is a photo of Roger Pepper, her colleague at the office where she works as a senior marketing manager for an up-and-coming fashion brand. Roger Pepper's face is abnormally long, made longer by the hipstery beard he's grown. His teeth are too perfect; all exactly the same size and so white they glow. He is holding one of those tiny espresso cups between his thumb and forefinger. Bleugh!

I shake my head, give her back her phone and continue walking. 'I met Roger Pepper last year at your Christmas do, remember?' I tell Imogene. 'He had a bit of vol-au-vent on the corner of his top lip. It looked like herpes.'

'He's got good banter!' Imogene retorts. '*And* he owns his own house. It's posh too. It has a bidet and everything. Imagine that!'

'Imagine Roger Pepper on his bidet? I will not.'

'Nora! Ew. Stop being facetious. Roger Pepper is lovely, you could do a lot worse.'

'He might own his own house with a bidet, but he has

zero banter. Even less than me and that's saying something! Seriously, he talked my ear off about Fitbit step counts, Imogene. *Fitbit step counts*. He went right into detail too, showed me all these little charts on his phone and all sorts. I told him I thought I was going to barf just so I could run to the loo and get away from him.'

'You did not! Good god, Nora.'

'What? I have trouble chatting to strangers at the best of times. I felt so awkward and so bored that my head almost popped off.'

'He was probably just nervous. You're so unreasonably fussy.'

I snort. 'It's not unreasonable to be fussy about *love*. Love is the biggest thing that happens to a person. I'm just waiting for my soulmate is all and I'm pretty sure Roger Pepper is not him.'

Imogene stops abruptly mid stride, lets out a massive huff and throws her hands up in the air. 'Aaaaaargh. Not this again!'

'What?'

'This soulmate bullshit. It's *such* an excuse!'

'Woah!' I fold my arms and step aside so a jogging man can get past us on the narrow path. 'An excuse for what?'

'For you to turn down any decent man who comes your way unless you feel some magical mystical spark.' Imogene does weird jazz hands as she says *magical mystical spark*. 'Magical mystical sparks don't happen in real life, sis.'

'They did for Mum and Dad,' I say quietly. 'And Mum told me it would happen for me one day too…'

I think back to a random night three years ago. I was going on a date with Timmo, my boyfriend at the time, a barman/amateur guitarist at a club where I had the odd gig as a singer. 'Never settle for less than your soulmate,' Mum had said to me earnestly as she swiped some Barry

M bronze glitter dust onto my eyelids, most of it falling straight onto my cheeks instead. 'Everyone is so sensible and realistic these days. No one goes after The Magic anymore! And it's right there for the taking, Nora. It's right bloody there.'

The Magic sounded amazing.

'Do you think Timmo is my soulmate?' I'd asked thoughtfully. 'How will I even know?'

'Oh, you'll know,' Mum had said mysteriously, her warm green eyes twinkling in the glow of her table lamp. 'You can just feel it. It might not be obvious at first and sometimes it takes a little while for your head to catch up with your heart. But you'll know, love… You just will. It's magic.'

Turns out Timmo wasn't my soulmate. The opposite, in fact. The only magic thing about Timmo was how quickly he disappeared after my parents died. He said my 'sad vibes' were 'stifling his creative exploration'. So I'm still waiting to feel that big thunderbolt.

'Mum and Dad were not the norm,' Imogene grumbles as we trundle onwards, passing the edge of the park green, where a couple of young families are having a kickabout. 'Dan and I didn't have a thunderbolt and look at us! Together for six years now and perfectly happy.'

Ugh *Dan*. Imogene's reasonably handsome but pretty condescending husband, who is in no way good enough for her.

'And anyway,' Imogene continues, 'even if thunderbolts and love at first sight were real, Nora, you're not even *trying* to date anymore.'

I don't have a comeback for that, because she's right. Last summer, I decided to take the soulmate situation into my own hands and declared it *the summer of a million dates* in order to get out there and be proactive about finding 'The One'. It was exhausting. Since losing Mum and Dad I've had trouble socialising in general and especially meeting new people. I thought diving in at the deep end with the potential reward of meeting my soulmate was a good idea… It was not. In fact, it was actually more depressing because even the most on-paper perfect guys were just not doing it for me. Forget thunderbolts! These guys had less fizz than a wet sparkler on bonfire night.

'I've dated every man in Brigglesford and the neighbouring villages,' I point out. 'It's not like I haven't tried. I went out on dates with total strangers twice a week for seven weeks!'

'And you barely gave any of them a chance.'

'I did! I literally gave everyone a chance.'

'For like, one date each. That Jonathan guy was lovely.'

'He didn't chew his food right.'

'What about that PE Teacher?'

'Oh, Alan? Yeah, he smelt like baked beans.'

'But you love baked beans.'

'On toast, not on a life partner.'

'And the hot, muscly Asian guy you went bowling with?'

'His favourite film was *The Next Karate Kid*, Imogene. He had *Karate Kid One, Two* and *Three* to choose from and he chose *The Next Karate Kid*. I mean, *come on*.'

'But your favourite bloody film is *While You Were Sleeping*!'

'Sandra Bullock and Bill Pullman together are cinematic art, it cannot be denied.'

Imogene tuts. 'Look, my point is that all those things that stop you from pursuing anything real with those men, they're all tiny, stupid, meaningless things. No one is perfect.'

Imogene's right. I probably could have gotten over those 'tiny things' *if* I had felt the thunderbolt Mum told me I was supposed to feel. But I didn't feel it, not even a little bit, so why waste anyone's time pursuing something that will inevitably turn into a big pile of awkward old nothing?

I explain this to Imogene and she pulls a face, then stops walking again and gives me a serious and frowny stare. She swallows hard and takes a deep breath as if weighing up what she's about to say next.

'Not wasting anyone's time is one thing, Nora,' she begins. 'And look, I don't want to upset you, but, well, since what happened to Mum and Dad, you've *completely* given up. On singing and writing your songs, on doing anything other than slobbing out in your pyjamas. You've even given up on, like, basic socialising. You have no friends anymore. You fumble and turn red whenever you meet anyone you don't know. You never used to be shy. Now you stay in all the time. You need to be out there. In the world. Living life! Not hiding.'

'I'm an introvert,' I retort, crossing my arms across my chest, forgetting, as I always do, that my boobs are way too hefty to do that comfortably. I plonk my arms back down at my sides. 'I *am* living my life, just, you know… indoors. I like staying in! It's delightful. I light scented candles, chuck on a fluffy blanket, make sweet, milky tea and read my books. I'm super hygge. There are loads of us out there! Hygge is a whole thing. Have you ever seen a night-time routine video on YouTube? That's me, only most of the time, not just at night. It's lovely. Plus, I *do* have friends. I have loads of online friends.'

Imogene rolls her eyes, as if online friends are mere bots and not actual humans behind the avatars. 'Well, I think you're depressed,' she says in a low, tentative voice.

What?

'I'm not depressed!' I protest. 'I'm fine! My life is just fine.'

'And you're happy with *just fine?*'

'I'm… fine with fine,' I say eventually, my heart starting to thud in my chest. I want to go home now. Back to my cosy bed, where everything is warm and easy, where I can do my untaxing work and watch my lovely movies and read my *Harcourt Royals* book series and fantasise about my future soulmate in peace and quiet.

Imogene stares at me for a moment, her eyes glistening with tears. 'I think... I think maybe you're becoming a little too comfortable in your grief,' she says, her voice wobbling a bit.

My heart dips. 'Comfortable? In my *grief*? What does that even mean?'

'It means that you finding problems with every man you meet, discarding them because there's no "magical thunderbolt" provides you an excuse to be alone, to coop up and to wallow in your misery because it's easier than getting out there and opening yourself up to any more pain.'

I feel hot tears immediately spring to my eyes. That was harsh. Why would she say something like that, today of all days?

'Shit, Imogene,' I mutter, my voice catching. 'Shit. I... um...yeah, I... I have to go now.'

I lean in to give Ariana a gentle kiss on the forehead before I turn on my heel and half walk/half jog out of the park. I wait until I reach home before I have myself a big old cry.

CHAPTER THREE

Gary

Dear Diary,

This is weird. I feel like a fifteen-year-old girl. Hmm. Maybe it would help if I didn't write 'Dear Diary.'

I'll just write… 'Hey.' Like The Fonz. Heeeeeey.

Gary, you are a dick.

Heeeeeyy.

Hey.

So. Here I am, on the advice of Ira, my therapist, writing a journal for the first time in my thirty-year existence. According to his expertise, this will help me to deal with this peculiar overwhelming feeling I've been having the last couple of months.

I guess I'm famous now and, to be honest, the reality of that is pretty fucking unexpected. I should feel happier than this, right? Success is what I wanted.

The fact that I'm not happy makes me wonder if I'm just an ungrateful asshole. I have everything I ever wanted. My new movie—my first ever leading role—has smashed box office records and now I've got scripts from every big studio stacked in my den waiting to be read. I'm no longer scrabbling for money, working at Eckerman's deli counter in Cedar Creek, and wishing I could find a way out of Texas. My Pops is proud of me. My girlfriend Tori is loyal and very sexy and way, way, waaaay out of my league. So why am I not wandering round with a stupid grin on my face at how fucking good I have it?

Because I'm a dick. I said this to Ira and he disagreed, but I pay him so… y'know.

I'm going away this weekend to try to clear my head. I'm taking Tori and Janet (the best, most gigantic dog you ever did see) back to Cedar Creek to make a surprise visit to my Pops. It'll be nice to get out of Los Angeles for a while and being at home might bring me back to earth; it's kinda hard to be an asshole around the man that raised you single-handedly.

Everything's so sunny and shiny here in LA and since *Justice of The Peace* came out last month, people are stopping me on the street and asking for autographs, suddenly interested in me, which, I gotta say, is unnerving. Aileen, my manager (and Tori's mom), told me it would happen, but I didn't quite believe it would. And then one day I seemed to go from being pleasantly anonymous to finding paparazzos hiding behind palm trees and taking pictures while I'm sticking as much burrito into my face as I can in one go.

I'm not complaining, because I know this is part of the job. But, still, it's unnerving, man.

Anyways, Ira suggested that, as well as having therapy and trying to spend more time outdoors, each day I journal three amazing things that happened, because writing them down will keep my mind focused on the positives, thus making me a happier, healthier human, instead of the brooding dork I naturally am inclined to be.

So these are my three amazing things for today:

1. My dog Janet straight up stole a huge raw carrot from the kitchen table and sauntered about the house with it in her mouth like it was a cigar. She had this expression on her face like she knew exactly what she was doing. I laughed so hard it made my nose run.

2. I start filming a new movie next week and I'm beyond excited. It's another action movie called *Nightcar*. The first day of a new shoot has this amazing energy, it's a crazy anticipation and all the hopes of what we're gonna make together. I can't wait to dive into a brand-new character for the next three months. Is it entirely embarrassing to write about how much I love acting? Yes. Yes, I reckon it is. But, fuck it, I do. I HEART ACTING.

3. I can't be sure because Tori wouldn't taste it to confirm, but I reckon that this afternoon I made the best grilled cheese sandwich that has ever been made by anyone ever. I did it in the skillet and used a mixture of sharp Cheddar and Gruyère and it was verging on, I don't know how else to say this… it was verging on sexual. Might have had a quarter chub. A fifth of a chub at the least.

I hope Ira doesn't intend to actually read this thing.

Okay. Well, I made it through my first official journal entry. Not quite sure how it'll help, but at least I can say I tried.

CHAPTER FOUR

Nora

I cheer myself up with a cheese toastie made with both extra mature Cheddar and Gruyère cheese for extra comforting cheesiness and stick *Serendipity* on the DVD player to distract myself from all of the feelings.

When Kate Beckinsale and John Cusack and their sweaty five-dollar note are finally reunited, I check my emails before heading over to the *Harcourt Royals* book forum I'm a member of. The small but passionate fandom is called The Crown Kissers and I visit pretty much every day because The *Harcourt Royals* romance books are my favourite book series ever, ever, ever. I discovered them last year online when I was looking for a book to take me out of my own head. I'd never heard of the author, CJ West, but the Goodreads reviews from other readers were all so ardent that I ordered book one.

I'm now completely hooked on this sexy, super-kitsch indie series about a princess called Esme and her secret affair with a commoner – a hot trumpet-playing, eco warrior, geek called Bastian who works as a stripper at a club called Dreamy Dix to pay his way through a marine biology degree. It's ridiculously steamy, kind of cheesy and totally tongue in cheek, but also swoonsome and addictive and surprisingly funny.

I look at the updated Crown Kissers forum posts – everyone is getting excited for the release of the next book tomorrow. There are lots of posts guessing at the plot and I love reading them. Every day for the past week I've been adding in my own ideas.

My favourite plot guesses always come from the user SunshineKennedy90291. They're usually totally outrageous and hilarious. Sometimes we chat on the instant messaging feature about *Harcourt Royals* books and, occasionally, if we're feeling a bit bitchy, other members of the forum who are getting on our nerves.

See? Imogene is wrong. I have friends. Sunshine-Kennedy90291 is my friend! Yes, her profile image is a picture of a sunset and, as far as I know, her surname is 90291, and, yes, we generally avoid sharing personal details in our messages because internet safety is very important, but we like each other's posts almost every day and she makes me laugh. Friend!

Sadly SunshineKennedy90291 isn't online right now so I shut down my laptop, head into my bedroom and reach my hand under the bed, feeling around for the old trunk I keep there. My hand accidentally comes to rest on the massive guitar case also nestled underneath. I haven't touched my guitar since the accident and I don't plan to ever again. I squeeze my eyes shut and ignore it, flapping my hand about until I find the trunk.

I drag it out and open it up, swiping through the collected sentimental junk of my whole existence: old birthday cards, gig flyers, photo albums and, creepily, three of my childhood teeth in an old matchbox. I riffle around until I find the blank DVD case. I press it to my chest for a moment before taking it through to the living room and placing the disc into the player. I plonk myself onto the sofa, curl my legs up beneath me and press play.

There's no fancy opening credits, no jaunty uplifting music by Hans Zimmer. This isn't one of my romcoms, but it *is* the most romantic movie I've ever seen. It's the video of my mum and dad's wedding.

I fast-forward through the shaky camera work showing colourfully dressed, excitable guests entering the church, and stop at my favourite bit. It's the moment that the vicar has just announced Mum and Dad as husband and wife and after they've kissed they both hold hands and start jumping up and down like a pair of idiots. The pure joy and excitement on their faces, entirely borne out of their love for each other, is daft and joyful and magical.

I finger my long black hair, thick and shiny just like my mum's. Then I softly touch my nose, slightly turned up at the end like my dad's. I rewind to watch again, but before I can press play, there's a knock at the door.

I frown. No one knocks on my door apart from the Tesco delivery person and I had all my loo roll and cheese toastie supplies delivered yesterday.

I plod over to the front door and open it to see Imogene standing there, a guilty look on her face.

'I'm sorry, sis,' she says. 'About before.'

''S'okay.' I shrug, forgiving her immediately. This is a sucky day for both of us.

She peers in and sees the still frame of Mum and Dad on my TV screen. She closes her eyes for a second.

I shift uncomfortably from foot to foot.

'Do you want to do something? Get out for a bit?' she asks me eventually.

I look over at my warm couch and think about Brigglesford high street and all the people who'll be out there, happy and revelling on a Friday night. 'I'm not sure...'

'Come on. Dan agreed to have Ariana for the night. We don't have to go into town. We could go to the pictures? We haven't been to the pictures for ages. Come ooooon. I'll let you choose the film. I'll even watch a romcom,' she says, miming a puking motion.

A dark room and a big-screen romance to get lost in actually sounds like one of the few things I feel like doing...

'I'm in.'

* * *

Brigglesford Cinema is located on a retail estate that also houses a giant Next, a giant Boots and an Italian restaurant that got a two-star food hygiene rating in the latest inspections. There's a lovely-looking Kristen Wiig romcom that I want to see, but the young woman at the ticket booth tells us that it's fully sold out.

'Ooooh noooooo,' Imogene says with mock dismay. She finds romcoms to be 'a vehicle for unrealistic fantasy.' Then again, her notion of true romance is when Dan gives her a five-second warning when he's about to let one rip.

'Do you have any other, um, r-romance films showing?' I ask, trying not to stutter in the presence of this unknown person.

'Nah,' the assistant replies. 'But there's this film you should definitely watch. It's called *Justice of The Peace*. It's epic. A real on-the-edge-of-your-seat thriller with a shocking twist, as they say.'

Who wants to watch a film from the edge of their seat? That doesn't sound comfortable at all!

'Ooh, what's that one about?' Imogene asks.

'It's about a young high-powered judge... and, get this... he's a vigilante in his spare time!' the assistant explains, eyes blazing with excitement at this whole concept. 'All the criminals in the county, the ones he thinks are guilty, he tracks them down and dishes out his own form of retribution! As if he's not already busy enough, being in his *own* court all the time!' She throws her hands up in the air.

Ugh. An action thriller. Men running around punching each other and crashing cars into the windows of innocent businesses. Great.

'That actually sounds amazing,' Imogene breathes. 'A vigilante judge!'

'It is.' The girl's eyes are wide and earnest. 'But it doesn't start for another hour and a half. I suppose you could go to the bar and get some drinks and some food? And seeing as you're here so early, I could upgrade you to some premier seats for free!'

'For free!' Imogene nudges me with excitement. 'Shall we do that?'

I mean, it's not ideal, but there's nothing else to do at the retail park beyond getting E. coli at Mama Romano's. And the taxi to get here cost a tenner. And it will be all busy and loud on the high street. And it actually feels unexpectedly nice to be out in the world with Imogene.

'Sounds brill,' I say eventually. 'Let's do it.'

'Drinks are on me,' Imogene declares with a little wiggle of excitement.

'*Justice of The Peace*,' the assistant says. 'You're going to fall in love with it.'

Yeah, I doubt that very much.

* * *

By the time we enter the movie theatre, we've had three glasses of wine each and, having not drunk for ages, I'm feeling more than a little tipsy. It feels quite nice to have this relaxed, happy warmth spread through my body. Although it's a manufactured feeling, it feels surprisingly like relief, which makes me think back to what Imogene said this morning. Am I depressed? I mean, I'm not dancing with joy or anything and I do, you know, cry quite a lot more than I used to…

Shit. *Don't think about that, Nora.*

I mentally karate-chop the thought away and take a sip from my bottle of water.

Thankfully, the lights dim then and the notice telling us to turn off our phones blares out through the surround-sound speakers. I peep around at the neighbouring seats. It's surprisingly busy in here, which comforts me that the movie we're about to watch might actually not be terrible.

I take a handful of the popcorn I bought, smacking my hand to my mouth and shovelling it all in at once, which is definitely the best way to eat popcorn. Imogene side-eyes me and glances at the popcorn, envy in her eyes. I offer it to her, but she says no. I feel bad that she's always on a diet. Her reasoning is that Dan married her at a size ten and she doesn't want to let him down by piling on the beef, which I think, frankly, is bullshit. Then again I'm not Dan's biggest fan. Imogene works full-time and still seems to do everything to keep their household running, looking after Ariana most of the time, while Dan takes on occasional freelance journalist jobs and barely helps at all. Not that Imogene seems unhappy, but still.

Taking another gulp of my water, I settle down into my seat as the movie finally begins. Cool, bassy electronica music sounds out all around us, as a wide shot shows the silhouette of a man set against the backdrop of a blazing orange dusk. He's holding a briefcase and walking towards a beat-up maroon-coloured car. I narrow my eyes. Something about the shape of the character's back looks oddly familiar.

'Who's the main actor in this, do you know?' I murmur to Imogene.

She shrugs vaguely, her eyes not leaving the screen.

'Shush!' comes a voice from behind me.

I turn around and give an apologetic shrug to the old guy looking irritated. Jeez, it's not like anything is even happening yet!

But then something does happen.

Something massive happens.

The camera pans around towards the front of the actor and all at once his face is lit up in the warm golden light of the fierce sunset. He's staring right into the camera, his charcoal-coloured eyes glinting. *He's staring right at me.*

He leans back against the car and smiles a devastatingly charismatic smile, brushing his slightly curly hair back from his glistening forehead before saying in a deep Texan drawl, 'I used to tell myself that I'd never let it get this far. But even as I was sayin' it, I knew, deep down, that I was full of shit. The truth is, I was always gon' end up here. And the trouble is, I'm not quite sure how the fuck I'm supposed to get back...' He tilts his head and gazes intensely into the camera.

My heart stumbles, my breath gathers in the back of my throat and I gasp sharply.

Oh my god.

OH. MY. GOD.

Holy shit.

It's him.

It's *him*!

My heart is thudding right out of my chest. My breathing quickens. I feel beads of sweat prickle along my hairline. I want to glance to my right to see if Imogene can hear me panting or has noticed that perhaps I am having some kind of medical emergency, but I can't take my eyes off the gigantic image of the stranger on the screen.

The character is now on his phone saying something to someone, but I don't hear a word of it even though the surround sound means the warm timbre of his voice vibrates right through my chest.

This is nuts.

This is ridiculous.

This is *not* how I imagined seeing my soulmate for the first time.

CHAPTER FIVE

Nora

I consider that maybe I am going crazy. I rub my eyes like a cartoon character and squint at the guy in the movie.

Yep.

Total, actual thunderbolt. I can feel it, right through my belly, just like Mum said I would.

And it's not because the man on the screen has the darkest, most intense eyes I've ever seen or shiny obsidian curls that are begging to be tousled or that his forearms are the kind of forearms that can make a person get horny over a damn *forearm*. It's not that... I... God, I feel like I *know* him. I'm staring at him on this ginormous HD technicolour projection and he's both unfamiliar and deeply, unerringly familiar.

I want to reach out and touch the screen and say 'Ah, there you bloody well are. Come on, let's go and start this thing finally!' Which is bonkers, I know. Who is he, even?

The rest of the cinema is deathly quiet while I sit there along with them all, my world tipping on its axis. Shit. I feel all fizzy. Am I actually having some sort of stroke? This being the anniversary of my parents' death has made it a particularly stressful day. Is this a strange new manifestation of my grief? What is going on?

I feel hot and weird and great and super super weird, but definitely great and excited. And hot. So hot. I have to get out of this stuffy room. I have to get out of here right now.

I grab my handbag off the floor beneath me and stand up quickly.

'Where are you going? What's wrong?' Imogene hisses, looking up at me in surprise.

The older dude sitting behind us grumbles, 'Please move, you're blocking my view!'

'Sorry!' I turn back to Imogene. 'Just need the loo.'

Her eyes float back to the screen as I scooch past everyone else on the row, banging a couple of them on the knees with my bag.

'Sorry, very sorry. Apologies!' I mutter, causing even more annoyance.

Once I've irritated everyone in the theatre, I push open the double doors and stumble, blinking, into the brightly coloured, artificially lit lobby of the cinema complex. I lean against a wall to catch my breath and try to figure out what's going on with me. I feel so hot. Bringing my hand up to my forehead, I check my temperature to see if I'm spiking a fever or something when my elbow bumps into a big cardboard cut-out, which then tumbles forward onto the floor.

'Oops,' I whisper, wrestling it back upright and noticing as I do that there, life-size, eye to eye with me is... him. Well, his picture, on a cardboard stand advertising the movie we were just watching. I reach my hand out and touch his dark cardboard curls, my heart starting to thud again. This feeling I have is much stronger than I thought it would be. Stronger than Mum and Dad could have ever explained.

'God he's hot, right?' the cinema attendant who

upgraded our seats earlier comes over to straighten the display. 'Not, like, your typical heart-throb, but just, really sexy and *manly*.'

I jump, quickly retracting my hand from the cardboard cheek and pushing it into my coat pocket.

'What is his name?' I breathe, studying his face like it's cake and I am starving.

The girl points to the top of the poster and taps it twice. 'It says it right there. Gary Montgomery.'

'G-Gary?' I ask, eyes widening. That's... unexpected. From the way he looks, I'd have expected him to be called Fitz or Ace or Maverick. I draw my bottom lip between my teeth. To be fair, his name could be Adolph Van Soggypants and it wouldn't suppress these crazy feelings I'm having right now. 'Hello, Gary Montgomery,' I beam up at him.

'Gosh, you're a strange person,' the attendant says matter-of-factly. 'Listen, don't try nicking the cardboard cut-outs all right? We spend a fortune replacing them. When *La La Land* came out, we had to hide all the Ryan Goslings because they kept getting pinched.'

'Of course I won't nick it!' I laugh casually, although I know my cheeks are turning red because it definitely crossed my mind.

'Gary Montgomery,' I say again with a wide grin.

'Okay... um... I'll leave you two alone,' the girl says, backing away, bewildered.

I continue to squint at Gary, trying hard to figure out if I've seen him in anything before, why I'm experiencing this full-on feeling of recognition, this colossal pull?

'Nora, what are you doing out here?' My thoughts are interrupted by Imogene's voice. I drag my eyes away from Gary. 'You've been ages. I thought you were doing a poo and then I remembered you don't like to poo in public places. Are you coming back in? You're missing the film. It's *gripping*.'

I point with a shaking hand to the life-size Gary Montgomery display. 'It's... it's him.'

'What? Who?'

I can barely formulate the words, my heart is thumping so hard in my chest. 'I think... I think this guy might... be my soulmate.'

As soon as I've said the words out loud, I know how outrageous they sound.

Imogene laughs flatly, like I've just told a shit joke, but then her eyes flick to my trembling hand and my serious expression. 'Are you pissed?'

I shake my head: no. 'I'm tipsy from the wine earlier. Quite a lot tipsy actually, but it's not that. I got this weird feeling as soon as I saw him and—'

Imogene's face falls into an expression of deep concern. 'Oh Nora... Fuck. This is bad. You're actually losing it.'

'I shouldn't have said anything. I know it sounds dumb. I just... I just...' I look at his face again and shake my head slowly. 'Just ignore me. I'm clearly going crazy.'

'Come on,' Imogene says gently, grabbing my hand and pulling me across the lobby. 'Let's get out of here.'

CHAPTER SIX

Gary

Hey,

The weekend back home was just what this country hick needed. I saw my old horse, Bess. She's not up to riding these days, but it was good to groom her and take her for a slow walk around the pen. I did everything I wanted to do; read the books I wanted to read, ate way too much pecan pie and shot pool with my old man. It was great for Tori to meet Pops, finally. I think he liked her. He told me she was way outta my league, and he ain't wrong. I wish he'd find someone of his own. Mom died giving birth to me (Ira is having a field day with this information) and Pops has never ever been on a date with another person. He swears he's not lonely, but I reckon he's lying.

I was thinking about things on the flight back to LA. It's funny, I always had this ridiculous idea that when you met the person you're supposed to spend the rest of your life with, you know right away. Like you see them and some funky chorus of angels sounds out in your head or your heart just about bursts out of your chest. Like there's this inherent knowledge that this total stranger is absolutely meant for you, like a big corny thunderbolt or something. I know it sounds absurd, but that's what happens when you grow up with a nanny who loved to watch every romantic movie in existence. Even when she wasn't really watching them, she'd have them playing in the background. That corny shit worms its way into a developing brain!

Anyway, my point is that I always expected to have this amazing moment. And then I met Tori and it wasn't like that at all. Our relationship was a slow burn. Thoughtful and considered and solid. I like that. It feels much sturdier than some frivolous infatuation. I like sturdy. Sturdy is safe. Sturdy lasts.

Okay, my three amazing things for today:

1. Pop's face when I showed up at the door. He was so happy. I cried a little. Just one tear though. One beautiful macho tear.
2. Argh. I'm cringing just writing this, but it was amazing so I gotta. Dustin Hoffman. THE FUCKING DUSTIN HOFFMAN sent me a note to say he enjoyed *Justice of The Peace*. What the hell is my life? Do I call him? Do I write him a note back? Will we become pen pals? Will I become pen pals with Dustin Hoffman? So much to think about.
3. My friend Seth sent me a script his girlfriend Olive wrote. Aileen reckons it's too small fry for me now that JOTP has done so well, but I love it. It's called *Chuffed*. It's an indie comedy drama and it's about a broken American family who discover they have a rich ancestor in the county of Yorkshire, England. They have to travel across the pond together to hear the will.

It's pretty small-scale, but it's so funny and the idea of playing Joseph, the asshole brother, sounds like so much fun. I have to convince Aileen to read it. I mean, I only did *Justice of The Peace* because the script was so good. Does that mean I have to do only big-budget movies now? I don't know. I'd like to do what I'd like to do, y'know?

Tori's calling me. Gotta go!

CHAPTER SEVEN

Nora

In the absence of anywhere else nearby, we find ourselves in Mama Romano's. For the first time in my life, I have zero appetite. In fact, I feel slightly pukey, which is useful, considering the dubious food prep practices at this place. While Imogene is getting us drinks from the bar, I peer around all the red leather booths filled with people tucking in to big plates of saucy gloop. They must not know about the two-star rating.

With still slightly shaking hands, I dig out my phone and google Gary Montgomery.

Gary Montgomery.

Three million results! Woah. I cannot believe I have never seen or heard of him before. I suppose I only use my Netflix account to watch old romantic comedies and I don't really read newspapers or go on social media a lot, beside the Crown Kissers forum. But there are so many articles and pictures of him here, I don't know where to begin.

This feels too weird. I thought I'd spot my dream man on a train, or on the street, maybe I'd save him from choking on a little piece of fillet steak at a high-end restaurant or our eyes would meet between the shelves of a dusty but super charming second-hand bookshop. Not in super HD vision at Brigglesford Cinema.

I immediately notice that Google says he lives in Los Angeles.

My shoulders slump. Los Angeles. That feels like such an abstract, distant place to me!

He doesn't appear to have any of the usual social media accounts, so I click onto his Wikipedia page and hungrily read his bio. It's not hugely long, but it tells me that Gary Montgomery was born in 1990, making him three years older than me. That he lives in the Venice Beach area of LA, was born and raised in Texas and that *Justice of The Peace* is his second major film. The first, a small indie film, won him a Critics Choice Award for best actor, and before that he was mostly in New York theatre, as well as having a few smaller parts in independent movies.

I feel a rush of pride, also a very peculiar thing to feel towards someone I didn't know existed until thirty minutes ago. Then I see an article slagging off his acting in *Justice of The Peace* as 'one note', which gives me a surge of rage on his behalf. Whoever wrote that is clearly a moron who is full of shit and knows absolutely nothing about anything.

Argh! Why am I getting so angry on behalf of a person I have never met? About the acting abilities of which I saw about three minutes' worth?

Taking a deep breath in an attempt to slow my racing heart, I click onto the Google Images page. There he is. Picture upon picture of Gary Montgomery. Mostly him at film premieres and some paparazzi shots of him eating a gigantic burrito in the same way that I eat popcorn – a full shovel and smack to the mouth.

There's a close-up still from his first film. I zoom in

even more. It strikes me once again how familiar his face looks to me. The intense darkness of his eyes, planes of his sharp jaw and his slightly wide, slightly too large nose. The cool pink flush to his cheeks and the upward curl of his stubby eyelashes. It's not the face of most other identikit stars you see in films. It's more offbeat, more intense, more arresting. I feel like I know those eyes. Like, really know them.

I click onto a picture of Gary Montgomery at some award ceremony. He's standing beside a tall, rangy blonde woman with a chic pixie crop and a stylish printed dress with billowing Victoriana-style sleeves. She is stunning. I open up the accompanying article. Gary Montgomery at the Screen Guild Actor's Brunch with Tori Gould, a noted make-up artist, Instagram influencer and the daughter of Gary's uber-successful Hollywood manager Aileen Gould. Gary and Tori have been dating for over a year and Tori accompanied him on his recent press trip.

My stomach flips in envy and sadness.

So that's that.

He's on the other side of the world and he has a girl-friend. I'm clearly going nuts. But that feeling I had in the cinema. The feeling I still have now, right in my belly…

Imogene swishes over with two Cokes, mine a full-fat that she was reticent to get me and hers a diet of course, and pops them down on the table. She takes an anti-bacterial wipe out of her handbag, wipes the rim of both glasses and takes a deep breath. 'I'm worried about you, Nora. You're acting very strange.'

'I'm fine,' I say, waving her away with a still trembling hand, my shoulders hunching up around my ears like they always do when she expresses worry about my mental health. 'Let's just forget about it. It was honestly nothing. Just having a weird day.'

'Um, no, it wasn't. You just said that the guy in that

movie, a *stranger*, was your one true love. That's ridiculous. Seriously ridiculous.'

'Just please forget I said anything.' I stir my straw around my drink and sigh. 'Please.'

'You don't *genuinely* think he's your soulmate?' Imogene presses. 'Do you?'

I pick up a green paper napkin and start pulling it into pieces. 'I just saw him and, I don't know, I felt like Mum said I would feel… Like I needed to be near to him. But I'm obviously just cracking up, right? And, like, even if he was my soulmate, it's not like there's anything I can do about it. He's in LA and he has a girlfriend, so that's that. There's nothing I can do. I'll just have to, I don't know, get over it? Ugh. This is so weird.'

Imogene shakes her head and tuts. 'Oh… how convenient.'

'What?'

'I said *how convenient*. I smell bullshit, Nora.'

'What are you talking about?'

'Well, you spent last year finding something wrong with every man in the greater Brigglesford area and now you tell yourself that a movie star might be your soulmate, someone so ridiculously, bonkersly out of reach that – surprise surprise – you don't have to do anything about it. You can just mope around, retreat into your "hoooga cocoon" even more and tell yourself that maybe you found the one special person you're obsessed with finding, but oh no! He's taken and, oh no! He's famous and OH NO, he lives on the other side of the world. And now no other man will ever match up? I mean who could match up to the most charismatic fella I, personally, have ever seen on a screen? He looks like if Adam Driver were a freaking cowboy. This is some psychological acrobatics, Nora, even for you. If it wasn't so sad, it'd be funny. But it's definitely sad.'

Her know-it-all face winds me right up. She doesn't

know everything about how I'm feeling, about how my mind works. Does she?

Is this psychological acrobatics? Is my mind playing mad tricks on me because I'm a bit more sad than I used to be? Am I like one of those women who fall in love with movie stars and boys in bands and prisoners on death row, people they can never have, people who can therefore never break their heart?

No. I'm pretty sure that's not it. It can't be. I'm not that person. I *want* to meet someone real. I *want* to have the magical kind of love Mum and Dad had. I want that more than anything else, pretty much.

'I don't think that's what's happening!' I say eventually. 'I don't have a single clue why I'm feeling this way, but I do know that it's a real feeling. People can't help the way they feel. And it's not *just* fancying someone.' I clear my throat. 'I... I felt a connection to him. I've never felt anything like that before. Never.'

Imogene blows the air out of her cheeks and runs both her hands through her hair. 'Okay,' she says eventually. 'So prove it.'

I blink. 'What? Prove what?'

'Prove that you're not bullshitting. That this isn't another excuse for you to close yourself off.'

I fold my arms and pull a face. 'And how do you propose I do that?'

Imogene places both arms flat on the table. 'Go to LA,' she says simply. 'Find Gary Montgomery. See if this "connection" you're talking about is as real for him as it feels for you.'

I start to laugh nervously. 'Shut up, Imogene. You're being stupid.'

'I mean it. See this delusion through.'

'I'm not delusional.'

'PROVE. IT.'

I shake my head very quickly. 'I can't afford to just pop off to America, I have—'

'I'll pay. Two weeks. Frankly, I'm sick of your excuses and I refuse to let you get away with them any longer.' She lifts her chin, face full of grim determination.

'I'm not making excuses! And what about my job? And how the hell am I even supposed to find Gary Montgomery?'

'Your job is remote so you can do that from anywhere. And surely if there is a "connection" with Gary Montgomery, fate will intervene, *right?* Mum and Dad were always saying how fate loves the fearless. You'll find a way. And, at the very least, it'll get you out of your house for more than a couple of hours…'

'I… I can't do that…' I say. The thought of flying to another country, where I know no one, to meet a movie star I've just seen at the pictures, makes me feel like I'm going to break out in hives. 'I can't go to *Los Angeles*. That's ridiculous. You're being ridiculous, Imogene. I know I am, but you are too. I'm not a stalker. Going to Los Angeles to track him down sounds super stalkery! I'm not that crazy.'

'Exactly what I thought you'd say.' Imogene smiles smugly.

Ugh. I hate how she thinks she knows me better than I know myself.

'Let me book you an appointment with the doctor on Monday,' she continues. 'I think you need to look at getting some counselling. Work your way through Mum and Dad's death, finally talk about what happened. Maybe get some medication or something.'

I get a sharp memory of Imogene's voice on the phone when I told her what had happened to Mum and Dad on the way to see me perform. I swipe the thought away with as much force as I can. Then I picture Gary Montgomery's strangely familiar face. My whole body warms up in a lovely, pleasant way, like I've just stepped into a big warm bath on an icy winter's day. I get a weird image of Gary and I swimming in a sparkling ocean, laughing at each other, our eyes squinting from the glare of the sun. It's so vivid that I can almost taste the slight sting of the salt water on my lips. I feel a hot ache of longing deep in my core.

'I'll do it!' I blurt out suddenly, causing a few of the surrounding diners to glance over to me in distaste, which is ironic considering they're all about to spend the rest of the evening with explosive diarrhoea.

'Good. I'll call the clinic in the morning. It's about time you—'

'No, no, not that. I mean I'll go to Los Angeles. I'll prove that I'm not delusional.'

Imogene's eyebrows almost shoot up into her hair. 'Fucking hell. Right… Okay then! But when he turns you down, and I love you and I think you're beautiful, but he *will* turn you down, Nora, then you'll come back here and you'll go to the doctors? Start dealing with… this.' She waves vaguely towards me as if to indicate the mess that I am.

I swallow and it feels sharp in my throat. 'Fine,' I say in a nonchalant voice.

'And you'll go on a date with Roger Pepper.'

'Ugh, really? No!'

'He's lovely,' Imogene protests. 'A real catch. He *actually* lives in this country and he *actually* knows who you are for a start.'

I take a deep breath. 'Fine.'

Imogene holds her hand out. 'Fine.'

I take her hand and shake it.

Um. What the fuck have I just agreed to?

CHAPTER EIGHT

Gary

Hey,

I guess that Tori and I just had our first fight. We've been together for just over a year and never fought before. Not once. I must be beat today, though, because I got angry and we just had a real live full-blown argument. I feel terrible.

Tori's mom has been talking about how it's time for Tori and I to get married. How we've been in a committed relationship for the right amount of time, and that it would be a great move for both of our careers, combining our audiences and, as Aileen calls it (I would never say this!), 'Star Power.' Barf. I thought Tori would be against the idea of me proposing in such an orchestrated, unromantic way. I thought she'd tell Aileen this, but she seemed big into the idea, which surprised me, I gotta say. She kept looking at me with these huge hopeful eyes like I was supposed to drop down on one knee immediately, in front of Aileen, and pop the question.

I mean, I want Tori to be happy. She deserves to have everything she wants. And I for sure wouldn't have any of the success I have if it wasn't for her. We met about a year after I moved to Los Angeles. I was the full budding actor cliché—waiting tables at a high-end restaurant and auditioning for shitty bit parts in commercials. I waited on Tori one night, we flirted a little and she asked for my number. I never expected her to call—she seemed way too fancy and accomplished to bother with some waiter wannabe, but she did call and we started hanging out as friends. Within a couple of weeks she introduced me to her mom Aileen Gould— one of the biggest managers in Hollywood. My friendship with Tori eventually turned to sex and because I'd been living with three other waiters/wannabes in a damp basement in Panorama City she invited me to stay in her Beverly Hills apartment for a nominal rent. Soon after that I signed with Aileen, started getting noticed and then, with *Justice of The Peace*, my career just skyrocketed. Thanks, entirely, to Tori. And everything has been great. Until today. After Aileen left the house earlier, Tori said that if I planned on proposing would I give her a heads-up about when I would do it because she would love to get someone to record the moment so she could share it on her Instagram account. Which I thought was a dumb idea, not to mention completely devoid of romance and sentiment. I told her that. And she got real pissed off and said I didn't respect the nature of her career when all she ever did was support me in mine. Which is probably true. I mean, I understand the makeup artist part of her job, but the Instagram Influencing, sharing every bit of your life online? Well, that flies over my head a little.

Anyway, we got mad at each other, there was shouting and now I'm in the den writing it all down in the journal so I can cool off a little. Jeez. I know we're both in the public eye, but there's got to be some private moments, right? Some magic? Proposing to Tori is something I've been thinking a lot about. But I can't just be hustled into it because it's a smart move for our careers.

I dunno. I guess I just need time to think about it.

All right. Three great things that have happened today:

1. Someone posted a clip of me on YouTube, acting in my college production of *Macbeth*. I've never seen it before and I am so bad. So, so bad. It made me laugh and cringe so fuckin' hard that I curled into a ball on the floor. Thank god I got more acting lessons.
2. I've decided I'm gonna learn how to surf. I sit and watch them all riding the waves out on the ocean and I feel jealous. They look so free out there. I want that.
3. Writing this has made me feel better. Huh. Ira's a smart guy.

CHAPTER NINE

Nora

I have very very mixed feelings about what went down last night at the pictures and afterwards at Mama Romano's. On the one hand, it's fucking batshit. I am fully aware that the scientific probability of even getting to meet Gary Montgomery, let alone talk to him, let alone my soulmate prediction being an actual real thing, is ridiculously low. Mum and Dad always said that fate intervenes when it comes to dreams, that it loves the fearless, but this feels like a bit of a stretch, even to me, the ultimate believer in soulmates, fate and the notion of one true love.

Then there's the idea of leaving my lovely, peaceful, safe, warm, cosy house and encountering, eek, other people, real-life people and real-life situations. The very thought makes all the muscles in my shoulders scrunch up and ache.

I stand up from the sofa and roll my head and shoulders in circles in an attempt to loosen the tightness.

California doesn't seem like the best place for an introvert to visit. I bet it's super loud there. I hate loud. I never used to mind noise, but after Mum and Dad, music, crowds, flashy lights, parties, all make me feel like my brain is itching.

I should definitely not go. It's a terrible, stupid idea.

I amble into the kitchen to make a cup of soothing hot chocolate when I get the same massively vivid image I had last night. The one of me and Gary swimming in an ocean. My hand starts to tremble so much that the teaspoon clatters onto the countertops. I picture his eyes and I feel this strange, desperate sense of urgency. Like I need to get to him as soon as possible.

Taking a few deep breaths to steady myself, I finish making my hot chocolate, making the executive decision to add extra whippy cream from a can, on account of my nerves.

I head into my bedroom, sit cross-legged on my bed and sigh.

I can't deny that the idea of a couple of weeks without Imogene's well-meaning but annoying micro-management seems like kind of a relief. And it would be good to have something different to think about for a while, right? To go to bed with something else in my head other than the constant replay of the moment the police called me from Dad's miraculously unscathed phone to tell me what had happened. I could do with a break from that chain of thought...

My phone vibrates, the screen glowing in the dim light of the bedroom.

Text from Imogene: *I've booked you a non-refundable flight for tomorrow night. I know it's super soon, but I'm not letting you wimp out of this. Check your email. I've sent the info there. You need to get an Airbnb booked asap. Less than $100 dollars per night. Dan would go nuts if he found out I was paying for accommodation too.*

. . .

Fuck. She's booked the flights? They won't have been cheap, especially at such short notice. Shit.

Non-refundable too.

That decides it... right?

I nurse the rest of my drink and head back into the living room, suddenly noticing as I do that so much of my life is me walking from room to room in this house. Not that it's a bad thing. Just... I don't think I had quite realised how much I do it.

I wonder briefly what it would be like to walk into a new room. A room with possibilities... It makes me dizzy with nerves. Ugh.

Settling myself in at the kitchen table, I crank up my laptop. I skim-read Imogene's email. The flight is leaving from Leeds Bradford airport at 9 p.m. tomorrow. Shit. That leaves me a teeny amount of time to prepare.

I dash off an email to my boss at Virtual Assistants 4U and let her know that I'll be in LA for the next couple of weeks but still online and available for work, albeit on US time.

My next task is to find an Airbnb within a reasonable budget for two weeks at short notice and I don't have a great deal of luck. Everywhere I find is either wildly expensive and fancy, or a treehouse, or twenty miles outside of LA, or the room is cheap but I'd be sharing with some dubious guy whose visitor reviews state that the house smells like mould and clammy balls.

I have a quick scroll of hotels, which are immediately out of the question due to the fact that most of them clearly cater for rich Hollywood types with endless budgets. And then I get a brainwave. Sunshine-Kennedy90212... She lives in LA, I think? Her profile picture on the Harcourt Royals forum is a sunset behind a sign that says 'Welcome to the City of Angels'. That's LA, right? Maybe she has some intel on Airbnbs that don't cost three months' wages.

I log onto the forum, scrolling through the endless posts from fellow Crown Kissers and GIFs filled with excitement for the release of the next book. I skip over these and go directly to my inbox to message Kennedy.

Oh good, the little green dot next to her name indicates that she's already online.

NoraHarcourtLove: *Kennedy! Weirdly, I'm doing a last-minute trip to LA tomorrow. It's very very very short notice, but do you know of any Airbnbs or hotels that don't cost the same as car?*

I take a deep breath before writing the next bit because I have gotten way out of the habit of meeting new people. But it would be such a shame to be that close to Kennedy and not attempt to meet up.

Also, maybe we could grab a drink while I'm there? My flight home is in two weeks, so I'm pretty flexible if you're free at all? Would be brill to chat all things Esme and Bastian with an actual in-real-life human! No worries if you're too busy though. Okay. Let me know!

She responds speedily.

SunshineKennedy90212: *Fun! Wow, this is exciting. Why are you coming to LA?*

NoraHarcourtLove: *It has recently come to my attention that the man of my dreams is living in LA. I think that he...*

might be my soulmate, lol. We've never met in real life. I know this sounds crazy and, believe me, you wouldn't be the first to think that. My sister is pushing me to visit LA in a bid to meet him and see if my instincts about him are right!

I neglect to mention that the man I'm referring to is a famous Hollywood actor.

SunshineKennedy90212: *You're right. That sounds absolutely crazy!*

I sigh, a hot flush creeping over my cheeks. Then I read Kennedy's next line and things start to brighten up.

It sounds just like something I'd do! I once learned how to play the trumpet to get the attentions of Paul Peter Macafferty, a very hot jazz musician in Silverlake, who looked a lot like Joseph Gordon-Levitt, but not quite as hot, obviously. Turned out he was only interested in dating men. You'd think that that's where I would back away politely, keep my dignity and let him be? Oh no. I turned up at Paul Peter's house wearing a trench coat and only a trench coat and when he opened the door, I let my coat fall open, lifted my trumpet to my mouth and played Mariah Carey's 'Love Takes Time'. I hoped that my killer body and whole-hearted blowing technique would convince him that maybe he could be interested in women too. Of course it didn't. He invited me in for an iced tea, wrapped a blanket around my shoulders and gave me the name of an excellent reflexologist who could help with my boundary issues.

And when I was in college, I had a crush on one of my journalism professors. I thought maybe she liked me back so I wrote an essay on how beautiful I thought she was and posted it under her office door. She told me she had absolutely no interest in me, that I was highly inappropriate and then she made me switch classes! Argh. We do dumb things for love, right?

I snort with laughter and continue reading.

Don't get an Airbnb! I think I've mentioned before that I live with my brother Brandon in Venice Beach, but we have a small spare room that you could totally stay in. I love the idea of having someone to talk all things Harcourt Royals *with. No one I meet in real life has ever heard of them!*

I would, of course, need you to sign a declaration stating that you are not likely to murder myself or my brother and that you will never bring meat or animal products into the house as we are a strictly vegan, whole food plant-based household. But, other than that, we're pretty easy-going.

Oh my goodness, what?!

NoraHarcourtLove: *This sounds amazing. How much would you charge?*

I wait nervously as the 'typing' symbol blinks on the screen. A reply pops up within a minute.

SunshineKennedy90212: *No charge necessary for a Crown Kisser, but... we were thinking of hiring a dog-sitter/walker for our darling Yorkie Winklepuff. But I'm just thinking that* *maybe you could help out while you're here and save me the task of finding someone for another two weeks. I've been slammed at work and Brandon is dealing with some other shit right now. Do you have any experience with dogs? He's a tiny little thing but quite spirited!*

I have zero experience with dogs. Zero. I consider writing that, but I can't let a tiny dog get in the way of what is looking to be an amazing offer of a free place to stay. How hard can it be to walk a dog? I'll just pop some headphones in so I don't have to talk to anyone and whip it around the block to do its business...

NoraHarcourtLove: *I have tons of experience with dogs.*

I type before even thinking about it.

SunshineKennedy90212: *Oh, perfect!*

She seems so pleased that I panic and double down in a major way.

NoraHarcourtLove: *My family bred dogs.*

I regret the lie as soon as I write it. *Bred dogs?!* Why did I even put that? Why not just put a tiny lie, like that I had a pet dog as a child? Why am I such an idiot? I consider telling the truth, but reversing now would make me look even crazier than I already do.

SunshineKennedy90212: *Are you kidding me? That's awesome! What are the chances?! I'll prepare your bed! Here's the address, text me when you land. This is so exciting!*

Eek.

Okay then.

This is actually happening. I'm actually doing this.

Shiiiiiiiit.

* * *

Because I've not gone on holiday since Mum and Dad died and I live in the constantly raining north of England where I mostly stay inside, I have a distinct lack of hot-weather-appropriate clothes. I yank an old suitcase out from the bottom of my wardrobe. The last time this case was opened was on a holiday in Greece I took with friends four years ago. Back when I had friends. I get a hazy memory of laughing with the other members of the band I was in at the time, everything colourful and vivid and sparkly. And then my heart sinks as I remember the period of time after losing Mum and Dad, all the texts and phone calls I ignored, the invitations I declined. Eventually the friendships fizzled and I was alone. Left in peace to watch my movies and read my books and not have to face anything I didn't want to.

I pull the crumpled items out of the suitcase one by one. The smell emanating from the case is of sun cream and happier, simpler times. I lay the summer clothes out on my bed. A bunch of sundresses, some jean shorts, an unopened pack of T-shirts, flip-flops, a few swimming costumes, a lovely gigantic wide-brimmed sun-hat. It's going to be weird to wear such skin-baring items. On account of the weather here, and boobs that want to greet everyone ten minutes before me, I tend to cover up most of the time. That's not going to be an option in Los Angeles. Where I am going. Tomorrow.

I sit down on my bedroom rug and take a few deep breaths to calm my heart as it nervously jumps about at the prospect of this pilgrimage. I pick up my phone and scroll onto YouTube to see if there are any new videos of Gary since I last looked… thirty minutes ago. Seeing his face, hearing his voice, will make me feel better about this whole thing.

Aha, there's a new interview on there! It's from a series called 'A Grown Man Answers Your Questions'. I've seen this before. It's pretty cute – an adult man answers questions from teenagers on every topic from making friends at a new school to body odour. I click on the link hungrily, my breath calming a little as I see his face smiling at the camera. It's not a professional video, it looks like it's been filmed on his phone. It seems odd seeing his face without a ton of production values thrown at it. No styling and make-up, no professional mic and lighting. Just him, looking slightly tired and with a heavy scattering of dark stubble on his chin. Wow. He is truly, truly hot. He introduces himself.

'I'm Gary Montgomery and this is "A Grown Man Answers Your Questions". Quick disclaimer – I'm thirty so technically a grown man, but I cancelled a meeting today so I could read my book, eat grilled cheese and drink beer in my underwear… so take my answers with a pinch of salt because I am definitely still working on getting my shit together.'

He reads books! And he loves cheese toasties like me! I feel my face go hot. Only a book nerd would cancel a meeting to read their book. In all of my visions of the nameless faceless man who would become my soulmate he was carrying a book. I wonder what kinds of books he reads. Will I get to ask him? Will we share a cheese toastie?

Gary opens a piece of paper and starts to read out the questions, providing insightful, sweet and funny answers. I laugh when he stumbles over a word, and get emotional when he gives a piece of advice on how to deal with feelings of overwhelm, telling the audience that it's totally normal to feel that way and that it's not weak to talk about it.

Purpose renewed, I click off the video, select a bunch of the old summer clothes I'm going to take with me. Then I grab some basics from my wardrobe – bras, knickers, jeans and tops and I pack them into the case.

Now, where's my passport?

CHAPTER TEN

Gary

Hey.

It's 10 p.m. and I've been learning lines for *Nightcar*
and running errands all day. I'm about to crash into bed,
but I wanted to add my three amazing things for today, so
I don't forget them.

1. I swam in the ocean this morning just as the
   sun was rising. The sky was purple and the
   water felt incredible. It was quiet and vast, and
   in a few weeks of feeling a little off-kilter, it
   was a perfect moment of serenity.
2. Janet took a visit to the dog salon to get
   groomed and they cut her too short – they
   pretty much shaved her whole body. She looks
   ridiculous. She is not happy about it. I am very
   happy about it.
3. I had a Middle Eastern Lyft driver today who
   also moonlighted as an Adam Levine tribute
   act. He offered to sing all of Maroon 5's

greatest hits for me. I accepted, which surprised him because he told me that people usually were in a bad mood and said no. He was great. Maybe even better than Adam Levine himself. I'm glad I said yes, it really perked up being stuck in LA traffic, although I now have those Maroon 5 lyrics stuck in my head: 'Look for the the girl with the broken smile. Ask her if she wants to stay a while.'

CHAPTER ELEVEN

Nora

Text from Imogene: *Are you there yet? What's it like? Dan thinks me pushing you to do this is a risky move, considering your mental health, but I really do think a dose of reality will do you some good. Also, I have emailed you an article about how using fantasies to replace real life is REALLY BAD FOR YOU. Please give it a read. Love you. Im x*

After an almost eleven hour flight, I'm here! I'm actually in actual America. And, holy heck, Los Angeles is as hot as a sausage. Feeling like this is all some weird fever dream, I drag my luggage out to the front of LAX and immediately start to sweat. It's 10 o'clock at night, but it feels as warm as a summer's afternoon in England. I stupidly assumed that because I was landing in the evening the weather would be cool.

I glance down at the jeans and woolly jumper I thought was such a good cosy call for the plane and mentally give myself a good talking-to for not packing a lighter option in my hand luggage. I feel the sweat beads prickle along my hairline as I open my phone, wait for it to adjust to the new time zone and open the Lyft app I downloaded this morning. Copying and pasting the address from Kennedy's *Harcourt Royals* forum message, I enter it into the app, glad of the fact that these things exist to help people like me to avoid minimal public interaction. I'm actually surprised and pleased by how much I managed to avoid awkward exchanges on the way here. Well, except for when my airplane seatmate asked me if I wanted his nuts and I almost choked until I realised he was holding out a packet of KPs.

Within minutes, a sleek and shiny blue car has pulled up right in front of me. A handsome Middle Eastern man climbs out and helps me to put my suitcase into the boot. Thanking him, I clamber into the car with a sigh of relief as the cool air of a fan hits me.

'Thank god for air con,' I mumble to myself.

'I know, right?' the driver agrees, smiling at me in the rear-view mirror.

I peer out of the window as we zoom down the highway. My hands tremble a little with nerves so I clasp them tightly together in a bid to keep them still. Oh my goodness, Gary Montgomery is somewhere in this city. He's probably at some cool movie party or at his mansion just pottering about completely unsuspecting. I smile to myself at the thought of meeting him and then catch a glimpse of myself in the rear-view mirror. My smile is more than a little creepy. And I'm thinking exactly the kind of thing a stalker would think while they plot their various stalking activities. Shit, am I... a stalker? Do stalkers genuinely think that they are the one true love of the person they're stalking? Because I genuinely think that Gary Montgomery might be my one true love... No. I'm NOT a stalker. All I want to do is meet him once. It's like if I saw him in a bar. And I went over to talk to him. Except that the bar is across the Atlantic Ocean and I flew all the way across that ocean to get to the bar. Anyway, if I meet him and he freaks out or tells me to get lost or just doesn't like me back, I will leave it at that and bugger off back home right away. I will remain respectful. That is *very* important. I will *not* be a creep.

'Are you all right? You look very worried!' the Lyft driver asks, his eyes meeting mine in the mirror.

I cough and shake my head quickly, the familiar new-person anxiety tightening my throat.

The driver continues to glance at me, expecting an actual answer because that is how conversations generally work for most people.

'J-just thinkin',' I eventually say in a weird American accent which is odd because I am from England and have never had an American accent in my life.

'First time in the US?' the driver asks. Clearly I am not the first person to come to America and slip immediately into a phoney American accent. I flush red.

'Yes.' I nod and look down at my knees, hoping that he gets the message that I am definitely not up for small talk.

He does not get the message. Instead he glances at my destination on his phone and does an excitable squeal. 'Venice Beach! Very exciting. You must be excited.'

'Yeah, um, I'm staying, um, with a friend,' I tell him, which isn't strictly true. I'm staying with two strangers and one dog who I'm expected to know how to handle like some sort of an expert.

'My name is Billy Fever.' The driver grins at me.

'That is *not* a real name!' Surprise and amusement make me forget my usual shyness for a brief second. Then I feel bad. Perhaps I've embarrassed him. 'Sorry,' I say in a small voice. 'That j-just popped out.'

The guy doesn't look offended though. He laughs too. 'You are right. My real name is Farooq Tabassum Hanania, but it is not catchy enough for my line of work.'

'Driving?'

'Oh no no no. I am a singer-slash-entertainer. This is my day job, but at weekends and on special occasions, as and when I am hired, I work as an Adam Levine tribute act.'

I sit up straighter in my seat. 'Are you for real?'

The driver smiles widely. 'Yes. I am very good at it too. Do you want to hear me perform? It will be a free performance as you are already here in the car.'

'Uh, you mean right now?'

'Yes. I can sing and drive at the same time. I'm a very talented man.'

I laugh out loud. 'Well, yes. I definitely want to hear you perform.'

Billy Fever gives a little whoop of delight. 'Today is a good day. I offer many people my free performance and they say no, but you are the second person who said yes today! I am on fire! I am, as they say, lit!'

I chuckle, leaning forward in my seat.

Billy breaks into a rendition of *Moves Like Jagger* and, no word of a lie, he is really really great. Maybe even better than Adam Levine himself! I get an urge to sing along and harmonise, an impulse I quickly push away. When he's finished, I tell Billy how great he is and he responds with an excited toot of the car horn.

'That is what the other passenger said too! I am having a very great day today. Would you like to sign up to my mailing list? I have twelve people signed up so far!' he says proudly.

It's taken me three years to clear my email of junk mail and old newsletters that I signed up for. But Billy Fever is the first person I've met in LA, the first person I've had a conversation with since the assistant at the cinema, plus he seems really nice.

'Why not,' I answer, and he hands me a little white

card with his website address and phone number printed upon it in blue ink.

'Just follow the link on my website to sign up.'

We continue our whoosh along the motorway as Billy treats me to another free performance, this time of *She Will Be Loved*, which makes me tear up a little, because the blissful look on Billy's face as he's singing it is the way I used to feel every time I performed.

We pull up outside the back of a few houses and I can't see much because it's fully dark.

'I believe number 34 should be through that little path there,' Billy says.

'Great, thanks.'

'I have rated you five stars, you have been a most delightful customer. Here, also, is a Hershey bar. They are my favourite thing about America and I think you will like them too because I have never met a person who doesn't like a Hershey bar.'

I take the bar with delight. This is the best cab ride I've ever had. I suddenly feel more positive about this whole thing. 'Thanks, Billy,' I say brightly. 'I will definitely give you five stars too.'

'Enjoy the City of Angels!' he says. 'I hope La La Land brings you everything your heart desires.'

'Me too,' I say quietly, before heading out of the car.

I step into a strong and abnormally warm breeze and set off towards Kennedy's house, the lyrics of *She Will Be Loved* dancing around my head.

CHAPTER TWELVE

Nora

I follow a little wooden sign that says Pleasant Beach Court and, heading down an orangey lamplit alleyway, I come to a side door. Number 34. This is it. This is Kennedy's house.

I roll and shake my shoulders which feel tight with the nerves and anticipation of meeting this person who is the closest thing I've had to a friend for the past year, but who I also barely know at all. I slowly blow the air out through my mouth in a futile attempt to slow down my jumpy heart. Then I wipe my fingers under my eyes to remove the errant mascara crumbs that always seem to be there no matter how many times I check. Brushing my sweaty hair out of my face, I paste what I hope is a non-psycho-looking smile onto my face. Then I reach for the doorbell and press it. It surprises me with a recording of wind chimes that's frankly much louder than it needs to be. Immediately, I hear the sound of frantic, excited barking from inside the house.

I take a shaky breath as I see a figure appear behind the glass door.

Okay, Nora. Don't embarrasses yourself. Don't melt into a puddle of shyness. Be confident. Be sure. Smile! This is a nice person. Just one nice person who is looking forward to meeting you. Kennedy is just a nice, friendly book geek, just like you.

The door opens to reveal the hottest woman I have ever seen in real life. Jeeeez. Without thinking, my eyes widen and I sort of lean closer to get a better look at her, because she looks like she's been lit with one of those skin-smoothing, eye-widening photo filters. Butterscotch blonde hair tumbles softly over her shoulders, a tanned, unlined, completely glowing face smiles at me, revealing perfectly straight, perfectly white teeth. Her nose is slightly short, which serves to add a sort of approachable cuteness to her face. She's wearing pale grey jersey jogging bottoms, a plain white vest that has not, unlike my white items of clothing, gone slightly pinky-grey in the wash. There's not even one tiny little tomato sauce stain upon her top. Shrugged casually over her shoulders is a floaty cream robe with little embroidered golden stitches around the edges of the lapel and pockets. This woman looks better ready for bed than I probably will on my wedding day. Her grin is warm and friendly, her eyes shining with excitement and curiosity.

'You must be Nora! I'm Kennedy!' She bows a little. 'Get in here!' Her voice is much less delicate than expected considering her general floaty and serene vibe. She pulls me in for a full-on hug, which immediately brings a lump to my throat. I can't remember the last time I was hugged by someone. Probably at Mum and Dad's funeral. Imogene and I tend to favour the odd arm pat or a brief kiss on the cheek. I swallow hard and awkwardly untangle myself from her embrace, only for her to grab both my hands and swing them about happily. I allow my hands to flop about in hers, because what the heck else am I supposed to do? 'You're here!' Kennedy exclaims, full of pep and cheerfulness.

'Uh, I am! Hi!' I respond, trying to match her energy and overshooting it so much that I sort of scream the words, causing Kennedy to jump back, startled.

Great start, Nora.

She giggles. 'You must be exhausted. How long is the flight from the UK? Nine hours, right?'

'It took almost eleven hours,' I grimace, brushing my hair out of my face, only for this mad warm wind to blow it around once more, so that my long hair covers my face like the girl in *The Ring*.

'The Santa Ana Winds are blowing!' Kennedy explains, reaching out and picking up my heavy suitcase up with very little effort. She must go to the gym all of the time. Hmm. Maybe we won't be quite as compatible in real life as we are online.

'Santa Ana Winds?' I ask, following her through the door and trying very hard to make conversation like a normal person. 'T-they talked about those in one of my favourite films: *The Holiday*. I forgot you guys have s-specific, named winds here. In the UK, wind is just, uh, wind.'

'The Santa Ana Winds are a katabatic wind,' Kennedy says knowledgeably. 'They're formed from high-pressure air masses coming in from the great basin.'

'Ah,' I reply, nodding. Why does Kennedy know so much about wind? And what the hell does any of that actually mean?

'The Santa Anas are a pain in the ass of every Angeleno. They cause flues and wildfires,' she continues as she carries my case through a Spanish-tiled hallway, occasionally looking back at me as she talks. 'Also, crazy things happen when they're in town. Mystical, magical, strange and weird things. You came at the right time to meet this guy! Last year, during a Santa Ana wind spell I was so horny that I slept with Erin, this woman I work with who I actually kind of despise. She's hot, but she's an awful human. She's actually kinda my work nemesis. But those dastardly magical devil winds. We were both working at the office late and I couldn't help myself.'

Magical devil winds? Windchime recording doorbells? And Imogene says *I'm* not quite in touch with reality?

Kennedy pushes open a set of white wooden double doors and holds out her perfect arm to present what looks to be a perfect home.

'Here's the living room!' she says brightly, plonking down my suitcase and demonstrating the space like an assistant on a gameshow.

I spin around, taking it all in. It's bloody gorgeous and much bigger than she made out over her forum messages. The floor is a scrubbed white painted floorboard almost entirely covered in a pale blue threadbare Persian rug. There are three small colourful ukuleles hanging on the wall, two plump cream sofas facing each other and a drift-wood coffee table in the middle of them, topped with a few chunky white candles and a burning incense stick that smells like jasmine and roses.

Kennedy catches me sniffing the air. 'Isn't it just gorgeous?' She points to the open stairway on the left of the room. 'Brandon's in bed, so it's the only time I'm allowed to burn my sticks. He hates the smell. Says it reminds him of musty old thrift stores, which he also dislikes. You'll meet him tomorrow if you're up before he goes to work. He's usually pretty busy, so don't be offended if he doesn't roll out the proverbial red carpet to give you the royal welcome. Royal, geddit? Like *Harcourt Royals*. Ha ha! Sorry. I'm a bit overexcited to have you here.'

I can't help but laugh. Kennedy looks like an actress on a glossy Netflix teen soap, but I can see that deep-down she's just as dweeby as she seems online, if not more.

'Brandon's happy for you to be here too, I promise!' Kennedy continues. 'He's just, well, he can come across as a little surly, you know? He's going through a heartbreak and his head's up his ass. But when he warms up, he's a sweetie, I promise.'

'That's cool,' I shrug, looking off to the stairway and making a note to hide in my room in the morning so that I can put off meeting this surly man for as long as possible. Encountering cheerful, friendly people like Kennedy is intense enough! 'You play?' I ask, pointing at the ukuleles on the wall.

'God no. I just like the way they look. I can play the trumpet, though. I was a total band geek in high school.

'Like Bastian in *Harcourt Royals*!'

Kennedy nods. 'Right! Yes. Good old Bastian.' She pulls me over to the end of the living room and dramatically swishes open a heavy cream curtain to reveal a double bed set up in front of a large floor-to-ceiling window, the outside so dark that all I can see is my slightly dazed-looking reflection. It's more of a cordoned-off area than a room.

'This is your room,' she announces. 'The curtains are super heavy: they're practically like walls. Here, have a feel.' She reaches over and picks up the curtain, miming and groaning as if it's a real struggle to lift. I follow her lead and lift the curtain up. It is very heavy. Not a door, but it's free and it's pretty and an amazing kindness of Kennedy to let me stay here.

Kennedy proceeds to chirrup away brightly as she shows me the rest of the house, bar the mysterious Brandon's room. The decor is all gorgeous, calming shades of cream, white and pale blue and natural materials like wicker and driftwood, which totally suits her serene, sunshiny vibe. It's clear, from the big heavy lamps and artwork dotted about the place, that Kennedy makes a decent amount of money, or her brother does. It strikes me that I don't even really know what she does for a living. I know it's something in television, but that's about it. We rarely talk about personal things on the forum.

I'm about to ask her what her job is when she grabs my hand like we are old friends and leads me to another set of double doors at the end of a narrow, but perfectly designed, kitchen and asks me a question with a very serious look on her face. 'So… are you ready to take a look at my little Winklepuff?'

I flush red. Her little *Winklepuff?* What the hell is a… Oh! Of course. Her dog. The dog I'm looking after in exchange for my accommodation. The animal she thinks I am an expert on when I basically know nothing about dogs, beyond arguing with Imogene because she always wanted to watch *Crufts* on our shared childhood TV when I'd have much rather have been watching *Gossip Girl*.

I nod fervently at Kennedy like I expect a dog person would. 'I can't wait to meet… that little guy!' I say, giving a thumbs up that is supposed to come across as enthusiastic and, I suspect, looks terrified.

Kennedy pushes open the double doors, exposing a small porch and a vast pitch-black, starry sky. I can hear the sound of waves crashing nearby and my heart does a little leap of excitement. And then, before I can consider anything else, I hear a low growl and a small tan and silver rat-like creature darts into the house, skids across the kitchen floor, jumps up and attaches itself to my leg like a koala bear. He's growling and I have no clue whether he's being amorous or intending to take a chunk out of my thigh, which, admittedly, has a fair amount of chunk to spare.

'Winklepuff! Down!' Kennedy calls out in a voice so exasperated, I get the impression she has commanded the same of this dog many many times before.

She nods quickly at me as if she's waiting for me to work my dog expert knowledge on her little Winklepuff. Shit. I should have at least done some type of research on the plane. The only real dog knowledge I have is based on an episode of *The Dog Whisperer* Imogene made me watch with her a long long long time ago.

I cough awkwardly, holding my leg out in front of me as this very determined Yorkshire Terrier clings on for dear life and growls.

'Uh, heel! Heeeeel,' I eventually say in an attempt at a deep and authoritative voice. I sound like a pissed-off podiatrist.

Unsurprisingly, Winklepuff ignores the command and starts to nibble at my jeans instead. I mean, they're pretty old jeans with raggedy edges but still! He is trying to *eat* them!

'Heel, now!' I say a little more loudly.

Nada.

Kennedy looks at me through narrowed eyes. I'm about to be busted. She's going to figure out my stupid lie and send me packing. I'll have messed this challenge up in under one hour, which would be embarrassing even for me, a master in messing shit up.

'This command always works in England,' I lie, my voice wobbling.

Kennedy nods. 'Yeah, it must be something to do with the accent.'

'Definitely,' I agree. 'Get off now, boy!' I say to Winklepuff, trying my best not to freak out as the little git slowly starts to hump. Ew. This is so gross.

'Hmmm… I'll grab one of his toys,' Kennedy suggests. 'Maybe it will distract him!'

As soon as she's gone up the stairs, I lean down to Winklepuff and plead with him desperately. 'Please don't ruin this for me! Just do as I say! Get down! Get off my leg. Heel. Heel now, boy.'

He clings on tightly and does another happy little growl.

'Come oooooon!' I beg, shaking my leg violently like I've just taken MDMA and fancy a spot of the Hokey

Cokey. 'Please, boy! If you just get down, I'll give you some ham as soon I can get hold of some, or whatever meat substitute you vegan dogs eat.'

Winklepuff's ears prick right up at the word 'ham'. He looks me directly in the eyes and lets go of my leg, plopping softly down onto the rug. Looks like we have a deal.

'Sit down,' I command, just as Kennedy walks back in with his toy.

Winklepuff sits neatly, staring up at me in anticipation of, I expect, some upcoming ham.

Kennedy's jaw drops. 'You did it! He listened to you! I usually have to give him a stuffed animal. Wow.'

I try not to look too surprised and shrug my shoulders nonchalantly.

'It's all about, um, confidence,' I blag. I picture the face of the dog whisperer. What did he keep talking about in that episode? Something about leaders. Alpha! That was it… 'You have to let them know who is the, um, alpha,' I add. 'I am the alpha.'

Kennedy nods slowly, eyebrows slightly raised. I know exactly what she's thinking. That the sweaty, meek-mannered, dazed as fuck woman declaring herself an alpha looks like the furthest thing from it. I know my vibe. Nerdy, vague, a listener rather than a talker, blushes at the mere idea of attention. Pretty much the *opposite* of an alpha.

Once Winklepuff is playing happily in the corner of the room with a stuffed elephant, patiently awaiting the ham I'm going to have to figure out how to get him tomorrow lest I break his trust, Kennedy offers me a chamomile tea. I accept gratefully.

While she measures out the chamomile from an actual bag of flowers rather than a teabag like I do, she casually explains to me that she works at a local TV station as a weather reporter.

'Ah, so that's why you're called Sunshine Kennedy on the Crown Kissers forum,' I say with a grin.

'Exactly! Next week I'm interviewing to become a junior afternoon news anchor. Hence your help with Winklepuff is truly appreciated. I'm in the running against a few people, including Erin; you know, the nemesis I slept with?' She rolls her eyes. 'And she's been there way longer than I have so I have a lot of practising to do before my initial screen test tomorrow.'

'Wow. A news anchor! That sounds literally terrifying to me. Being watched by all of those people.' I shudder at the thought. How did I ever spend all that time singing on stage without puking in fear?

Kennedy laughs out loud and shrugs a shoulder. 'I've been presenting the weather for five years now, so nerves are a distant memory. My mom read news for a local station in Ohio, where I grew up. She always wanted to be the next Katie Couric before she had Brandon and I. She "strongly encouraged" me to major in Journalism at Northwestern, so she's super invested. God, she's so excited, she's been calling every day to discuss current events and politics with me in preparation.'

I ignore the envious heart dip that occurs whenever anyone talks about their parents. 'It sounds like a dream job for you,' I say.

Kennedy's smile falters for the briefest of milliseconds, so brief I wonder if I imagined it, before she says, 'It's an exciting opportunity, that's for sure!'

We carry our mugs through to the living room and sit down.

'How long are you staying for?' Kennedy asks. 'You can stay for as long as you like, you know? Don't mind Brandon. He'll object probably, but he doesn't mean it. Like I said, he got dumped recently, so he's in a weird place, bless his heart. Besides, he's always at work or up in his room writing.'

'Writing?'

'Oh, I think he's writing a screenplay or something? He's always holed up in there tapping away. Anyway, don't worry about him. He'll soon warm up. Just know that you are very welcome here.'

'That's really kind of you, thank you. My flight home is in two weeks. I hope that'll be enough time to figure out this whole Gary thing.'

Kennedy splutters her Chamomile tea, a little of it dripping off her chin. 'Your dream guy is called *Gary*? That's a plot twist.'

I sit up straighter. 'I know! It's not a typical romantic hero name. He looks more like a Maverick or a Jonny or, well, a Bastian.'

'Gary or not, he must be fucking hot if you've come all this way to hook up with him. Have you got his picture?'

I think of the hundreds of Google images I've scrolled through. 'Not on me,' I say faux-sadly.

Kennedy does not seem sceptical of this, considering that it is pretty much possible, these days, to get a picture of every person on earth within five seconds.

'It's so romantic,' she breathes instead, clasping her hands to her chest. 'Like when Bastian and Princess Esme saw each other across the procession crowd for the first time and knew in an instant that they were meant to be.'

'It's kind of crazy, though, right?' I say. 'Coming out here. It was my sister's idea, actually.'

'It's totally crazy. But brave. And what have you got to lose?'

My dignity? My mind? My ability to ever trust myself again? Gary? I look down at my thumbs and try not think of all the things at stake.

Kennedy gives a ginormous yawn and covers her mouth. 'Gosh, I'm sorry! I'm totally beat! I should go to bed.'

'Absolutely,' I say. 'I appreciate you waiting up for me. You go to bed.'

'Are you sure you have everything you need?' Kennedy asks, already standing up from the sofa and stretching her arms up in the air before bending from side to side. 'You know where the bathroom is, make yourself at home and help yourself to breakfast and tea in the morning! I left a set of keys on the hook by the door. Oh, and make sure you close the blinds in your room. Brandon's truck is parked outside of there, so it's blocking the view, but once he leaves for work, it's pretty public. And I apologise in advance if you hear me snoring. I have a deviated septum and a propensity for thick mucus. Sorry, that's TMI. Okay. Sleep well…'

I nod quickly. 'Thank you! I'm shattered too. I'll probably just crash.'

Before she heads up the stairs, Kennedy turns to me. 'Let's do dinner tomorrow, okay? I'll be out researching a news story, but I'll be back in the afternoon and we can get to know each other a little more. I'm dying to find out what this dream guy thinks about you coming all the way out here for him. He must be so flattered!'

Um…

CHAPTER THIRTEEN

Gary

Hey!

My friends are in town! Seth and Olive have come to stay to get a little sunshine and escape the madness of their jobs in Manhattan. I didn't realize I'd missed seeing anyone from the old days in NY until Seth showed up and told me my hair looked 'stoopid and ridiculous.' To be fair, he is completely right. It's much longer and fluffier than it used to be and now I have tiny, delicate brown highlights weaved throughout to 'add dimension' to the black. It's very Hollywood and looks good on camera, but in real life I look like if Liberace joined a 90s boy band. And, for the record, if it were up to me, I'd shave it all off and be done with it. But Aileen says she'll fire me if I change a hair on my head, and I have no doubt she means it. Especially not now that a men's hair product company want me to be the face of their line.

Jeeez. 'Face of their line.' Who even am I? Hopefully, a couple of weeks with Seth and his girlfriend – the sweetest English woman – will bring me right back down to earth and soften this unglued feeling I've been having lately.

Okay, Seth is telling me not to be such a rude asshole and get him a beer at once.

But before I do, here are my three amazing things for today:

1. Seth is the happiest I've ever seen him. He and Olive are always laughing at each other and with each other. It's so damn great to see. Tori and I don't really laugh like that with each other. It's just not something we do. She is a truly amazing woman and has a million other qualities. But I can't help but wonder what it must be like to be with someone who makes you laugh until you cry. Exhausting, I expect.

2. Only two more days until the shoot starts for *Nightcar*. I cannot wait to get on set, meet the other actors and just dive right into my character. I love acting, man. It's the only thing that makes me feel truly free. I step into the body, the world, the mind of an entirely different human and somehow I can escape my own shit and fly away for a while into someone else's emotional experience. It's cool.

3. I'm in the middle of reading this awesome book and I am actually excited to get back to it once everyone's gone to bed. It's kinda weird because, after getting my degree in English Literature and having all the fun pretty much sucked out of books, my usual reading taste these days is pretty standard Lee Child, John Grisham fare. But I found this book at a second-hand bookstore in Malibu and, I'll admit, I opened up to the first page with the intention of a little light mocking – the cover was a semi-clothed hot couple wearing huge

bejewelled crowns. I mean, come on! It was the first book in a series called *Harcourt Royals* and written by an author I'd never heard of – someone called CJ West, which is clearly a pseudonym. Ten minutes had passed before the store owner said, 'Dude, are you gonna buy that or just read the whole damn thing right there, crowding up my store?' I was surprised to find that by the end of the first chapter I had become fully hooked. I'm now reading book four in the series. It's insane and salacious and kitsch and over-the-top romantic, but it makes me feel happy and ridiculous when a lot of my life feels so serious right now. It's pure fucking fun, and who in their right mind turns that down?

CHAPTER FOURTEEN

Nora

Text from Imogene: *What is it like there? Are you okay? Is the person you're staying with a Catfish?! Have you been murdered and I am sending this text to a ghost? Dan found out how much the flights cost and is having a shit-fit at me. So I really hope this trip sorts out your head and makes you realise that it's time to make some massive changes. Im x.*

As always, I have weird dreams the whole night through. In so many of these recurring dreams, I am on a big stage, dressed in something glittery and bursting with the power that comes from having command of a whole room of strangers. I used to *love* that feeling; seeing the happiness that would come over people's faces when I sang phrases that they connected to, when I reached notes that seemed like they ought to be impossible to reach. In the dream, after I've finished singing, things always move into a dark, cool afterparty, full of memories of what it was like to have friends to hang out with, people who I could talk to without melting into a puddle of bashfulness and introversion. And then, with no warning, everyone at the dream party just starts to cry, like properly full-on sobbing. I ask them what's wrong, but nobody will tell me. It's super unnerving. I always, always wake up feeling relieved that I'm not in a room full of crying people after all, but also sad and puzzled that I'm no longer able to access the feeling of joy and power I used to get from performing my songs for an audience.

This morning, I awaken from one of these dreams completely soaked in sweat and with a mouth drier than sand-topped crackers. Why is it so hot? I blearily open my eyes. God, it's mega bright too. What happened to my blackout curtains that I spent two whole days' wages on?

Oh.

I am not at home.

I am in Los Angeles.

America.

My belly kerplunks with nerves. Today I have to make a masterplan on how to track down Gary Montgomery. Gary Montgomery the movie star with a girlfriend who is hotter and more accomplished than me in every conceivable way.

I push away the voice in my head that asks me what the fuck I think I am playing at and try to keep focused on Imogene telling me that I was full of shit and that my weird instinct about Gary is nothing more than an excuse to be alone forever. Which it is absolutely, definitely, categorically not. Nope. She asked me to prove it and I will.

'I am not full of shit!' I mumble to myself, blindly feeling about the bedside table for my glasses before remembering that they're still in my washbag on the other side of the space. I grab my phone and hold it right up to my face: 10.20 a.m. Kennedy said everyone left the house before nine, so I am here alone, which is good considering Kennedy's warning about her surly brother.

I sit up in the bed, blow the air out through my cheeks

and furiously fan myself with my hands, because this room is super warm in spite of the air-con box currently whirring on the wall. I look down at my body and realise that I must have chucked off my pyjamas at some point in the night because I'm now wearing nothing but a pair of bed knickers, which are, for the uninitiated, knickers so big and raggedy and overwashed that they are only good for when you're in bed alone (which, for me, is always) or are enduring a particularly heavy flow.

With a small roll and stretch of my stiff shoulders, I cross the room and grab my glasses out of my washbag, sliding them on to my face. Aha, lovely vision restored. I spin around back towards the bed, only to realise that, in my jet-lagged state last night, I completely forgot to close the blinds. To my absolute surprise and horror, the massive floor-to-ceiling windows that I so admired last night open onto a view of magnificent sandy white beach filled with people, many of whom are definitely staring at me as I stand there, gawping, mouth open, boobs akimbo. A beautiful and glowing Swedish-looking couple are pointing at me through the window, their two glowing identikit teenage children are holding up phones to capture this less than stellar moment.

I frantically place my hands across my bosom, which is a futile gesture because I am a size 36 DD and it would take many more hands to give me even a centimetre of privacy. I grab my pyjama top off the floor and pull it over my head, face flaming with embarrassment.

'Shoo! Shoo!' I shout to the Swedish-looking family, who are now waving at me and beckoning at me to join them out on the beach. What the hell? The mum is pointing at my knickers and pulling a sad face.

'They are bed knickers!' I explain through the glass. 'They are not for public consumption!' And then I ask myself why I am even trying to explain myself to these perv strangers through a window. 'Go away!' I say, gathering up my courage to raise my voice. 'This is a private abode. I clearly did not know that the window overlooked a bloody public beach. Shoo now!'

With a flaming face, I speedily roll down the blinds. I can see the shadows of the Swedish family still out there, unmoving. That is the creepiest bunch of blondes I've ever seen in my life and that's coming from someone who has watched every season of *The Real Housewives of Beverly Hills*.

I shudder and head through to the kitchen to find coffee, marvelling again at how gorgeous and perfectly considered this place is. As I open the door to the kitchen, Winklepuff immediately dives out and climbs onto my leg once more.

'Ham!' I say sharply, which works immediately, the dog plopping off my leg and sitting obediently before me, his tongue slightly poking out.

I open the fridge to see if there is, on the slimmest possible likelihood, actually any ham. But, of course, there isn't. I find a Tupperware box full of tofu and pull out a cubed piece, waving it at Winklepuff hopefully. I swear he curls his top lift in disgust.

'I hear you,' I say, taking a sniff and wrinkling my own nose. 'If you remain chilled, we'll go out later and find you some of the good stuff. There must be a deli nearby.'

Winklepuff's ears flicker upwards at the word 'deli', which again is very odd. Then he scratches at the door to the little yard at the back of the house. I let him out and see if there's anything available for breakfast. I search the fridge, rummaging through more tofu, some weird dried mushrooms and a gigantic bottle of something called Kombucha. Hmmm. I'll just grab something later on when I walk Winklepuff. I feel pretty sick with nerves anyway.

I eventually manage to find some coffee at the back of a cupboard filled with every herby, fruity or superfood tea that has ever been invented. Then I grab my notebook out of my room/bed area and sit down at the reclaimed wooden kitchen table. Time to figure out what the hell I'm supposed to do next.

I write *Nora Loves Gary* at the top of the page with a heart instead of the 'o' in the word 'loves'. And then I scrawl a million hearts around the edges of the page. I never doodled hearts in school because I never really had big crushes on guys, seeing as I empirically knew that none of them were my soulmate, and the one time I did get a crush he ended up going out with Imogene anyway.

I underline *Nora Loves Gary* three times. Then I think hard. And then I think some more. First things first, I have to actually meet him. If my instincts are right and he is my soulmate, then surely he will have the same reaction to me as I had to him?

I catch sight of myself in the full-length mirror resting on the wall opposite. My face is pillow-crumpled and red, my pyjama top a little tight on these unwieldy boobs, my bed knickers are, well, bed knickers. Hmmm. Maybe he won't have *quite* the same reaction.

Opening my phone, I pull up Tori Gould's latest Instagram post. It's a picture of her on a beach doing a perfect yoga handstand in a bikini, every last bit of her exactly the way it ought to be. I feel a mixture of envy and guilt at the fact that I'm basically creeping on an innocent woman's boyfriend. I emphatically don't believe in going after men who are already involved. But... what if Tori is missing out on finding *her* true soulmate because she's wasting time with mine? If I think about it like that, then maybe I'm actually doing Tori a favour. Right? And, like I said, if he isn't responsive to me then I will respect that and go back home and, ugh, go on a date with Roger Pepper like I promised Imogene I would.

Okay. The first step is to find out what his schedule is. And who else would know that but his manager?

I open up Google and search for Gary Montgomery's manager's contact address. It's a management company based in West Hollywood and has a public telephone number. Simple!

I press the number and clear my throat. I'm going to tell Gary Montgomery's manager that I am an old friend of his and that I'm looking to get back in touch.

The phone rings twice before it's picked up by a youngish, bored-sounding guy.

'H-hello,' I say brightly, gathering up all of my courage and trying very hard not to stutter and mumble. 'M-may I speak to Aileen Gould, please?'

'Who is calling?'

'Nora Tucker.'

'One moment please.'

Yes! Wow. They're putting me right through. I must actually hold some natural gravitas in my tone. This is going to be easier than I thought.

I hear a few clicks and then a scratchy but purposeful voice.

'Aileen here, how can I help you?'

'Oh h-hi!' I say cheerily. 'I'm looking to get in touch with Gary Montgomery. I'm an old college friend and I was just wondering if—'

'Let me guess. You were *just wondering* if I could tell you his schedule? His phone number? His address so you can turn up at his home unannounced to surprise him?'

'Um, well, yes! Thank you. That would be amazing. Thank you so much, Ms Gould.'

I hear a muffling over the phone as Aileen hisses to someone else, 'It's another fucking creepy girl trying to get to Gary. Can you please do a better job of screening, Andre? Christ!'

'I'm not some creepy girl!' I gasp with unjustifiable indignation. 'I am Gary's old college friend!'

'Oh, are you really? So what college was that then?'

'The University of Texas at Austin,' I say, thankful for my extensive googling of Gary.

'What year?'

'The 2011 graduating class,' I respond confidently. I remember seeing that Gary had always been in plays in college. 'I was actually in his drama group,' I add. 'Although, of course, I saw him around campus when he wasn't in his classes studying for a m-major in English Literature.'

'Oh!' Aileen says, her tone of voice changing. 'You clearly do know him. Sorry for being suspicious. Since *Justice of The Peace* was released we've had a lot of calls from people pretending to know Gary. Were you in *Romeo and Juliet* with him? I would have liked to have seen that. I imagine he made a wonderful Romeo.'

'Yes! He was an amazing Romeo. Perfect!'

'Ah, well that's very interesting of you to say because Gary Montgomery was never in *Romeo and Juliet*. He was in *Macbeth*. If you try to get in touch again, I will call the police.'

The call is ended from the other side. I stare at the phone screen, my mouth open in shock.

The police? My god, that woman was so aggressive. I can't help but feel pleased that Gary is clearly being protected, but still... Argh! Frustrating to the max.

I let the phone drop onto my lap and sigh.

Thinking that this might be tricky was a massive understatement.

CHAPTER FIFTEEN

Nora

I eventually get dressed, only to discover that the clothes I hastily packed from my summer holiday a few years ago no longer fit.

At all.

I mean, I knew I had gained a little extra chunk on my trunk, but not enough to be bursting out of these threads as much as this. Maaaan. I always buy clothes that are too big for me, I like being comfortable and hidden. But all those cheese toasties must have had an expanding effect. I don't mind being fatter, I think the softness suits me, but it's not like I have enough money to get new, roomier stuff and I can hardly ask Imogene for more cash when she's already given me so much.

I stand in front of the full-length bathroom mirror examining the fourth item I've tried on – a French-style blue striped summer dress with buttons all the way down the front. They're so tightly buttoned around the boobs that they've flattened and pushed up my breasts so much that my cleavage is almost touching my chin. I look like a provincial buxom wench. And this dress is not even the tightest of the clothes I've brought. The two pairs of shorts are just shy of full cameltoe, my swimming costume can now only be worn with an extreme wax job and the previously baggy vests roll up to expose my pale belly more than is necessarily decent.

Replacing my glasses with contact lenses, I peek out of the bathroom window to catch a view of the gorgeous expanse of beach outside. I take in the people swimming and running and hanging out in such a carefree way. They're all showing plenty of skin, in tiny dresses and butt-flossing bikinis. It seems no one has baggy clothes here. These clothes will be fine. They're not perfect, but it's not that anyone will really notice me anyway. My invisibility superpower will be in even greater effect in a place surrounded by such glamorous, beautiful people.

Once I've brushed my hair and pulled it into two plaits at the sides of my head, I feed Winklepuff his plant-based, gluten-free kibble and make myself another cup of tea. All the while, I think hard about what my next move should be. I just need to get details of Gary's location. I could creep on Tori's Instagram and zoom in on the backgrounds of her pictures and try to figure out where she is. Then I could race there and hope she turns up again and then leads me towards Gary Montgomery.

That's a stupid idea.

And then, like it is sent via Cupid himself, a really brilliant idea just darts into my head. All I need to do is phone Aileen Gould again. But this time, instead of pretending to be an old college friend, I need to pretend to be someone actually in the movie industry. Someone who is interested in Gary for a part. A big-budget part that any manager worth their salt would hate for him to miss out on.

Hmmm. I'll definitely have to do an American accent so I sound authentic. I practise in front of Winklepuff. 'How you doin'? Get me a burger! He's such a jock, right? Greg. Creg. You wanna piece of me? Like, totally, as *if*.'

Winklepuff blinks at me and curls his lip slightly, which I take as a positive sign considering that most of the morning so far he's been trying to a) mount my leg again and b) destroy my favourite comfy flip-flops.

I take a deep breath and practise a few more American words and phrases. 'Let's go to the drive-in moooovie. Tomayto. Tomaaaaaaaayto. Why doncha take a look in the miiiirrrror. Mirrrrrrrorrr. Okay, I think I'm ready.'

I pick up my phone and head out onto the porch, settling myself down onto the wooden bench, Winklepuff following me and perching at my feet, anticipating the ham I keep promising him. I dial the number once more. As it's ringing, I mentally push myself into the body of someone much more aggressive and successful. Someone who doesn't mumble and stutter. I close my eyes and channel Imogene, along with a touch of Gordon Ramsey if he was American.

'Hello, Gould Management, how may I assist you today?'

'Get me Aileen Gould, right a-fuckin-way,' I spit out in my best, confident, get-shit-done, Hollywood player American accent.

'Excuse me?' comes the guy's voice.

'Aileen Gould?' I try. 'Listen up, why doncha?'

He clears his throat. 'Okaaaay. Who, may I ask, is speaking?

Shit. I can't give my real name again. Then, because I've been reading the new book and it's the only option that pops into my head, I give the name of the author of the *Harcourt Royals* books instead of my own. 'CJ West,' I blurt. 'My name is CJ West, okay?'

Argh. What if this guy has heard of Harcourt Royals? No, no. It's a very niche book. The chances of him having heard of it are very slim.

'One moment.'

A five-second silence.

And then, 'Aileen Gould speaking.'

Yes!

'How you doin'?' I say, as if I don't give a single shit how she is. 'My name is CJ West and I'm interested in Gary Montgomery for a real big project.'

'You and everyone else in Hollywood,' Aileen snipes.

God, this woman is mean. I need to impress her.

'Yeah, I'm the assistant to Martin Scorsese,' is what pops out. Shit. He's the first director I could think of. Scorsese's a pretty big play, but it's too late to backtrack, so I march on. 'Um… yeah. He has asked me to personally reach out and organise a meeting so that ol' Marty may discuss this p-project.'

Aileen is quiet for a moment and then she sighs. 'I know it's you again.'

'What? Who am I? I am Marty Scorsese's assistant.'

'Your American accent is terrible.'

'What are you talkin' abooout? As if! Forget about it!' I am sinking. I am sinking so fast.

'What's your real name?' Aileen says. 'Andre didn't write it down and I'd prefer to have it for the police, WHEN I CALL THEM ABOUT YOU.'

'I'm CJ West!' I say in panic. 'I gotta big-budget movie to shoot! Hey!'

The phone clanks down on the other end and I groan with frustration.

'What am I going to do now?' I ask Winklepuff sadly. 'I thought my American accent was great. Indistinguishable!'

'I guess it was, for a 1940's New York gangster,' comes a deep, bored-sounding voice from the front doorway.

I look behind me to see a stocky man leaning against the door frame. His blonde hair is messy, his face is kind of drawn and his eyes are bloodshot. He's watching me in a mixture of badly concealed amusement and aversion. This must be Brandon. He looks as grumpy as Kennedy implied he would.

'I'm Brandon,' he confirms. 'I came in through the side door and heard you out here. What the hell was that crazy phone call about?'

Oh god.

'You... um, y-you heard the whole thing?'

'Oh, I heard every word,' he says, his tongue poking out slightly between his lips.

Shit.

Brandon strides over towards me and sits on the other end of the bench, his thick thighs taking up so much of the room that I have to scooch further down.

I cough. 'It's nice to meet you,' I say in my most normal, not a psychopath voice. 'I wasn't expecting to see you. Kennedy said you w-wouldn't finish work until late.'

'I'm in set design, so the hours can be odd. Is it a problem that I'm here? At my own house?' His eyes flick down at my escaping breasts, the corner of his mouth upturning slightly.

I lift my chin, trying my hardest not to just run over to the beach and bury myself in the sand, never to emerge. 'No, of course not. I-I never said that...' I stutter. 'I, um, really appreciate you letting me stay here.'

'I didn't get much of a say in the matter.' Jeez. He is *prickly*.

He stares at me, his bloodshot blue eyes are stony and severe. I do not like him.

After a moment of excruciatingly awkward nothingness, Brandon sighs and stands up from the bench. '*Great* chat. Okay, well, I'm only back to grab my tennis racket and my laptop. I'll be out of your hair soon, stranger.'

'I didn't... and I'm not a stranger. I'm, um, Nora Tucker. I'm q-quite nice and reasonably normal! Ha ha.'

'I'm sure.' He pauses for a second. 'And CJ West is, what, your secret alias?'

Of course. He heard me give a fake name on the phone. I cough. 'It's... erm... Yes. It's, well, it's complicated.'

His mouth twitches and he lightly kicks his foot against the porch fence. 'Is "it" something to do with the "soulmate" you're here to meet? The one you've never actually met in real life?'

'Kennedy told you about why I'm here?' I ask, my face flushing red before I remember that Kennedy does not know that the Gary who is the object of my mission is America's hottest movie star, Gary Montgomery. She thinks he is just some random non-famous Gary. Which means that all she will have told her apparently dickish brother is that I'm here to connect with a normal man who I have normal feelings for, which is perfectly reasonable and normal behaviour.

'Of course she told me,' Brandon says. 'She may be blasé about who she lets stay in our house because she's sweet and open-hearted, but I prefer to gather a little more intel.'

'Oh.' I nod over and over while Brandon stares at me with narrowed eyes as if trying to force me into spilling some dark secret, some reason why his sister shouldn't trust me.

'I have no secrets!' I blurt out eventually, immediately covering my mouth with my hands.

Brandon snorts and pushes his blonde hair back from his face. 'Everybody has secrets.' Then his blue eyes glint and he mumbles, almost to himself, 'Especially the people you least expect.'

Am I supposed to know what he's talking about?

'Yes. Right.' I say as if I do.

Winklepuff interrupts this odd moment by eagerly scrambling up Brandon's legs. Brandon picks him up and scrunches up his face while Winklepuff frantically licks it. He ruffles the dog's head and sets him back down onto the porch floor before striding back into the house, only to return less than a minute later with a tennis racquet-shaped case, a gym bag and a laptop.

'Take it from me,' he says, his expression cold. 'You're kidding yourself if you think soulmates are anything more than a construct developed by commercial gift companies preying on googly-eyed mooning idiots.'

My mouth opens and closes angrily as I try to form a response to this horrible and blatantly untrue statement. I'm not a googly-eyed mooning idiot. Mum and Dad were not googly-eyed mooning idiots. The surge of rage in my chest pushes me to stand up for myself. What a cynical, rude, grumpy person this guy is. The polar opposite of his lovely sister.

'What is *wrong* with you?' I ask, shooting up from the bench. 'Haven't you got a heart?'

He shrugs and half laughs at me. 'I suppose not, no.'

And with that, he turns on his heel, jumps off the porch steps and heads down the beach.

What the *hell* was that? I blow the air out from my nose and notice that my heart is beating faster than it has any right to. Ugh. What a prick. People aren't rude to me very often. They mostly don't seem to notice me, which is exactly as I like it. To have someone be directly rude to me as an adult woman is very disconcerting. And then, as if to top everything off, Winklepuff crouches right by my foot and pushes out a tiny plant-based turd.

This trip is not going well. At all.

CHAPTER SIXTEEN

Gary

Hey.

Being famous is weird, man. I mean, I always suspected it would be, everyone knowing your face and your business and being suddenly interested in you. I hoped that my acting would be good enough to make a mark, to have my name known, but I didn't expect it to happen so fucking fast. Neither did anyone else, to be honest. I remember Aileen telling me when I first signed with her that this business was a long game and that most people making a living being an actor have over thirty IMDB credits to their name. I had two at the time.

Speaking of Aileen and fame being completely weird, she just called me and opened up the conversation with the words 'You better be careful.' Which is a real ominous thing to say at any point in a conversation, not least the very beginning of one.

'Uh, what?' I'd replied, wondering if she had accidentally dialled my number instead of someone she had some altercation with, which wouldn't be the first time.

But no. She meant me.

'I've had a whole bunch of women calling recently, trying to get in touch with you, saying they knew you at school, college, old jobs, that kind of hokey shit.'

'Who? Did you give them my number?' I asked. I was never Mr Popular Jock at college, or school for that matter, but there are a few friends I'd be up for reconnecting with. People who knew me before this strange success are in short supply, and hanging out with Seth has made me realise that I could definitely do with a few more of them.

'Creepers, stalkers, weirdos, that's who. This can happen when charismatic, talented men get famous,' Aileen said knowingly.

'How do you know they're not for real?' I'd asked.

Aileen made an exasperated noise. 'Because I tested them!'

'Tested them?'

'Asked them real questions and trick questions. Rooted them out like sneaky little rats. One of the broads calling was British! She put on some hokey Yank accent, and – get this – she said she was Martin Scorsese's assistant. The brass balls of these chicks.'

'Are you absolutely positively sure she *wasn't* for real? Because you know how I feel about Martin Scorsese.'

'Trust me. You're a great artist, darling, but Martin Scorsese isn't casting for anything right now.'

'Oh,' I'd said, feeling vaguely disappointed.

'Yes, *Oh*. So be careful. That's all I'm saying. I don't want anything bad to happen to you.'

'Because I make you so much money?' I'd joked.

'Because I love you, even if you are a pain in my ass. And Tori is finally fuckin' happy because of you, miracle of miracles. And these fangirls, honey, they can be real bunny boilers. I've heard all kinds of horror stories, you don't even know. You don't *wanna* know.'

'Good job I don't have a bunny.'

'You have a dog.'

I thought of Janet. And how she's so goofy and trusting. If any nefarious fan or stranger with a vendetta wanted to coax her away, they wouldn't have to try too hard beyond holding a brightly colored ball within a five-meter radius. So, yeah, at that point I assured Aileen that I would keep an eye out for any creepers, stalkers and weirdos. I have no idea how on earth I'm supposed to actually do that; people don't exactly introduce themselves as such, do they? I'm not that worried, to be honest. Fans are part of the business and I signed up for this, didn't I? And Ira told me that I needed to work on my inclination to worry too much about bad things happening in the future. He says that because my mom died giving birth to me, I've grown up constantly expecting disaster to return to my life and that I need to learn how to live in the present. Hmmm I wonder how am I supposed to live in the present if I'm constantly on the lookout for creepers, stalkers and weirdos? I'll ask Ira at our next session, like it's a totally common thing to ask.

I'm about to take Janet for a walk and so here are my three amazing things before I go.

1. Aileen might be nuts, but she and Tori believed in me when no one else did and on the eve of shooting my next project I feel real grateful for that.
2. Seth and Olive are having a ball in LA. We're mostly just kicking back with beers and snacks (Seth insists on meatball pizzas). Olive's having meetings with managers who are loving her script and I'm still trying to get Aileen to read it so she can see how perfect I would be for the part of Joseph. I don't care if it's not the lead part. The script is so damn funny. Having Seth

and Olive stay is great. I wish they lived here all the time, but they seem pretty wedded to New York. Besides, I'm not sure Tori is as enamored with them as I am. She told me last night that she thought they were a little 'much' because they're forever telling jokes and trying to get each other to laugh. I reassured her that they would be returning to Manhattan in a couple weeks and then everything would be back to normal.

3. Yesterday I managed to stand up on my surfboard for ten whole seconds without falling into the ocean. It wouldn't have been so embarrassing if some odd blonde Swedish-looking family were staring and pointing as I eventually toppled into the water. Anyway, I am proud of those ten seconds and I'm going back out again later for another lesson. I already can't wait. I feel like I can breathe out there.

CHAPTER SEVENTEEN

Nora

Text from Imogene: *God, you need to reply to my message, Nora! What time is it there even? I need to know you are alive and safely arrived on American soil. Also I have emailed you a list of therapists and some grief support groups you can contact when you return. I know I said that if Gary Montgomery is really your soulmate you don't have to do anything I say ever again, but we both know that Gary Montgomery is NOT your soulmate and that you're there to see that for yourself and snap yourself out of this. So it seems prudent to start preparing options for how we're going to get you into a better place once you return home. Text me back! Gotta go. Dan is peeved because the light from my phone screen is keeping him awake. Im xx*

After Brandon leaves, I respond to a glut of messages from Imogene. Her insistence that I am entirely wrong about everything just makes me more determined to create a better, more concerted plan for meeting Gary. So I spend the rest of the morning researching and googling and making spider-graph suggestions of where I might encounter him. I use Kennedy's printer to print out paparazzi photos from restaurants he seems to frequent. I print out a couple of maps and the address of Gould Management, as well as a few screenshots of any of Tori's Instagram posts that feature Gary. I also find a forum full of celebrity sightings and write down all of the places that Gary has been spotted. When I'm done, I fold up all the papers and neatly tuck them in between the pages of my notebook.

In the afternoon, I take Winklepuff for a walk and feel ever more suspicious of his supposed vegan lifestyle when he drags me towards a local deli, sitting down neatly in front of the door as if he has been there before. I head in and get him some good ham and myself a cheese toastie, although it's nowhere near as good as the ones I make myself; the cheese is all plasticky and the bread is full of seeds. Yeuch.

Outside the deli, Winklepuff sits obediently, his neck arching, seemingly jonesing for some meat.

'You know just what this is, don't you?' I say, taking out a small piece of pork from the waxed paper. 'It's ham.'

At the word ham, he rolls onto his hind legs and starts to beg.

'Very curious,' I say with narrowed eyes, feeding him pieces, which he gobbles up as if it is the elixir of the heavens, licking his chops afterwards.

I walk a now very satisfied dog through the bustling beachside street, stopping every so often to pour some bottled water into a little fold-out bowl Kennedy gave to me. The vitamin D hitting my skin, along with the smell of salty sea and sweet candy floss from a nearby truck, brightens my mood and starts to distract me from the shit-show that was this morning.

It's like a whole other world here. Everyone is tanned and smiling and active and most of them look so joyful and colourful. It's a pretty stark contrast to the drizzly greyness and drudgery of Brigglesford. As expected, no one even glances at me, which makes me feel much better about the world's tightest dress and its awe-inspiring effect on my boobs. I am, frankly, imperceptible compared to the people I've seen knocking about so far, including a woman wearing nothing but gold body paint on her top half and a guy in his twenties casually riding a unicycle and wearing a bowler hat.

I've been meandering about for an hour or so when my face and arms start to tingle. It occurs to me that I'm a complete idiot who did not put a high enough factor of sun cream onto the very, very pale English skin basking in this relentless Californian sun. I glance down at my arms to see that they are super pink. Eek. I pull out my phone and take a quick look in the camera screen. My face and nose are cherry red. Damn. I need to get indoors as soon as possible.

I hurry back with Winklepuff, who is obeying every order I give him now that I am officially his meat dealer. I quickly stop at a cute little cart selling flowers and plants and buy a small bunch of daisies for Kennedy. Then I dart into a grocery shop and grab a bottle of white wine for when we hang out later. Of course I have no plans to tell her about who Gary *really* is, but a few glasses of wine will help me to feel better about deceiving someone who has shown me nothing but kindness.

As I let myself into Kennedy's house, sweaty and knackered, I realise pretty swiftly that I needn't worry about revealing my real reasons for being here. Oh no. Kennedy is standing in the middle of the living room, and laying in a scattered circle on the floor around her are the Gary Montgomery research print-outs.

Kennedy is holding up my notebook, open at the page where I have written *Nora Loves Gary* along with approximately two hundred and fifty-three hearts of various sizes.

'I think we need to talk,' she says, waving the note-book in her hands, her eyes wide and looking more than a little frightened.

Shit. If my face wasn't already mega red from sunburn, it would be blushing furiously by now. My body stiffens with mortification.

Kennedy is just staring at me, her mouth slightly agape. She takes a tiny step backwards, away from me. She clearly thinks I am creepy and dangerous.

Wait… Why was she going through my private stuff? Is… is *she* creepy and dangerous? I take a step backwards too and narrow my eyes.

Kennedy must read my mind because she pinkens and gestures towards my bedroom area, the heavy curtain now flung open. 'I only went in there to lay out some welcome to LA crystals for you!'

I glance at the bed and there, laid out in the shape of a heart, is an array of small, differently coloured rocks.

'I moved your notebook to make room for the crystal arrangement and I must have held it upside down because all of… *this*… fell out…'

I open my mouth to say something, anything, but nothing comes. I have no reasoning that sounds anything less than seriously wacko.

This looks bad. This looks really really bad.

Kennedy gently picks up my printouts and places them on the coffee table in neat rows. Photos of Gary, printed out from the internet, his university graduation info, his IMDB page, articles, maps and screenshots of Tori's social media. Shit. I *absolutely* look like I'm preparing to murder Gary Montgomery. Like I'm plan-ning to put all these pics and papers and printouts up on a corkboard with some connecting coloured string and words like 'die!' and 'I will soon have my revenge!' scrawled all over it in blood-red lipstick.

Kennedy clears her throat. 'I can't believe I'm asking

this, but… is this… is this guy, this soulmate you're here for… is it, um, is it Gary Montgomery, as in *the* Gary Montgomery? Like, the star of the biggest movie in the world right now? The guy who looks like a sexier, more dangerous version of Adam Driver? Wow. How on earth did you meet him online? Wait, did you even meet him online? Why do you have all these unsettling printouts? I have so many questions! Are you here for more nefarious reasons than you led me to believe? And, wait, why is your face so red? I'm so confused. Who *are* you? Are you even the Nora I know from the *Harcourt Royals* forums? My god, are you even a Crown Kisser?'

I look down at my flip-flopped feet, which are still puffy from the flight. Winklepuff is gazing up at me with devotion, his belly full of illicit ham.

There's no backing out of the truth. If I have any chance of not getting kicked out of this house or, worse, ruining my budding friendship with Kennedy forever, I need to come clean about the real reason I'm here.

I take a big breath and muster up every ounce of courage I have.

'I *am* Nora Tucker, a true Crown Kisser, a genuine *Harcourt Royals* s-superfan, Bastian-Esme shipper and I… well, yes I, erm, think my soulmate might be Gary Montgomery. The movie star. He, um, he actually doesn't know I'm here. And the reason he doesn't know that is… because we've n-never met. Not online, not in real life. He's never even heard my name. I saw him in a f-film at the cinema a few days ago—'

'*Justice of The Peace*?'

'Yes, *Justice of The Peace*. And when I saw his face, I just felt the strongest sensation go through my whole body. Like he was the one single person on earth that I was supposed to b-be with.'

'Ho-lee shit,' Kennedy breathes. 'I don't mean to be rude, but you do know that pretty much everyone who has seen *Justice of The Peace* has a huge crush on Gary Montgomery? I mean, he's no Joseph Gordon-Levitt, but everyone has a thing for him right now.'

'I don't think it's just a crush!' I protest with a sigh, stepping towards Kennedy and feeling relief when she doesn't take another fearful step back.

As clearly as I can, I explain to her about how I've always believed in soulmates. How my mum and dad were soulmates, how they were so truly, deeply happy because of each other, how they were joyful pretty much every day because they got to hang out together. I tell her that I think my life has a chance to be magical if I could have what Mum and Dad had. I tell her that Imogene thinks that my coming here and getting rejected by Gary is the only way to end this delusion. How she thinks that me feeling a film actor might be my one true love is just an excuse for me to never give anyone else a try, to exist in a state of grief and depression forever and ever until I die surrounded by romance novels and DVDs, literal comfort blankets and the crumbs of too many bags of crisps.

When I've finished my impassioned explanation, Kennedy plonks down on the sofa with a gentle thud. 'Wow. Your sister sounds like a lot.'

'She's great,' I say, also sighing and plopping down beside her. 'But she has some pretty strong opinions and she truly thinks I'm delusional. But I promise you, Kennedy, I'm not some crazy creep. Yes, I really do think that I'm supposed to meet Gary. And I know that the theoretic likelihood is that Imogene is right and that this is me maybe having some sort of mental break. And I know that it seems like a bit... no, a *lot* of a stretch that someone like me,' I gesture at my too tight clothes and bright red sweaty face and swollen legs and general shy, ordinary-girl package, 'is supposed to be with someone like him.' I wave a hand towards one of the myriad photos lined up on the coffee table, where Gary is smiling confidently into the camera, his dark, clever eyes flashing sharply, his smile exuding charisma and warmth. 'I'm fully aware of that. But I have to try, you know? If I'm right about how I feel, then I can't give up on meeting him. And if I meet him and he doesn't feel a spark with me, then I will respectfully leave him alone for ever. But I have to see…' I slowly exhale, my mouth in an O shape. That's got to be the most words I've said to anyone who isn't Imogene in over a year. It's pretty overwhelming.

Kennedy nods and bites her lip. 'In *Harcourt Royals*, Bastian never gave up on Esme,' she says quietly. 'Even though everyone in his life told him that a princess would never even look at a poor but super-hot stripper-slash-marine-biology student like him.'

'Hmmm, maybe I've read too many of those damn books,' I giggle. 'They're giving me notions.'

'No such thing as too many *Harcourt Royals*,' she grins. 'True.'

Kennedy peers at me, perfectly shaped blonde eyebrows furrowed. 'So… what about Gary Montgomery's girlfriend?'

I groan, my head flopping back against the sofa cushion. 'I know. I hate myself for even slightly eyeing up another woman's fella. But I just have this *feeling*. It's so strong, like nothing I've ever felt before. I can't ignore it. If I do, I might regret it forever and I, well, I already have enough issues to be getting on with. I have to do this, at least to know that I tried.'

'You brought wine?' Kennedy asks, pointing at the wine on the floor, where I abandoned it along with the daisies when I first came in.

'I did,' I say with a shrug. 'It's a white Rioja. The man at the shop said it was lovely. And the flowers are to say thank you for letting me stay here when y-you're so busy with work and preparing for your big anchor interview. I understand if you want me to leave now, though.'

Kennedy shakes her head quickly, turning towards me and grabbing both my hands. 'Are you kidding me? This whole mission is one of the craziest things I've ever encountered and I once saw Lady Gaga licking a storm drain on the Santa Monica Boulevard. There's no way you're leaving, girl. I'm hooked in now. You're totally batshit and, frankly, I'm fascinated, no offence.'

'None taken. It *is* bonkers.'

'You're really doing this?'

I give a tiny nod. 'Yes. I'm going to try. I'm pretty terrified, to be honest.'

Kennedy shakes her head at me and scrunches up her face. 'Hmmm. I think we should open that wine,' she muses before pointing at the selection of Gary-related print outs and notes on the coffee table. 'And we definitely need to get this shit into some kind of order.'

CHAPTER EIGHTEEN

Nora

Text from Imogene: *What is it like in Los Angeles today? Is it really hot? Is everyone absolutely stunning? I wonder if I should have come with you... I'm feeling like I kind of dumped you in it. I know I sent you off to do this out of frustration, but I'm wondering if I've been too hasty with your mental health. It's pissing it down here. Dan is grumbling because the guttering has overflowed and I didn't remind him it needed clearing last month. Oh, I saw Roger Pepper today in town. He really is lovely, you know. You could do a lot worse! Something to think about while you're away and HOPEFULLY getting to grips with reality. Ariana sends you a kiss, as do I. Oh and that pic you sent – the sunburn on your face is horrendous. You look like that time we went to that spin class in Sheffield and you sweated so much they surrounded your bike with towels. Ha ha. Lots of aftersun. And lots of make-up. Love, Im xx*

The hour of day is truly ungodly when Kennedy shakes me awake the next morning. We absolutely thrashed through that bottle of wine, as well as a bottle of shady-tasting 'organic' peach wine. I'm pretty sure that's what's responsible for the fact that my entire body is now protesting at having to do anything other than lie completely still. My brain feels like it's having a boxing match with my skull and my tongue is the tongue of a woman who really needs to go hard on the mouthwash as soon as possible.

'Wha timeziiiit?' I groan as I open my eyes to see a perfectly coiffed Kennedy standing over me, eyes sparkling. She's dressed in a stiff-looking blouse and sharp blue skirt suit, her long blonde hair tied neatly into a perfect chignon. She looks the absolute opposite of the floaty, relaxed version of her I've seen over the past couple of days. She pulls uncomfortably at her blouse collar before smiling a big toothy smile and I feel a long-missed sense of gladness that I have an actual real-life friend for the first time in God knows how long.

We ended up hanging out and nattering until one in the morning. I can't remember the last time I wasn't tucked up in bed with a hot chocolate and asleep by 10.30 p.m., hoping against hope that I would finally sleep the whole night through. I get a flashback to last night: me telling Kennedy about my life in Brigglesford. How I mostly do my job and watch romantic comedies, read my books and fantasise about the joy I will feel when I find my soulmate. I remember Kennedy drunkenly clasping my hands and shouting that I didn't need a man to find joy. I absolutely agreed with this notion, which she ignored, proceeding to vow that she, Kennedy Cooper, would help me to rediscover my *own* joy. Whatever that means.

'It's 6.10 a.m.,' Kennedy states as if this is a normal time.

'You look so different!'

She gestures to the outfit. 'I'm actually in the office

today – this is how I dress at work. I have my first round of screen tests, so I'm leaving early to do some more prep work, but that's not the reason I'm waking you up... I'm here because... I have some *great* news for you!'

I slowly sit up in the bed and wince as my head protests. What on earth could possibly be worth waking up at this time for?

'What is it?' I ask, covering my mouth to spare Kennedy from the morning tongue.

Kennedy perches on the side of the bed and hands me her phone. The screen shows a page with an address in Los Angeles. 'This is where Gary Montgomery will be shooting his new movie, *Nightcar.*'

I gasp, fully alert now. The pain in my head increases, but suddenly I don't care. 'How...? How do you know this?'

'I was thinking about this picture.' She points to the wall by the bed. I splutter and cough when I see it. Shit, I had forgotten that last night we had drunkenly Blu-tacked all my notes and printouts onto the wall because Kennedy said if I was going to do this, I should lean into it and do it properly. I get a fuzzy memory of us clinking our glasses of peach wine together and declaring the wall the 'Creepy As Fuck Soulmate Procurement Wall'. Which makes sense because it definitely IS disturbing. Really, really disturbing. I notice one particularly massive colour printout of Gary's face. My goodness, he is so extraordinary-looking.

'Which picture?'

Kennedy gets up from the bed and walks over to the Creepy As Fuck Soulmate Procurement Wall. She taps a printed screenshot of Tori Gould drinking an iced coffee in front of a small coffee cart. I remember this one because I felt envious of the caption:

'Accompanying my love G to Pre-production costume fittings. Any excuse to see him dressed up.... Or not dressed at all.'

Which I thought was a bit of a smug thing to say in all honesty.

'What about it?' I ask Kennedy.

'I recognise that coffee cart and that tall, funny-shaped building in the background,' she says. 'I once dated a set caterer called Andre the Avocado Guy who worked at this very studio. I completely recognise it and this is the address. Gary starts shooting today!'

'What? How do you know *that*?'

'I searched on Twitter. I typed in the name of the studio and a background actor had tagged them and said he was excited to start work on *Nightcar* tomorrow. Which is today.'

'Oh my god!' I gasp, eyes wide awake now. 'How on earth did you know to do that?'

'I'm a journalist,' Kennedy laughs, affecting a silly stance, hands on hips. 'I've been training my whole adult life for this shit.'

'You are brilliant.'

'Tell that to my bosses, would you? Okay, I gotta run. Help yourself to anything in my closet. Best way to get anywhere in this city is with taxi cab apps– I'll text you the address. And keep me updated on what happens. First days on a movie set are usually crazy – everyone's distracted and getting their bearings, so you have more chance of sneaking in. Just act like you belong! It's served me well my whole career.'

I blink, hardly able to believe what is being planned right now.

'The Santa Ana winds are pretty wild today...' Kennedy says, her hands clasped together against her chest, eyes twinkling. 'Which means that even the most unexpected things could happen.'

Oh my god.

Today.

I am going to find Gary Montgomery today.

* * *

Before I can even focus on what the hell my plan will be, I have to answer all the Virtual Assistants 4U emails I'm behind on, as well as organise a client's calendar for the next week, book flights for the CEO of a subscription box company and do some social media posts for a Scottish carpet shop. I do all of these things from bed because I am still in the midst of a peach wine hangover. The last thing I need right now is to lose my job; apart from recent evidence to the contrary, I consider myself to generally be a sensible and reliable person.

When I've sped through my tasks, I glance at the poster of Gary on the wall. Today I'm going to try my very best to see that face in real 3D vision. Real life, actual Gary Montgomery. Will sparks fly? Will the chemistry be so palpable that neither of us can resist it and we have to immediately make love? Will he laugh at me and tell me to get the fuck away from him, proving that Imogene is right about me? Will Tori see me and kick me really hard in the legs?

Argh, no, don't think about bad things, Nora. Think about the possibility of making love to Gary Montgomery again. That's better...

I lean back against the headboard and have a little daydream of Gary pulling me into his trailer and tearing off my clothes and us having frantic sex up against the trailer wall and when it's done, Gary says, 'Wow. That was... wow,' and I say, 'I know.' And then he says, 'I think I loved you before I met you,' and I say, 'I will love you forever, Gary Montgomery.' Or maybe I'll even call him Gar or Gazzo, depending on what the mood is. I am fully aware that this is a highly optimistic version of what might be about to happen, and the fact is that to even get to him will likely be a task and a half. But if I don't believe that something good might somehow, someday finally happen for me, then what the hell am I even doing here?

Climbing out of the bed, I head to the bathroom and, clipping up my mess of dark hair with a crocodile clip, rinse my face with extra-cold water. That trailer sex daydream got me all hot and bothered. I peer at my face. It is still redder than a bloody post-box. My nose is slightly peeling. Yep. I'm going to need all of the make-up.

While I'm brushing my teeth, I think about what I might get to talk to Gary about. I need to think this through so that I don't completely embarrass myself and blurt out that I think I love him, possibly scaring him off before he gets the chance to see that we might be perfect for each other. Safe topics. Books, music, cheese toasties because he mentioned liking those in that YouTube video…

I drop my toothbrush in the sink with a clatter as a really fantastic idea occurs to me. Aha! I will make him one of my amazing cheese toasties. That would be quirky and romantic and will definitely catch his attention without being too full-on. It sounds like something Zooey Deschanel or Kate Hudson would do in a romcom. It's cute! I would keep it super casual, though. See how it goes, get the lay of the land and if he seems receptive, which I think he might, I will mention that I just so happen to have the equipment to make him the most perfect toastie he has ever had. Is that weird? No. I mean, I would love it if someone tried to woo me that way. It's a cute idea. Right? Hmmm…

I think so…

I'm just going to do it.

I head into the kitchen and start wiping down the small George Foreman grill I find in a cupboard. I will pack this up, take some proper plates and cutlery and then on the way to the lot I'll buy my sourdough and two types of cheese, plus some Maldon salt and freshly ground black pepper. I hope they sell English cheeses around here. I might have to find a speciality cheese shop. Do people even eat cheese in LA? I hope so, for their sake, because the alternative doesn't bear thinking about.

Winklepuff licks my ankle in encouragement. I'm touched. I refill his water bowl and after he has had his fill, I pick him up and we do a little dance around the kitchen. He yawns happily, giving me an unobstructed whiff of his terrible breath.

'Yikes, Winklepuff,' I say. 'Halitosis much?'

He responds by licking the side of my face, which, while disgusting, makes me laugh. Hmmm. Dogs might be cooler than I expected. Winklepuff is like a teddy bear, only alive and a secret meat fiend.

I start to twirl with Winklepuff clasped to my chest. 'Can you believe? The answer has always been love and cheeeeese,' I sing to him as we dance. 'Love and cheeeeese for Nora, please. Finally found just what I neeeed. Love. And. Cheeeeese. No cheeeese for yoooooou, cos' your breath smells like poooo…'

'You're genuinely odd, aren't you?'

I jump at the voice coming from behind me, pulling Winklepuff tighter to my chest. I turn around to find Brandon standing there, a tote bag that says 'What The Hel – Vetica?' slung over his shoulder. Shit. I thought he'd left already? Kennedy told me he leaves the house every morning at seven thirty. I yank down the old *Friday Night Lights* T-shirt I'm wearing as a nightie, glancing downwards to make sure that it is, in fact, covering my vulva. It is, but only just. Which means that Brandon almost certainly got a peek at my bum while I was dancing with Winklepuff. Note to self, get fully dressed before leaving my bedroom area. At the very least, remember to wear bed knickers.

'You s-scared me,' I say self-consciously, continuing to

pull my T-shirt down as far as it can go with the hand not clutching Winklepuff.

To his credit, Brandon's eyes remain on my face. 'Hmmm,' he says. 'Some people act oddly in front of other people for show, for attention. Especially in LA, where everyone's just desperate to be noticed. But you're the real deal. A genuine, bona fide oddity. What was that song you were singing to my dog?' He reaches out and takes Winklepuff from me, as if I've done something wrong.

'What song?' I say nonchalantly. 'I wasn't singing.'

He bites his bottom lip. 'I believe I heard the phrase *love and cheese?*'

This guy is the worst. 'Oh. Nothing,' I say quietly. 'I was just, erm, humming. I'm looking forward to the day and sometimes I, you know, tra la la when I'm looking forward to something.'

'Tra la la? Right. So what exactly are you looking forward to?' he asks, seemingly unaware that this is a deeply uncomfortable moment and that the only reason I haven't run away is because I'm scared to expose my nether regions any more than I possibly already have done.

I shrug. 'Uh, because it's sunny and…'

'It's always sunny here,' he scoffs.

Gah. Why is he so rude? Just because he's been dumped, it doesn't mean he has to make everyone he encounters feel bad too. I lift my chin and look him in the eye. 'I-I'm hoping to meet my soulmate today, if you must know. I'm looking forward to that. Okay?'

Brandon smirks a little and looks me up and down. 'You really think Gary Montgomery is gonna leave his smoking-hot, professionally successful girlfriend for… *you?*'

Shit. Kennedy must have told him that the man I came here for is Gary Montgomery. When did she even do that? It's only 8 a.m.! Why does everyone get up so early in this city? Argh. I mean I know he's her brother and they're super close but still… My cheeks burn with humiliation.

I shake my head firmly. 'I… I don't think that Tori Gould is right for him. It's just a very strong feeling I have. If I'm wrong, then fine. I'll be on m-my way.'

Brandon gently plops Winklepuff onto the floor and crosses his arms. 'You don't even know her. *Or him.*'

I nod. He has a point, of course. 'Well, technically you're right. But that's exactly why I'm here in Los Angeles. I mean, he has every right to m-meet me and decide that there is zero connection there, right? That's all I'm doing. Just finding out if this hunch is more than just a hunch.'

He laughs at me. But not in a friendly way. In a mean, judgy way that really makes my chest burn.

'Stop laughing at me,' I say, two hands glued to the T-shirt's hem.

He doesn't stop. He just laughs more.

'Look,' I say, when I can no longer bear this entire situation, 'just because your girlfriend dumped you, and, frankly, I can't blame her, doesn't mean that you have to spread your cynicism and misery around to everyone else. So please leave me alone.'

Brandon blinks and then frowns slightly. I blink too. I can't quite believe I said that. I didn't even mumble or stutter too. Shit, Kennedy told me not to mention Brandon's recent dumping in his presence. She said it was a total sore spot. Where did the balls to say that even come from? It actually feels quite empowering. I remember that feeling. I hold his gaze. I don't feel like backing down. He is horrible.

Brandon's eyes harden. He stops laughing and clears his throat. 'Please get dressed properly while you're staying here.' His eyes scan my body, his lips curling slightly as they rest on my chunky thighs and rounded belly.

'Nobody needs to see that in the morning, or any time for that matter.'

I storm past him and into my area, not even caring if he can see my fat bottom as it wobbles away.

He can kiss it for all I care.

* * *

When I hear Brandon leave via the slam of the back door, I exhale angrily and pummel my pillow in a bid to get some of this furious energy out of my system. I've not felt this sort of rage in a very very very long time. Not even when I think about how terrible the *Gossip Girl* finale was.

I head to the bathroom for a long cool shower, spending extra time shaving my prickly legs in case my wildest most-out-there dream does come true and Gary is moved to take me right there in his trailer.

Wrapped in a fluffy navy towel, I head into Kennedy's room and rummage through her closet to find something that might be suitable for the important task ahead. Although Kennedy suggested I could wear her clothes, the truth is that she is at least three sizes smaller than I am. The pickings are slim, even if I'm not. I do find a pretty green and peacock blue paisley maxi dress with an elasticated bandeau top half and a roomy flowing skirt that comes down to the ankles. I pull it over my head, and while it's a little snug across my boobs, it's respectable enough. I look in the mirror. The colour brings out the green flecks in my hazel eyes and enhances my best feature – my abundance of dark wavy hair.

I pad back into my bedroom area and start applying make-up. My mostly indoors Brigglesford life doesn't ever call for make-up and so I'm a little out of practice. I try to think back to what I did when I was out performing gigs every night. I was a dab hand back then, easily managing to get a full stage make-up look done in about ten minutes. I push the image of me all dolled up and singing on a stage, laughing and joking with the other musos, firmly out of my mind because it gives me an odd little ache in my chest.

Taking a deep breath, I start with foundation, hoping that I can cover this extreme redness as much as possible. Hmm. Not bad. It looks a tiny bit chalky, and the peeling on my nose seems not to want to go away. But the redness definitely looks a lot calmer. I frame my eyes with a smudge of grey kohl at the outer corners and dab on some coral-tinted lip balm. Then I open the new highlighter I managed to pick up for cheap at the airport duty-free. All of the models on Instagram wear this stuff. It makes their skin look all dewy and glowing and gleaming and their cheekbones super high and chiselled. My softly rounded cheeks could use a pop of this for sure. I squeeze a blob of highlighter out onto my fingers and dab it carefully onto the high points of my face like I saw the models do in the Instagram videos. Along my cheeks, above my brows, a little on my nose and then I smear what's left on my Cupid's bow. There. That's nice. I turn my head this way and that in the mirror. The highlighter makes me look nice and gleaming and shiny like an Instagram person!

I glance at my phone and notice that it's already 11 a.m. Eek. I really need to get a move on if I'm going to find my cheese toastie supplies and get to the studio set before lunch. I spritz a little of Tom Ford's *Black Orchid* onto my throat and wrists – a perfume that Imogene says is perhaps a little too bold for me, but makes me feel brave. I slip on my ballet flats, grab hold of my favourite turquoise tote bag and then pop a newly obedient Winklepuff into Kennedy's stylish leather dog carrier, which is fancier than any bag I have ever owned. Winklepuff's head pokes out of the top of the bag and I make a note to pick up some extra ham on the way to keep him sweet.

'Right! Let's go do this, buddy,' I say to the tiny dog in a confident voice that belies the nervous fluttering in my heart.

I can *do* this.

Can't I?

CHAPTER NINETEEN

Gary

Hey.

Today is the day. First day of shooting on *Nightcar*! I'm so psyched. I'm nervous to meet everyone and wondering whether I'll be good enough, but I just have this feeling that it's going to be one of those days I'll never forget. This is a short journal entry as my call time is in about ten mins and I want to check over my scene lines one more time.

Three amazing things:

1. I get to do this for a fucking job!!
2. Tori has agreed to read the first *Harcourt Royals* book so she can see why I've always got my head stuck in one. She thinks that I should probably not be photographed reading a sexy novel with half-naked bodies on the cover, that it wouldn't be great for my 'image'. She read the blurb and said it sounded corny. She's right. Those books are so, so corny, in your face corny. They lean in to the corn. They're

also hilarious and super weird. That's why I can't stop reading them.

3. The best of the three amazing things: Pops texted me this morning. He met a woman at the local farm supply store. Her name is Tammy and he says she is 'real nice,' which is about as big a compliment as you could ever get from my father. He didn't tell me much more than that, but he texted a smiling face at the end of the message and he has never used an emoji before in his damn life.

CHAPTER TWENTY

Nora

Apart from this mental wind that keeps blowing dust into my eyes, everything is going smoothly so far. I like to think that maybe fate is giving me a helping hand, leading me to this day. I remember both my parents used to quote a romantic poet called James Russell Lowell, who said something about fate loving the fearless. I haven't exactly been fearless since their death, but that's what I'm doing now, right? I'm trying so hard to be fearless. Will fate help me along? Please, please let it.

With the help of Google Maps, I managed to find my cheeses in a little artisan shop on a road called Abbot Kinney Boulevard. I got a gigantic block of Cheddar and a medium one of crumbly white Cheshire cheese too. They also had a deli meat counter, so I was able to get a massive stack of ham to keep Winklepuff in check.

While I was in the cheese shop, another customer, some guy with a very pointy nose, got mad because Winklepuff was in there, even though he was neatly and hygienically ensconced in his fancy carry bag. Plus, the customer before me took a dog in and that dog wasn't even in a bag, which definitely isn't hygienic. As the grumpy customer tutted and grumbled and complained to everyone else in the shop, I had a little daydream about what would happen if I just grabbed a wheel of Camembert and splatted it on his pointy nose. All the other customers would clap me for stopping his mean-spirited 'no pooches in the cheese shop' rant and maybe the owner of the shop would gift me free cheese for a year, which Gary and I would eat every night with a little teensy glass of sherry like Frasier and Niles, while telling each other about our days and then making saucy love in our aqua-coloured swimming pool.

By the time my daydream was over, the customer had gone, red-faced and hissing at me. I ignored him, absolutely determined not to let another man wind me up today.

Now out on the sunny street, I order a Lyft which, to my disappointment is not driven by Billy Fever the Adam Levine tribute singer. When the Lyft drops me off around the corner from the movie lot, I thank the driver, climb out of the car and make sure my dress is aligned and neat, that my hair is smoothed down and tucked over one shoulder and that I don't have a ton of mascara under my eyes from where I've been constantly rubbing the dust out of them.

I've already developed a plan for what I'm going to say at the entrance to the movie lot, if someone asks to see my credentials. I am going to pull out my blocks of cheese and I'm going to say that I am making a delivery for the catering company. Thanks to Kennedy's internet research skills and her relationship with Andre the Avocado Guy, I know that the studio's catering company is called Yum Hollywood and that the head of catering is called Julie Pleppi. It *has* to work.

As I cautiously approach the outside of the lot, I'm surprised by how dull and industrial it looks. I don't know what I imagined – something more colourful: sequinned showgirls and men with cigars maybe? One thing that *is* expected is how busy this place is. All sorts of people, mostly wearing T-shirts and jeans, rush around from various outbuildings to other various outbuildings looking harried and distracted, muttering into walkie-talkies and occasionally staring at iPads or clipboards filled with millions of papers flapping about in this hyper wind. No one looks very glamorous at all, so I actually fit right in.

I expect there to be some sort of security people at the entrance gates, but I glance around and there is no one fitting that description nearby.

Fate loves the fearless! I take a deep breath and march into the lot with my chin up and purpose in my step. I have zero clue where I'm going. I just know that I have to find the trailers. Kennedy said that they're usually labelled with the names of whoever inhabits them.

To my delight, but not to my surprise, no one really pays me any attention as I walk through the lot. I *knew* my invisibility superpowers would come in useful for this. One woman nods a vague hello in my direction and says, 'First days are a killer, right?'

'Oh, yes, uh, such a killer,' I reply in a shaky voice and hurry past her, happy that this particular first day on set means that no one can spot an interloper, because they're all probably still strangers to each other. My feeling of achievement at having actually made it onto the lot is briefly replaced by a little dart of worry. I imagine Gary and the other actors wouldn't be too happy to know that people can just randomly walk onto their set. I mean, at least I don't have disreputable intentions, but some other person totally could! There are all sorts of stalkery people out there!

Winklepuff wriggles about in his bag. I stroke his head and soothe him with a little ham-based sweet talk. He licks my hand once in response.

I round a corner to find a quieter area housing a long row of grey-coloured trailers, both big and small. They have little name signs taped up on each door, just like Kennedy said they would. I'm almost there!

I walk past a few taped with names of actors I vaguely recognise. The gravel crunches beneath my feet and I use my arm to wipe the sweat from my forehead. I eventually pass by the biggest of the trailers and – oh my actual goodness –there's a piece of blue paper, tacked up on the door, Gary Montgomery's name upon it.

Shit. This is it. This is his trailer! There's a lengthy window along the side, covered by a cream-coloured blind. I spot a shadow move inside. Gary! He's in there *right now*. Oh god, that's him, right there, so close!

My heart starts pounding in my ears and all moisture disappears from my mouth.

Is this it? Is this about to happen?

I think this is it.

This is the moment of truth.

Fuck.

I take a deep, steadying breath and then knock on the trailer door with a trembling hand.

A few excruciatingly nerve-wracking seconds later, the door is pulled open and standing there, staring right at my face for the first time ever is…

… *Nicolas Cage?*

'Oh, Nicolas Cage!' I exclaim because he is very very famous and he is right in front of me and all of my powers of 'act like I belong' melt into a big uncool puddle of gormlessness.

Nicolas Cage. *Actual* Nicolas Cage narrows his famous eyes at me. 'Who are you?' he asks, full of suspicion.

Shit. He just knows I am an interloper. He can just tell. He's probably dealt with tons of interlopers in his time.

'Um… Um…' I stumble.

Nicolas Cage closes the trailer door slightly as if to protect himself. He's going to rat me out. Argh!

And then I get a brainwave and remember my cover story. 'I-I'm from catering,' I say, trying to stop my voice from wobbling. 'Yes. Julie sent me. Julie Pleppi, owner of the catering firm Yum Hollywood.' I pull out my pack of Cheshire cheese and wave it about for proof.

'Yeah, I know who Julie is,' Nicolas Cage drawls in his Nicolas Cage voice.

'I've come to t-take your lunch order,' I say quickly.

Nicolas Cage smiles then and the full weight of his megawatt charisma and hair plugs almost make me swoon.

My left eye suddenly prickles with the remains of some wind dust from earlier on. I squeeze it shut in an effort to stop the stinging. Then it occurs to me that it looks like I am winking at Nicolas Cage.

He looks slightly surprised before casually winking back.

'Cool. Lunch,' he says. 'Yeah, so I'll take a poke bowl with salmon, it has to be line-caught salmon, mind you. I'll have a vitamin water, three oranges, an egg-white omelette, a mushroom coffee with MCT oil stirred in. Not too hot, all right? The last one burned my tongue and an actor without his tongue is severely incapacitated.'

I nod quickly, most of what he's saying making very little sense to me.

He pauses and frowns. 'You're not writing this down?'

'I will remember,' I say, tapping my head and knowing that I will not remember a single fucking thing apart from the fact that I am talking to Nicolas Cage.

I'm about to walk away without much more ado when Nicolas Cage asks, 'What's in the bag, kid? It's moving.'

'Uh…' I glance down to Winklepuff's bag wriggling about, thankful that the mesh window that reveals his adorable face is hidden from Nicolas Cage because, although I'm sure lots of people on movie sets have dogs with them, I'm pretty certain that a person in a catering department definitely wouldn't.

'It's a chicken,' I tell him in a panic, my voice breaking and squeaking like a thirteen-year-old boy. *A chicken, Nora? A chicken?*

'A live chicken?' Nicolas Cage raises an eyebrow.

Shit. He doesn't believe me.

'Yeah, um… Gary Montgomery. He likes his chicken fresh.'

Nicolas Cage nods slowly and looks into the distance thoughtfully. 'Wow. These up-and-comers, huh?'

'I know,' I say with a conspiratorial eye roll.

Nicolas Cage leans against the trailer doorway. 'And you have to uh…' He mimes a cutting throat motion across his neck and looks at the wriggling bag.

'Yes,' I say, shaking my head sadly.

Nicolas Cage purses his lips together for a moment. 'What did you say your name was?'

'I didn't…'

He gives me a hard look. 'What's your name, kid?'

'CJ West,' I blurt and start quickly backing away, because Nicolas Cage looks very distrustful of me and my live chicken sacrifice story and I feel like I'm about to get busted. I need to get to Gary before that can happen. This might be the only chance I get to meet him. 'Bye, Nicolas Cage, sir,' I shout, heading down the lot as speedily as I can before breaking into a jog. 'Coffee not too hot,' I call back in a panic. 'ATM oil! A multivitamin! I've, uh, got you covered.'

He watches me take off through narrowed eyes and my forehead breaks out into an almighty sweat. Dammit. Why did Nicolas Cage's trailer have Gary's name on it? They must have switched trailers or something. I start to read the trailer signs again, frantically searching for Nicolas Cage's name. I pass three trailers before I stop and glance up.

And he is there.

Gary.

Less than five metres away.

Not on a movie screen or a laptop or magazine page or in my head.

He's staring at his phone and slowly heading towards the trailer that I assume must actually be his.

It's funny: he's shorter than he looks on screen but still tall enough for me to have to tilt my face up if I were to kiss him. The perfect height. *He* is perfect. I can only see his face in profile, but there's a half-smile lifting the corners of his lips and whatever is making him smile like that, I am grateful for.

My heart lifts and that overwhelming feeling I got when I first saw him at the cinema increases by a gazillion percent. That feeling that I know him. My heart swells and yearns as if my entire life, all those thousands of small moments, has been leading to today, to this moment. To meeting him and him meeting me.

Still gazing down at his phone, Gary steps up into his trailer and closes the door behind him. I shake my head to clear the daze that seems to have settled over me, freezing me to the spot. I'm going to go and knock on the door. Holy crap. Please let me be right about this. Please *please* let me be right about this.

I begin to walk towards his trailer, towards what could be my future, and in that moment I know that even if Gary doesn't return my feelings that I'll be forever grateful I was lucky enough to find my one soulmate. And I will love him for as long as I breathe air into my—

'Argh!' I yell and jump as someone unexpectedly places a heavy hand on my shoulder. I spin around quickly to see a gigantic, barrel-shaped, shaven-headed man in his late forties, wearing a too-tight black suit and holding a walkie-talkie to his mouth. He looks royally fucked off. The badge on his jacket says 'Security'.

Oh, this is not good.

I waddle away from this menacing-looking man so quickly that I end up sort of running backwards, the momentum of which means I fall backwards.

I drop my tote bag and watch in horror as it skids across the tarmac, the cheese, the knives and forks, the ham and bread rolling out onto the dirty ground. Instinct makes me clutch my Winklepuff carrier to my chest to protect him, meaning that I don't break the fall with my arms.

OUCH. My butt.

The big man strides quickly towards me and looks down at me through narrowed eyes. 'Where is your ID?' he asks in a super deep and very strong Australian accent.

I scramble onto my feet, quickly scooping the *Harcourt Royals* book I brought with me in case I had to wait around for Gary, the cheese, ham and cutlery, minus one knife which I can't seem to find, back into the tote bag. I poke my head into Winklepuff's carrier to check if he's okay. He looks as startled as me but, thankfully, uninjured. I dust off Kennedy's dress and rub at my elbows and my legs and my bum.

The man is staring at me, his nostrils flaring, awaiting my answer.

I panic. 'My-*my* ID, you say?' I squeak. 'Where is *your* ID, sir? Maybe that is the true q-question here.'

He frowns and points to the very clear lanyard hanging around his neck. 'Where. Is. *Your*. ID?' he asks again, his big stubbly jaw making him look even more intimidating. 'You need to show it to me right now. We've had an alert questioning the legitimacy of your employment here.'

Oh Nicolas Cage, you dirty narc.

'I… forgot it?' I say weakly, my bashed bottom starting to throb with pain and Winklepuff growling and grumbling in his carrier. 'It's okay, pup,' I whisper to him, lifting the mesh flap so his head pokes out and I can give it a reassuring ruffle.

'You forgot your ID on the first day, did you?' Gigantic man says drily.

'Um, yes. I left it, uh, in my bathroom.' I smack my hand to my head. 'Silly me... I'm so embarrassed.'

'Hmmm. Well, Mr Cage wanted to confirm that a young woman named CJ West was in fact working in the catering department.' He taps a meaty finger to his head. 'In preparation of this shoot, I memorised a list containing the names of every verified employee on this movie and *CJ West* is not on that list. That, coupled with the fact that you "forgot" your ID, leads me to believe that you are an intruder. Come with me, young lady.'

Yep. I am well and truly busted. Fuck. I was so close to Gary! If Nicolas Cage hadn't asked me what was in my bag, I might already have been in Gary's trailer right now, making cute jokes with him before we snog frantically and maybe bone.

The security man marches me back down the lot, away from Gary. We pass Nicolas Cage, who is standing at the door of his trailer with his arms crossed, slowly shaking his head at me. He had to go and ruin everything. I am so resentful of him that I flip the bird. He flips it back with a little chuckle. Ugh. I will never watch *Face Off* again, which will be hard because it is an excellent movie.

I spot the security man's name badge. John Alan. Ugh. He looks just like the kind of man who has two first names.

'John Alan. Please don't call the police,' I try asking in my most polite voice, as he drags me past what looks to be a group of extras, all staring at me, gleeful at the spectacle. 'I'm not dangerous. I just wanted to see Gary Mont-gomery because...' I trail off and clamp my mouth shut because how am I supposed to finish that sentence? I just wanted to see Gary Montgomery because I think he might possibly be my one true love? Somehow I don't think that explanation will help my cause.

'Nick has requested that we remove you from the lot and that we don't press charges since you're clearly a very troubled young woman. And would you stop winking at me, I've just told you we're not going to press charges.'

'I'm not winking!' I protest. 'It's the dust from these devil winds, getting into my eye.'

John Alan ignores my explanation. 'I will not be seduced. Not again... Don't make me change my mind about letting you go without consequences.'

'Okay, okay. Thank you for not pressing charges,' I mumble as I am marched right to the front of the lot, receiving a mixture of curious and disgusted looks on the way.

I hear one of the bystanders ask, 'Where did she come from? How did no one spot her?'

Another says, 'Thank you, John Alan.'

'Back to work, everyone!' a woman with a headset eventually calls out as John Alan pushes me out onto the street and closes the big cast-iron gates behind me, securing them with a gigantic lock that he quite frankly should have used this morning. It's lucky that I, a sane person, was the only one who got in.

'Nicky Cage might be a soft touch these days,' John Alan says, snapping his walkie-talkie into a holster strapped around his waist and folding his arms over his massive chest, 'but I, John Alan, am not. If I see you around here again, I will not hesitate to call my old colleagues at the LAPD.'

Oh god.

I nod quickly, hoick Winklepuff's carrier and my tote bag onto my shoulder, and run the hell away.

CHAPTER TWENTY-ONE

Gary

Hey.

Okay, so I said in my last journal entry that being famous is weird. Well, I'm doubling down on that statement. Because it appears that I have an honest to goodness *stalker*. One of the other actors I'm working with on *Nightcar* said it's a rite of passage, but, I gotta say, it's given me the heebie-jeebies. Because this woman actually turned up at the lot where I'm filming! God knows how she got past security in the first place, but she did, and by all accounts she was pretty smart, if a little unhinged.

According to Nick, she said she was going to sacrifice a chicken for me?? Apparently, she had odd shiny stripes painted on her cheekbones and the end of her nose and she was winking a whole lot. Nick's actually the one who suspected that she was a fraud and called Security. He said he saved my life, so now I have to forgive him for making us switch trailers because mine had better water pressure than his.

I vaguely saw the back of this strange prowling woman as Security escorted her out and something about the shape of her, I don't know… I had this weird urge to run after her, to pull her away from the huge guy manhandling her and then I realised that this woman was obviously pretty crazy and that interacting with her would surely make things worse. I did feel like I'd seen her before though… I wonder if she's been following me for a while and this is just the first time that someone caught her? Aileen did warn me. Fuck.

As I was going back into my trailer, I spotted something glinting on the floor outside my door. It was a knife. While it was only a blunt butter knife that clearly couldn't do any real harm, Security have classified it as a weapon. And because of that, the studio have assigned the security guy to be my bodyguard for the duration of the shoot. So now I have this beefy, grumpy-looking, Australian ex-cop tailing me wherever I go, which is necessary, I guess, but not ideal. His name is John Alan and something about that name just makes me irrationally annoyed.

Tori seems to be enjoying the drama of it all. Seth and Olive find it hilarious that someone maybe planned to attack me with a blunt knife. They keep saying that I'd butter be careful.

Feeling tired and on edge after such a weird-ass day, but I suppose the point of Ira assigning the journaling and doing the three amazing things was that you have to find things to be thankful for even if you are more than a little freaked out.

So here goes:

1. I'm aliiiiive. I was not killed via butter knife and I did not have to watch a chicken get sacrificed before me.
2. My co-stars are great. Despite my lack of concentration this afternoon, they were truly

supportive and gave me complete understanding when I needed extra takes.

3. I have a surfing lesson at dusk and afterwards Seth and Olive are joining me on the beach for a cookout. If anything will make me feel better, that will. Even if Olive did suggest we use plastic cutlery so as not to trigger me.

CHAPTER TWENTY-TWO

Nora

By the time I've made it a few blocks away from the movie studio, the tears are at full pelt. I feel humiliated and stupid and sad. This is why I never go anywhere or do anything, because if I just stay inside and watch lovely movies and read lovely books, then I won't have to feel this horrible feeling, like I can't breathe, like bad things will always happen when I'm involved. This is what happens when I step out of my safe, warm cocoon. Disaster!

I mean, I now legitimately have beef with Nicolas Cage and no doubt the security team will tell Gary all about me. I was so close to him and now he will know I was there and he will think I'm some crazy chicken-killing oddball. The very thought of it makes my whole body itch with humiliation.

While Winklepuff finishes his wee, my Lyft driver pulls up and pips his horn. Scooping Winklepuff back into his carrier, I get into the car.

'It is you!' the driver says. 'My future number one fan! I notice you signed up for my mailing list. I am very grateful to you.'

I wipe the tears from my eyes and see that it's Billy Fever. The Adam Levine tribute singer.

'Oh hey!' I say, trying to inject enthusiasm into my voice. Trying not to sound like someone who just got chucked off a Hollywood film set for trying to make covert contact with a celebrity. 'It's lovely to see you again.'

'Why are you crying? Did this dog bite you? Is Aunt Flo in town? Did you watch a tear-jerking movie and it jerked your tears? You are so sad.'

I shake my head. 'It's nothing. I've just got some dust in my eye from the wind.'

He looks at me in the rear-view and pulls a sympathetic face. 'Your eye does look unwell.'

'I know,' I say, rubbing at it again. 'This wind is mental, though.'

'Do you have any further appointments this afternoon?'

Apart from having to explain to Kennedy how today went and have her stupid brother laugh at me some more? 'Um, no.'

'Then I will drop you at the local CVS, so you can get eye drops. I will not allow my number one fan to go blind.'

'Okay… that's really nice of you. Thanks.' I nod, trying hard not to burst into tears again, my insides still in knots of shame.

'And then perhaps I will drop you off at a nice beach that is accepting of dogs?' Billy suggests. 'They sell very nice ice creams there and I feel this will cheer you up.'

I glance down at Winklepuff, who has been so well-behaved during this morning's escapade. He deserves a run on the beach. And ice cream is always useful in times of upset.

'Thank you, that sounds great,' I say, smiling weakly at Billy Fever in the mirror.

'You are welcome,' he replies. 'I am the best Lyft driver

in the whole city. And until we get to the CVS, I will sing to you, for *free*.'

'Oh, it's okay, you don't have to do—'

'I got the mo-o-o-o-o-o-o moves like Jagger!…'

* * *

My eyes filled with soothing eyedrops and having been regaled with the tale of Adam Levine's upbringing in Los Angeles and his break into the music industry, I arrive at the dog-friendly section of the beach. Billy Fever was right – it's really lovely, vast and clean, and not at all crowded like the tiny dog run outside of Kennedy and Brandon's house. The air smells like salt and sun cream. The waves on the turquoise ocean are huge and frothy. There are people surfing and dogs running around happily. No one knows who I am. No one knows what just happened.

I try to settle my breathing, which is shaky from all the crying, and I walk down onto the beach. I slip my shoes off and sink my feet into the soft gold sand, wiggling my toes deep into its warmth. Taking Winklepuff out of his carry bag, I plop him down beside me, only for him to zoom off at excitable speed across the golden powder, his fur blowing about in the gusty wind. I watch him running about and wonder whether I should just get a flight back home. This morning couldn't have gone much worse and, while I still *feel* I'm supposed to meet Gary Montgomery, it also appears more likely that Imogene was right. And maybe that what happened at the movie lot was the dose of reality I needed in order to rethink my whole life. The thought of that makes me want to burst into tears all over again.

Keeping an eye on Winklepuff, I head towards the ice cream stand Billy Fever recommended: *Bud's Ice Cream*.

The guy manning the stand looks like a blonde, surfer version of Jason Momoa. He's in his early twenties, with his shoulder-length hair wrapped in a red bandana. He is shirtless and his bronzed, muscled body almost makes me exclaim aloud. I have never seen a body like that up close and in real life. I start to sweat again. I am so out of practice interacting with people that when I encounter someone this muscly with their top off I actually cannot function properly.

'Uh, hello, may I want an ice creams for me?' I blurt, trying unsuccessfully to repress the hot blush I can feel flooding my cheeks. I don't even fancy him. He is just glistening in a way that is almost pornographic. His shiny, aggressively sexy abs, plus the events of the past few days are, frankly, too much for me to process. I sigh heavily. 'Aaaaaargh,' I mumble to myself, burying my face in my hands for a moment.

When I emerge from my hand-face cocoon, the young guy has looked up from the magazine he's reading – something with lots of pictures of surfboards.

'Woah!' he exclaims, his pale blue eyes meeting mine. 'You look seriously uncentred, bro.'

His Californian surfer accent is so exaggerated it's almost as if he's doing it as a joke. He pronounces Bro like Brah. I squint slightly to see if he's going to laugh and admit that that is not his real accent, but his face is blank. He really does talk like Bill and Ted!

I brush my hair out of my face and clear my throat and try to look at his eyes rather than his nipples or his belly button or his very very low-slung shorts. 'I've had a weird morning,' I say.

'Yeah, Santa Anas'll do that to you.'

'Devil winds,' I reply with a small, awkward smile.

'They are way gnarly, but the swells are rad when they're in town.'

The swelzarad? What's a swelzarad? I nod politely in response.

'What'll it be then?' the guy asks when it's clear that I've not much more to say for myself.

'My friend sent me here,' I tell him. 'He said your ice creams would cheer me up.'

The guy nods knowingly as if lots of people are sent here on friends' recommendations, which wouldn't be a surprise considering that he looks like he was carved out of bronze.

'So, can I please have…' I squint my eyes at the menu board behind his head… 'A rocky road ice cream cone with chopped walnuts on top,' I say, checking behind me to make sure that Winklepuff is all right. He's fine, running in very fast circles, then racing towards the ocean but scooching back just before his little paws get wet.

'Just rocky road or special rocky road?' the guy asks. 'You look kinda stressed, bro. Your eye is fuuuuuucked.'

I rub at my eyes. The drops seem to be helping a little bit, but my left eye still feels really dry. 'What's the difference between the rocky road and the special rocky road?'

His blue eyes sparkle. 'Well, the special one is, you know… totally special.' He stares at me, smiling and nodding very slowly.

'Okaaay?' I say. 'Um, are they the same price?'

'For you they can be. You look like you could catch a break.'

Behind me, Winklepuff starts barking at the ocean. It appears his scooching didn't work and he's now furious because he's got a little sea water on his paws.

'Um, thank you. Great, okay,' I say distractedly. 'I'll have the special rocky road please.'

I call Winklepuff over to me. He ignores me. I call out *Ham* instead and within seconds he is at my side. While my ice cream is being prepared, I reach into my bag and pull out a little piece of ham, which Winklepuff takes happily and swallows without even chewing.

'That's high-quality ham and you're not even tasting it!' I grumble to him.

'Here it is, dude.' The ice cream guy hands over what looks like a pretty normal, non-special ice cream with some chopped nuts sprinkled on top. 'Enjoy...' he says pointedly as I pay. 'And I hope your day improves, man.'

'Thank you,' I say, finding myself impressed with how much pride he takes in his product and also his perfect abs. 'I will try my best.'

CHAPTER TWENTY-THREE

Nora

Text from Imogene: *What are you doing today? Ring me when you get a chance. I'm starting to feel really guilty about sending you to do this. You're not in the right place mentally and I should have known that. I was just trying to help. Dan says I shouldn't interfere and maybe he's right. Is he right? Have to go. Got a Pilates class and work is going to be very busy, plus I still need to get Ariana ready for preschool. I am like a hamster on a wheel! Im x.*

Well, golly flipping gosh if I'm not feeling much, much better. I'm still trying to figure out what made the special ice cream any more special than just a regular cone, but also it doesn't really matter because after today's humiliation I finally feel very chilled out. Very, very chilled out. I barely feel anything about the fact that I left my home and my life to fly solo to Los Angeles, America, and am now on some random beach with a secret meat-eating dog, scraped elbows and knees having been thrown off a movie set where I was trying to meet the famous man I think I'm in love with.

Instead, I'm casually sitting here, smothered in high factor sun cream and reading the brand-new *Harcourt Royals* book while Winklepuff darts around with no signs of slowing down. I'm hoping that if I just let him go for it, he'll tire himself out and will behave for the rest of the day.

I settle back into my book and read about Esme and Bastian's latest sexy and drama-filled conflict. Oooh, a sexy journalist posing as a sexy new bartender at Dreamy Dix, the strip club Bastian works in, is flirting with him. What a surprise, she knows all about the rare white-clawed crayfish, which Bastian is extremely interested in, what with his marine biology obsession. This sexy woman is clearly conning him just to get a news story about Princess Esme.

'Oh holy heck, stay well away from her, sweet, sexy Bastian,' I mutter to myself, rubbing my already sore eyes because, weirdly, the words on the page keep blurring in front of me.

My stomach gives an almighty rumble and I realise that it's three o'clock and I've had no lunch because my great cheese toastie plan was thwarted by Nicolas Cage. I get a vision of Nicolas Cage flipping me the bird as I flipped him the bird and at the thought of how fucking weird it was I burst into laughter. I picture his face and the fact that I told him that Gary liked his chicken extra fresh. Then I think of seeing Gary, just five metres away, and how my heart ached for him. How close I was to actually speaking to him before that stoopid John Alan fella ruined it all. And then I laugh even more because I'm suddenly feeling incredibly, oddly giddy.

And *hungry*.

I really am hungry. So hungry. I don't think I've ever been this hungry before. I reach into my tote and grab one of the blocks of cheese, which has softened grossly in the heat of the sun. I try to find the knife, but it's nowhere in my bag, so instead I tear the wax paper open and take two gigantic bites, leaving behind little teeth marks.

'Ew, take a breath, girl,' says a sleek man walking by with a sleek greyhound on a sleek silver chain lead.

Which just makes me laugh more. 'You are!' I shout back at him, which is a terrible comeback, but right now I simply do not care. That ice cream really did make me feel better about all of the things!

The sleek man hurriedly drags his sleek dog away as if I plan to take a bite out of both of them too.

I shrug and pick up my book again and am just sinking into the next chapter when I hear a blood-curdling scream. I jump up in shock and look down the beach to see a tall woman wearing a baseball cap a few metres away yelling at Winklepuff, who, oh my god, is *humping a very large golden retriever*? Oh shit. How did this even happen? How did he even get up there? That dog is massive! Did Winklepuff *climb up* the other dog? I don't understand the logistics.

'Stop that!' the woman yells at the dogs, frantically flapping her hands in their general direction.

I scramble up and quickly jog over to the fracas, wobbling a little to the left as I do.

'Winklepuff get down, right now! Get off that golden retriever!'

The blonde woman squeals again. 'Ewwww! Is this your dog?'

'No, I'm dog-sitting him!' I explain. 'Winklepuff! Down! Ham! Ham! Deli ham!' My stern calls do nothing. I pull some ham out of my bag and wave it around in the air. 'Come get it,' I say.

Winklepuff fully ignores me. He is having the time of his life and the golden retriever seems psyched about the whole thing too.

'Get him off of her!' the blonde woman yells again.

'This is horrible.'

I reach forward to grab Winklepuff, but both he and the golden retriever growl and snarl at me.

'Argh!' I jump back in fright. 'I can't do it. They're snarling. They seem to want their privacy!'

'Crap. They're fucking now,' the woman says. 'They're going to be stuck together for at least twenty minutes. Great. My boyfriend is gonna go nuts. His precious Janet, deflowered!'

'Your boyfriend's dog is called *Janet*?' I giggle, looking at the woman for the first time. She removes her baseball cap, revealing a shock of short white blonde hair.

My heart lurches because I recognise her perfect sharp-featured face and large long-lashed doe eyes. Oh my goodness. This woman is Tori Gould. Gary Montgomery's fiancée! How is this happening? Why am I meeting her? Is this… is this *fate* telling me not to give up on my mission? Or fate telling me to stay the hell away from this woman's boyfriend? Winklepuff's new beau must be Gary's dog. Called Janet. Arguably the finest name I ever heard for a dog in my life.

I try not to let on that I recognise Tori because, while she's a well-known make-up artist on Instagram, she's not regular-person famous. It would be odd for me to know who she was, especially as I am very clearly not the kind of person who understands anything about hair and make-up and fashion.

'He's had her for years,' Tori says, her voice the sort of mid-Atlantic/vocal fry heavy drawl that all the fancy kids had on *Gossip Girl*. 'He's gonna go nuts. I mean, at least she consented, but what if she gets pregnant? We don't have time to deal with puppies! Plus she's a pure-breed. She's only meant to "be" with other golden retrievers.'

'Dog eugenics,' I mutter under my breath.

'Excuse me?' Tori frowns, slightly.

'Oh nothing.' I pull myself together because I am both feeling and acting very weird and this woman has done nothing wrong apart from fall in love with the man I strongly suspect I'm supposed to grow old with. 'Well, I really hope Janet doesn't get up the duff.'

'Up the what?' Tori gives me a horrified glance.

'Pregnant.'

'Oh. Yes. Me too. I couldn't bear having to deal with a whole litter of stinky Janets loping around and making a mess. Yuck.'

'Right. Of course.'

I wait for her to say something else, but she doesn't. And I don't because I'm not good at small talk most of the time and especially so when said small talk is with a woman whose boyfriend I, just this morning, was fantasising about having sex with.

I avert my eyes while the two dogs continue to enjoy themselves. Tori sits herself down delicately onto the sand, brushing errant grains off her perfect ankles. With a sigh, she takes her phone out, lifts up the screen at an angle and snaps a selfie, before tapping something out onto the screen. I bet she's instagramming.

I sneak open my phone and take a look at her profile which I have bookmarked on my home screen. There's the selfie she's just taken right this minute! You can see a little bit of the dress I'm wearing in the background. I read the caption: 'An idyllic LA Beach moment, walking my beloved dog and catching some rays. Covered in SPF of course!! #LAMoments #sunshinefordayzzzz #LaMerTheSPF #doglover #dogownersofinstagram'

Idyllic LA Beach Moment? Hardly. But, then again, I suppose that is the point of an influencer: to present a perfect life even when your dog is getting screwed by another dog and the whole thing is truly gross. And actually pretty funny. I give a little giggle. I'm feeling very giggly in general right now. Much more than usual.

Tori looks up at me with pursed lips, before her eyes run slowly over Kennedy's dress, which, yes, is a more than a little tight around the boobs. She takes in my red face and gammy eye and raises her eyebrow just the tiniest bit, but enough for me to notice.

She goes back to her phone, ignoring me, and although all signs point to Tori Gould not being the kind of person I would want to hang out with, I mentally tell myself off for jumping to that conclusion so quickly. It would be much too easy to cast her as a villain. The truth is that *I* am the villain in this whole scenario. I am the one hoping that her boyfriend will be my boyfriend, my husband, the fella who will grow crispy and wrinkly with me before we eventually die at exactly the same moment, holding bony hands and staring lovingly into each other's rheumy eyes.

Winklepuff and Janet don't look to be ending their affair any time soon so I go and grab my unattended bag from further down the beach, wobbling again and wondering why I feel so light-headed – I must be dehydrated from the heat. I return and sit down beside Tori, taking a big gulp of water from my bottle while we wait for the dogs to finish. She's busy on her phone, so I grab my book again and, before I flip to find the page where I left off, Tori glances over and frowns.

'Oh, my boyfriend has that book. I'm trying to read one of them at the moment, but it's ridiculous, no offence.'

My mouth drops open and I take in a sharp breath.

'*Harcourt Royals?*' I stutter. 'Your boyfriend reads the *Harcourt Royals* series?'

'Yeah,' she shrugs and rolls her eyes slightly, continuing to tap out on her phone while she's talking. 'He's always got his nose buried in them. I'm more of a *Vogue* girl myself.'

I force a straight expression onto my face. 'Cool. Cool,' I say as casually as I can manage, which is hard, considering that my heart has started beating very very quickly. Oh my god. Gary Montgomery is a *Harcourt Royals* fan? Fuuuuuuuck. What are the chances? Such a small number of people have even heard of the series. And he is one of them? If this isn't a massive freaking sign that I am doing the right thing being here, that I should pursue this, that fate loves the fearless, then I don't know what is.

Shit, I mean, what are even the chances that I would bump into Tori Gould today? That Winklepuff would choose *Gary's* dog, out of all the dogs on the beach, to make public love to? It's insane. Actually insane.

Oh my god, I wonder if Gary's on the *Harcourt Royals* forum under a fake name? I wonder which bits of the book make him laugh and I hope it's the same bits that make me laugh. This information almost completely eliminates my embarrassment from this morning. Even if John Alan told Gary about me, even if I did almost get arrested, even if I am losing my mind, I *have* to keep going. This is an undeniable sign! Wow. I can't wait to get back and tell Kennedy about my discovery! As I'm picturing her face when I tell her that Gary Montgomery is a fan of the little indie book series we are also fans of, Tori makes a little squeal of relief.

'Thank fuck for that,' she drawls.

I follow her gaze to find that the dogs have separated.

'Finally,' I agree, calling Winklepuff over as his tongue lolls shamelessly out of his mouth.

He flops towards me, while Tori ties a rose gold lead around Janet's chunky neck.

'You, um, should probably give me your boyfriend's number,' I say breezily.

Too far.

Tori frowns as a happy and tired Janet pants beside her. 'Um, why would I do that?'

'Uh, you know, in case Janet gets knocked up. Winklepuff would deserve to know. It would be his, um, paternal right. Right?'

'I don't think that's a thing,' Tori replies as if I am a moron, which I absolutely am.

'I think it is... legally,' I try.

Why am I pushing this? Shut up, Nora.

Tori pauses for a moment and gives me an enquiring look. 'Do you know who I am?' she asks eventually, her eyes squinting before she quickly slips on a pair of sunglasses to hide them. 'Who my boyfriend is?'

I affect a blank face. 'You are Janet's mum and your boyfriend is Janet's dad?'

'Hmmmm. We'll just take your number,' she says.

That's something, I guess.

I type my name and number into Tori's shiny gold phone. When I'm done, she pulls at Janet's lead.

'This was... weird,' she declares, returning her baseball cap to her head and heading off down the beach.

'Yep, it very much was,' I say. 'Bye, then!'

She throws her hand up in a dismissive wave without looking back at me.

I clip on Winklepuff's lead. His eyes are sparkling as we trot back down the beach. 'That was extremely gross, Winklepuff, but, I've got to say, I appreciate it. If it wasn't for you, I'd never had discovered that Gary actually reads my beloved *Harcourt Royals*. I'm doing the right thing being here. I have to be!' Winklepuff looks up at me blankly. 'You don't care, I get it. All you care about is Janet. But, either way, thanks for being such a filthy git. It has really helped me. You're definitely growing on me, buddy.'

As I walk past the ice cream man, he holds two fingers up in the peace sign. 'You're looking a lot more chilled now, dude,' he says happily. 'That's dope! Ha ha, do you get it? That's dope!'

'Ha ha,' I say, nodding as if I do get it. 'Yes, definitely. Take care!'

What an odd guy.

CHAPTER TWENTY-FOUR

Nora

By the time I've relayed the events of the day and my disaster at the movie set, Kennedy is wriggling with disbelief, her jaw hanging open.

'I've got to be honest,' she says, 'I'm kind of surprised you even got past security…'

'But you told me to act like I belonged! That everyone would be distracted.'

'And I was right, I guess. Wow.'

She makes me a chamomile tea and I tell her all about Nicolas Cage and how he ratted me out AND flipped the bird at me (to which she shrieks with laughter), about seeing Gary and feeling the same pull that I felt when I first saw him at the pictures. She covers her mouth with her hands when I relay the experience of John Alan kicking me off the lot and threatening to get the LAPD on me. When I tell her about meeting Tori Gould, her eyes widen in astonishment and when I reveal that Gary Montgomery reads the *Harcourt Royals* books she jumps up from the sofa.

'He reads *Harcourt Royals?*' Kennedy shrieks, which is

exactly the reaction I was unable to express myself at the time. 'For real? For real real? Holy shit! That's crazy!' She does an air punch, which looks weird considering the stiff blue work suit she's still wearing. Ha ha. This is an even better reaction than I had expected. She is properly psyched for me.

'It's a clear sign, right?' I say. 'Fate.'

Kennedy nods quickly. 'Hmmm. And you met Tori Gould too! Wow. What is she like? I actually love her Instagram. She always seems so authentic.'

'Yeah, I wouldn't bank on that transferring over into real life.'

'Really?'

'Yep.'

Kennedy plops back down onto the sofa and strokes Winklepuff on her lap. I was so afraid of telling her what he had gotten up to with Janet, but when I did, she seemed pretty non-plussed. 'Oh, he does it all the time.' She shrugged. 'He has, as they say, hoes in every area code.'

I kind of wish she had told me before. But then I suppose if she had, I might never have met Tori and been reassured that this weird crazy thing I'm doing is the right thing. I feel much less wobbly than I did at the beach – maybe I was getting a little too much sun – but I still feel more than a little giddy about what I've discovered.

'I'm going to spend the rest of the night making another plan to get to Gary,' I tell Kennedy. 'I've got so much to do. Do you mind if I use your printer some more? I have things to add to the Creepy As Fuck Soulmate Procurement Wall.'

Kennedy bites her lip. '*Or...* Instead, you could let me take you out, show you this immoral lil' town. I could do with a break myself, to be honest. Work has been real heavy, what with the fight for anchor position and then, of course, there's the whole...'

'Whole what?'

Kennedy's mouth clamps shut. 'Nothing.'

I shake my head. 'I shouldn't, really. I might have learned more about Gary, but this morning went so terribly that I should probably stay here and figure out the next step. Plus, I got really light-headed at the beach. I feel much more steady now, but what if I have a spot of sunstroke? And anyway, I'm not really the "going out" type.'

'What does that even mean? Of course you're the going out type!'

I shrug my shoulders. 'I just like staying in. I don't know if you've noticed, but I'm not the most outgoing person.'

Kennedy gives me a disapproving glance. 'You're a little shy, yes, but still! Where is your joy, girl?'

Joy sort of stops meaning as much when your beloved parents die and it's all your fault. That's the thing with grief, it feels like you can't fully experience happiness the way other people do. It's like, no matter how much you think you're healing, you've constantly got a griping stomach ache, a painful itch, a fractured bone that makes everything good you experience feel a little less good than it might otherwise have been.

I don't say that out loud because I only met Kennedy for the first time in real life a few days ago and, well, the only person I've ever talked to about Mum and Dad is Imogene and even those conversations make me feel like I'm going to throw up.

'Being with my one true love would bring me joy!' I say eventually, my heart panging as I think about how truly happy Mum and Dad were with each other. How happy I could be if these crazy feelings and instincts I'm experiencing are correct. How glad they would be if they knew I had managed to have what they had… 'That's why I need to stay in and plan. Plus, my eye is all scratchy and red from Santa Ana wind dust. Plus, I have Virtual Assistants 4U work to catch up on. PLUS, I need to get up early to call my sister while she's on her afternoon break at work.'

I think of Imogene's messages and how every time she mentions Dan it's because he's being a dick in some small way. I want to check she's okay.

Kennedy pouts a little and blows her soft blonde fringe out of her eyes. 'Listen. You're here for a couple weeks, right? If you're going to think properly and come up with a good next move, then surely you need to give your brain a little rest, especially after a day like today. All the best ideas come to an open, relaxed mind and that's a fact.'

'But I—'

'You can't come to LA and not experience the debauchery.' Kennedy folds her arms sternly. 'Come on, let's go get drinks, dance, meet new people. All of those good things. I said I would help you to have a joyful time here!'

'Meet *more* new people?' I can't help the look of horror that contorts my features.

Kennedy laughs at my expression. 'Come on. Staying in is cool, but it's also great to let off some steam, right? This mission of yours is so… *intense*. It's not healthy for it to be the only thing you do, the only thing you think about. Get this – if you come out with me, I promise to help you with your Gary Montgomery sleuthing tomorrow, okay? I have some work to do on my audition in the morning, but after that you will have all of my journalistic tools at your disposal. I'll even go through every member of the *Harcourt Royals* forum and see if any of the Crown Kissers might be Gary under a secret name. You know I'm one of the moderators, right? I have privileges! It's pretty dicey legally, but *technically* I could get access to everyone's real name and address…'

'You would do that? There are almost three thousand people in that fan group!' I gasp. 'You could get in serious trouble.'

'I'm a journalist, I can cover my tracks. And the head admin of the forum, RoyalsStanAngel28 is super easy-going. And, for the record, there are two thousand eight hundred and ninety seven Crown Kissers in that fan group,' Kennedy corrects me, even more of a *Harcourt Royals* fangirl than I am. 'I mean, approximately. But I don't mind that. I want to help. Mostly I am also trying to bribe you to come hang with me. It is my duty as your host to show you a good time. I couldn't forgive myself if you returned to the UK having stayed in this one house every night.'

'If I meet Gary, maybe I'll get to stay here a little longer...'

'Hmmm, definitely! Even more of a reason why you should get to know this town. So, are you in or are you going to make me beg some more?'

I roll my eyes, although secretly I'm pleased that she obviously likes me enough to want me to join her and her friends. She is much, much cooler than me and my ego is suitably flattered. 'I have to go and do a couple of hours work first. But after that... I'm in.'

'Yay!' Kennedy starts shooing me away towards the bathroom. 'Go ahead, go do your work. I'm gonna go and work out. Oh, and there's this restaurant that Joseph Gordon-Levitt was photographed at last week. I want to try it! Ooh, there's some Olaplex in the cabinet above the sink, make sure you put some on – your hair is very crispy. You really should wear a hat in this heat! Yay! We're going out ON THE TOWN!'

Argh.

* * *

I manage to focus enough to catch up on most of my outstanding tasks and emails for work and make a plan for the next few days of admin assignments. After I've showered, I smother my body in an aloe vera gel that Kennedy suggested on account of my continuing mega-redness. I catch a glimpse of myself in the bathroom mirror and realise that all my freckles have properly come out. I can't remember the last time I saw my freckles! I like them.

I put some more eye drops in my eye, dry my hair in the bedroom area, and am delighted that – thanks to Kennedy's suggestion of using that Olaplex stuff – it is now looking as glossy and silky as Imogene's always does. I grab my jean shorts and pull them on, breathing all the way and grunting a bit as I wrestle to button them up. I pair them with a pearlescent white T-shirt of Kennedy's, which, on her, looks big and baggy but on me looks like a cool form-fitting top.

Feeling the nervous beads of sweat start to form on my head, like they always do when I'm about to interact with strangers, I head over to the full-length window and gasp in astonishment at the candy-coloured pink and purple streaks painted across the sky as the sun sets. The beach has cleared considerably, leaving a few people milling about, taking photos of the sky and the palm trees, or sitting on colourful blankets, reading books or cuddling with loved ones. Further down the beach, way in the distance, there's a man on a surfboard, wobbling slightly but holding himself up as a wave brings him to the shore. When he gets out of the sea, he starts dancing excitedly and the two people he's with grab him into a bear hug. It makes me smile and I feel a small pang of longing, which is odd because the idea of surfing has never appealed to me before.

When I've finished getting ready, I spritz out a little cloud of perfume and walk through it before heading out of my area and into the living room. Kennedy, looking amazing in a tight purple dress, is frantically typing something on her laptop. When she sees me, she slams down the lid and stands up.

'Just working on my news story in case I get shortlisted for anchor,' she explains. 'I'm trying to choose between two. A story about this guy who restored a 300-year-old piano and donated it to a middle school *or* a story about an Ocean Park goose and a cat who have become BFFs...'

'They both sound like lovely stories.'

Kennedy sighs. 'Not exactly thrilling, but, hey, it's the junior anchor position. These are the kind of stories I'd get, so that's what I should audition with. They save the really meaty smart stuff for the prime-time anchors. Anyway, your hair looks *great*!'

I flick my newly tamed hair around my shoulders daftly. 'Thank you! It's that stuff you made me put on. It's amazing. Do my eyes still look really gammy?'

'*Gammy*?'

'You know, gross and red.'

'A little. But they're better than they looked before... so, are you ready to have some fun?' she asks, standing up from the sofa and grabbing a small black purse from the coffee table. 'Find some joy?'

'I think so. But I can't drink too much or stay out too late, okay? I really need to focus tomorrow.'

'Of course,' Kennedy says, linking her arm through mine. 'Let's go!'

CHAPTER TWENTY-FIVE

Nora

Text from Imogene*: You met Nicolas Cage?? You got kicked off a film set? Shit. What do you mean you saw Tori Gould and you are determined to prove me wrong? Please turn your phone off silent. I need to hear your voice to check if you are all right. Ring me. I don't care if it's a weird time here. I am okay. Just the same old stuff happening! I hope you're all right. I can't quite tell… Im x*

So this is what it's like to have a bona fide girls' night out with an actual girl friend! I've never done it before. I mean, I went out a lot when I was gigging and was even starting to get a solid circle of friends – mostly other musicians and venue staff. And then the accident happened. Of course, I've attended online Facebook parties and forum meetups and enjoyed them very much. But this way is scarier.

We're at a rooftop bar on nearby Abbot Kinney Boulevard. It's not a particularly tall building, but the view out over the glittering city, set amongst a backdrop of hazy purple sky, is mind-bogglingly pretty. And the bar itself is gorgeous; all glass tables, firepits and white outdoor sofas filled with the most attractive collection of people I've ever seen in one place. In the centre of the space is a small, glistening turquoise pool with teeny floating candles bobbing gently along it. It's pretty clear that I stick out as someone who doesn't belong, with my noticeably bigger than a size zero body, very tight jean shorts, sun-dried face and still squinting dusty eye. But that feeling of anxiety is blurred considerably by the Patrón Silver tequila shots Kennedy keeps ordering for us, which I'm especially grateful for when we bump into a few of Kennedy's co-workers and I have to make excruciating small talk with them.

One of the co-workers is the nemesis Kennedy talked about – a gorgeous, tiny red-headed woman called Erin, who actually seems much nicer than I expected and tells me that my hair reminds her of Penelope Cruz, which is maybe the nicest thing anyone has ever said to me.

I watch Kennedy and her co-workers chatting and it's weird; she acts so differently around them. She's nowhere near as floaty and chilled as she's been back at the house and she definitely doesn't make any of the geeky comments she's been making to me online or in real life the last few days.

I ask her co-workers, Miles, Helen and Erin, whether they've read the *Harcourt Royals* romance books too and the three of them look at me as if I just suggested we take a turd in the pool.

'Ha!' Helen, who looks a lot like Lucy Liu, only hotter, says. 'Who even has time to read fiction in this political climate? Long-form essays are about as frivolous as I get.'

I'm about to say that obviously Kennedy does because she's a massive *Harcourt Royals* nerd when she sort of nudges me in the ribs, giving me an almost imperceptible shake of the head. Her cheeks pinken slightly and she swiftly changes the subject to local municipal elections and their candidates.

The conversation about local elections and other 'newsy' topics leads me to drink my alcoholic beverage faster than I ordinarily would do. And then, in the middle of a conversation about a recent *NY Times* profile on some woman I've never heard of, Erin, who has been intermittently checking her phone, squeals out loud.

'What is it? What's going on?' everyone asks, jostling over to see what's on Erin's phone and why it's making her so excited.

'I'm shortlisted for the anchor position!' Erin reveals with a huge white-toothed grin, her dark red painted lips glistening under the lights. 'Me and one other person, apparently.' She looks at Kennedy pointedly.

I gasp and am about to suggest that Kennedy checks her email, but she's already on it. After a few seconds of pressing on the screen, she starts to jump up and down, which is impressive in the spindly heels she's wearing. 'I'm shortlisted too! Oh my goodness! Wow!'

I join Kennedy in jumping about. 'This is so so so amazing!' I cry happily, the alcohol making me feel loose and extra excited. 'They are going to love your goose and cat story. How could they not? Everyone loves interspecies friendships!'

Kennedy's face falls and I very swiftly realise that I wasn't supposed to say that. Shit. Was that supposed to be a secret?

'Oh, that sounds adorable,' Miles chuckles, pressing his hand to his chest in an exaggerated sort of way.

'You're not *really* going with "cute animal story", right?' Erin asks, doing actual air quotes with a slight smirk on her face.

Shit.

Kennedy shrugs a shoulder, her cheeks colouring from pink to red. 'I mean, it's the kind of story they always give the junior anchors. It's what they want, right?'

Erin snickers. 'At least give me a little competition, babe. You know I like a challenge.'

They stare at each other for quite a long time and I cannot tell if it's in anger or sexual tension. Either way, it is super uncomfortable for the rest of us.

'Well, what story are *you* auditioning with?' Kennedy asks eventually, her shoulders slightly hunching up.

'And why would I tell you that?' Erin laughs, tucking a shiny red strand of hair behind her tiny ear. 'Let's just say it's got a *little* more substance than a duck and a cat.'

'It's a *goose* and a cat,' Kennedy corrects, lifting her chin.

Helen and Miles giggle along with Erin and I'm pretty sure that these co-workers are not very nice after all. And I've gone and made Kennedy's happy news into something sour.

I knock back the rest of my drink. This is why I should not leave the house. I just fuck stuff up.

Kennedy smiles beatifically at the rest of the group. 'Well, it's been great bumping into you guys, but we have somewhere else we need to be.'

With her head held high, she starts walking towards the door and for a second I think she's going to leave me behind on account of my drunken, bean-spilling mouth. But she turns around and holds out a hand towards me. 'Come on, Nora. We have somewhere else to be.'

'Oh!' My heart dips in relief.

I turn and awkwardly wave at the bitchy co-workers before grabbing Kennedy's hand.

'Where else do we need to be?' I ask her as soon as we reach the warm, busy street.

'I don't know! I just made that up to get out of there,' she replies as we stumble along. 'This place will do.'

She drags me into the very next bar we come across, a

place lit with a flashing neon sign declaring itself to be called 'Trash'.

I follow Kennedy through a swinging door to a narrow, longish room filled with tables of people drinking from jugs of beer and chatting over a soundtrack of Miley Cyrus. The bar is small and surrounded by a crowd. At the end of the room is a small stage with a tinselly backdrop. Maybe it's a comedy club...

Either way, it couldn't be any more different than the place we've just come from. For a start, while the clientele still contains an abnormally high ratio of good-looking people, it does not look like a *Vogue Interiors* photo shoot. The chairs are upholstered in well-worn, raggedy hot pink fabric and the walls are crammed with pink and purple neon signs that say things like 'Send Nudes', 'The Future is Now' and 'Spring Break Forever'.

One thing that is the same, however, is that almost every person in here – men and women – turn to admire Kennedy. I mean, it's fair enough: she looks like she looks, and even with my Olaplex'd hair and my juicy denim-short-covered butt, I am drowned out by her light. Kennedy doesn't even notice the appreciative glances. She's more intent on the bar, ordering us another round of tequila shots and a jug of beer, which sounds like a pretty lethal combination considering the fact that I'm already more drunk than I have been in a number of years.

'I'm not sure I should drink any...' I trail off as Kennedy narrows her eyes at me, her serenity clearly upended by what just happened.

'We're celebrating the good news! Plus, you told Erin my story idea. You owe me. You are drinking with me.'

I can't really argue with that. I shrug and we each take a shot before carrying the rest of the drinks over to a table by the stage.

'Erin is The Worst. I cannot believe I slept with her. Ugh. Did you see how smug she was? How arrogant?'

'I'm so sorry for spilling the beans.'

'No, it's fine.' Kennedy sighs and rubs my arm, before taking another glug of beer, indicating that I should do the same. 'I mean, maybe she was right. Maybe I need to find a meatier story to focus on. My mom actually said the same thing…'

'What do *you* think?'

'I guess I want to increase my chances of getting the gig…' She shrugs. 'And I thought light stories would be what the producers wanted from me… Anyway, I will focus on that tomorrow. For now, let's celebrate the good news!'

She holds a shot glass aloft. I do the same.

'To you smashing the junior anchor audition!' I say.

At the same time, she says, 'Gary Montgomery reads *Harcourt Royals!*'

We knock back our drinks and I'm pretty sure that I am now completely and utterly drunk. So much so that when an older, very tanned guy in a glittering blue shirt with white spiky hair arrives on the stage and announces that it's karaoke time and Kennedy suggests we do a song, I don't immediately dismiss the suggestion out of hand.

The muchos alcohol I've ingested is definitely taking the edge off what I'm sure a sober me would classify as terror. The last time I sang in front of anyone was at the showcase gig I forced my parents to attend. The one they never made it to. Since then I've avoided stages the same way I avoid sweetcorn, new people and any kinds of competitive sport – with a deep and abiding focus.

'Come on, it'll be fun,' Kennedy urges, her eyes sparkling. She tops up my beer glass. 'Find your own joy, girl!'

I take three big gulps and, all at once, Kennedy has dragged me onto the little stage with her and is talking into the ear of the glittery-shirted tanned man.

What am I doing up here? I feel a bit sick. I should go

and sit back down and let Kennedy karaoke alone, but then she shoves something cold and heavy into my hand. I look down and see that it's a microphone. Some small part of my heart lifts in excitement. I used to love having a microphone in my hand. I remember now. I used to revel in that growing bubble of anticipation, in those moments before I would see the audiences' faces change from non-plussed to impressed. I had this need to show the people around me that I had real talent, that I could sing my stories and they would want to listen to them.

The crowd blurs in front of me, an abnormal proportion of attractive people swimming in and out of focus. I shouldn't be up here. I should be at home doing Gary planning. But before I can second-guess what is happening, the music starts. Kennedy has chosen Adele's 'Rolling In The Deep'. With a bellyful of liquid courage and my new friend by my side, I start to sing.

As my voice booms out over the microphone, my cheeks lift into an irrepressible smile. I'm singing. I'm singing for an audience. I missed this. I missed it so much.

On the second verse, I turn to smile at Kennedy and notice that she's no longer singing. She's staring at me with an open mouth.

Kennedy leans into me and yells into my ear, 'You are incredible. This one is yours, Nora.'

She quickly hands her microphone back to glittery shirt man and hurries to our table, and instead of feeling scared, I just want to get lost in the music, in the silly drunkenness, in my voice and how oddly surprising it is to me that it is still there, as if it's been waiting to be let out.

And so I sing. I sing like I've not sung in two years.

CHAPTER TWENTY-SIX

Gary

Hey,

I am journaling for the second time in a day! Ira, what have you done to me, you sneaky old dog.

My very peculiar and unsettling day completely turned around into something awesome and it's now 1.30 a.m. and I can't seem to get to sleep. So here I am to 'write it out.' Again. I don't want to forget how I feel tonight…

I just got back from an impromptu celebration dinner because two excellent things happened this evening. The first one is kind of insane: Aileen called me up and told me that I have been invited to do a handprint ceremony at the Chinese Theatre in Hollywood in a few days. I asked why the short notice and Aileen assured me that these things always move quickly, which makes a nice change from the snail's pace the rest of the industry moves at. It feels ridiculous to be doing an actual fucking handprint ceremony. BUT Cary Grant did it, Marilyn Monroe did it, the cast of *The Big Bang Theory* did it. And so I'm going to take my opportunities when they come knocking and do it too.

The second reason for the celebration dinner is that tonight I was at the beach with Seth and Olive and they witnessed me riding my first full wave without falling off the board! They only came so they could laugh at me when I choked, but IN THEIR FACES! This dude has been practicing his fucking ass off. I mean, it was a tiny wave and I wobbled the whole time but… I did it! What a high! My whole body was buzzing. I'm already eager to get back in the ocean and do more.

So Tori, Olive, Seth and I have celebrated this evening with a champagne dinner and it was an all-round epic night.

Oh, a couple of other amazing things to add to the three I did earlier…

1. Janet came home from her beach walk with Tori in the best mood I've ever seen her in. Her tongue was lolling, her eyes were sparkling and she just kept bounding around the house and rolling over onto her back like a total happy fool. I'm so glad she and Tori love each other so much.

2. On the walk home from the restaurant tonight, we passed this bar and from inside we heard a woman singing and I swear she had the most incredible voice I've ever heard. It was sweet and sort of raspy and strong. It made the hairs on the back of my neck stand up. I suggested we go in and check it out, but poor Tori had a stomach ache from all the food we ate, so we headed on home. Still, that voice was one of a kind. Even in Los Angeles you don't come across a gift like that too often.

CHAPTER TWENTY-SEVEN

Nora

I get off the stage to a deafening round of applause. It's a sound I've not heard in such a long time and it sends a bolt of elation right through my body. I'd forgotten how performing makes me feel. It makes me feel *free*. Like when I'm in that space, there's just me and the music, my head is clear and quiet, my heart is calm. I miss that feeling. Like I can fly!

When I reach the table, Kennedy stands up and pulls me into a massive hug, but we're both so pissed that we sort of topple to the side, a fall only being prevented by the fact that we are situated right by a wall. We get an attack of the giggles and start jumping up and down again. I am not a person who giggles and jumps around quite so much. It's a nice, daft feeling. I worry for a second that all the jumping will make me puke, but no, I am fine. Just quite drunk.

'That was unexpected,' comes a voice from behind me.

I turn around and my good mood dips when I realise that it's Brandon or, as I've been calling him in my head, Horrid Brandon on account of his horrid personality. He's dressed in a navy T-shirt and grey cargo pants, carrying his tote bag, which is filled to the brim with books. He reads? I soften towards him slightly, but still, ugh, what is he doing here? It is a girls' night out!

'Brandon!' Kennedy yells happily. 'You're here!'

I look between them, my face contorting into a squinty-eyed frown. Kennedy *invited* him? Why on earth would anyone invite the most miserable man of all time to a fun night out? Even if he is your recently dumped brother.

'Wasn't Nora amazing?' Kennedy asks Brandon, shaking her head in astonishment. 'Who knew she had that big old voice tucked away in there!'

'You're really talented,' Brandon says, a surprised look on his stern face.

'You should be a singer!' Kennedy remarks as we all sit down at the table, a round of drinks appearing from a nearby group who enjoyed my performance.

I can feel my cheeks turn red. 'Nah.'

'You could get paid for it,' Kennedy says. 'Seriously, you should get a manager, or do a show, make it a career...'

Making a career out of singing and writing songs is firmly off the table. The only reason I just got up on that stage is because the tequila has significantly blurred the painful memories and numbed the absolute nausea I usually feel at the mere thought of performing.

I plaster on a cheery smile and hold my glass of beer aloft, turning to Brandon and firmly changing the subject. 'Did Kennedy tell you her good news?'

* * *

Later on, back at the house, Kennedy fusses over Winklepuff, who is wiggly with happiness at our return, barking happily and running around in little circles. 'You are the goodest, most well-behaved dog in all of California,' Kennedy slurs, lying through her teeth.

I slip off my shoes and try not to fall immediately asleep on the sofa, not least because I have a tendency to drool and I do not want that shit on public show, drunk or not.

Brandon heads into the kitchen and grabs three cold beers out of the fridge. As he offers one of the bottles to me, I notice his hair is slightly sweaty and mussed up, like he's just got out of bed. It makes him look friendlier somehow. I really really really shouldn't drink any more, but Brandon is looking so cheerful and not like he wants to kill me, so I take the bottle from him to be polite.

Kennedy leans sleepily against the white painted bookcase and gives us both a sort of odd tender look and then does a massive stretch and yawn so big it looks like she might unhinge her jaw.

'Guys, I'm beat,' she tells us, cuddling Winklepuff to her chest and burying her head into his fur. He snorts with delight at the attention.

'You don't want a beer?' I ask, realising that I have already accepted a beer and will therefore have to sit here with Brandon on my own. I mean, tipsy Brandon is definitely better than the awful version I've encountered over the past couple of days, but still. Awkward.

'No, I have to work on my audition story in the morning,' she says, placing Winklepuff back down. 'I should definitely get to sleep… You two kids have fun!'

Argh. I was the one who was supposed to be sensibly going to bed so that I could get up early and research Gary stuff. Now Kennedy is already loping up the stairs, sort of bopping into the wall with each step upwards.

'Bye then…'

I smile awkwardly at Brandon, who does a half shrug in return. It's funny, now that he's not scowling, I realise that he is a good-looking guy. It's a little more of a traditional, gentler kind of good-looking. In contrast to Gary's intense eyes, dramatic curls and large, slightly wonky nose, Brandon has lighter, bigger eyes and the same shiny blonde hair as Kennedy. His nose is the nose of a Roman statue and he clearly works out because each time he lifts his beer bottle I can see his arm muscle pop a little bit underneath his shirt.

'Shall we take these outside?' Brandon suggests, gesturing to the bottles and then in the direction of the porch. 'I've got a surprise for you.'

A surprise? Oh! What could it be? An apology for being so mean to me? An admission that soulmates are not a fabrication invented by googly-eyed mooning idiots? Gary Montgomery's address?

Taking more energy than I would like to expend, I get up from the sofa and follow Brandon out onto the front porch, Winklepuff trotting along at our ankles, his little tail wagging giddily.

Outside, we take a seat on the porch bench and I smile because it really is gorgeous out here. It's past midnight and still warmer than most days in the north of England. I can't see the sea, but I can hear it gently lapping back and forth in front of us. The entire beach is empty and, above, the sky looks like the kind of diamond-dotted sky you would only ever see in a movie.

'I'll be back in just a moment,' Brandon says, handing me his bottle and scooting back into the house.

When he returns a few seconds later, he's carrying a Tupperware box, a couple of duck-egg blue plates and some paper napkins.

My stomach rumbles. I had thought about getting a drunken snack because we were supposed to eat out but ended up drinking in the karaoke bar instead. I did raid the fridge, but all that was in there was some kumquat and kombucha and I have zero idea what either of those things are. I must do some grocery shopping tomorrow.

Brandon sits back down on the bench and opens the Tupperware lid to reveal a mound of soft, charred pastrami.

I gasp. It smells amazing.

'I have a mini fridge in my room.' Brandon laughs, using a fork to put some pastrami and pickles onto two plates. 'Kennedy thinks it's for me to store the sparkling water I'm addicted to, and mostly it is, but I also keep secret meat in there.'

'Kennedy doesn't know you're not vegan?'

He does an exaggerated guilty look, his mouth stretching into his cheeks. 'She'd be so disappointed in me if she knew. So do not tell her.'

I appreciate that Brandon is opening up to me and that he's provided possibly the best midnight snack I have ever had, but I feel a tad weird that he's asking me to keep something from Kennedy. Then again, I've been feeding her dog ham and I've been keeping that from her, so I can hardly take the moral high ground.

Below us, Winklepuff rolls back onto his hind legs, paws in the air, begging adorably.

Brandon feeds him some pastrami. 'He loves beef. Not as much as ham, which he usually prefers, but I like pastrami more so that's what he gets,' he says.

I laugh as I finally realise why Winklepuff responds so acutely to the word ham.

Brandon asks what's so funny. I tell him that I have also been feeding Winklepuff secret ham.

'Dogs are not supposed to be vegan,' Brandon declares, laughing at my confession. 'Their teeth are made for meat. You definitely can't tell Kennedy now you've admitted to me that you are a fellow ham enabler.' He smiles and it transforms his grumpy face into a warm and friendly one.

I take another bite of pastrami, sighing happily as I do,

and have a sip of my beer, before leaning back into the porch bench with a sigh.

'So…' Brandon says eventually. 'Gary Montgomery, huh?'

I feel my entire face go red; like, actually feel it warm up.

'Kennedy didn't tell me, by the way,' Brandon adds. 'In case you were wondering.'

I feel a rush of relief. 'Oh. So how…?'

'Well, there was that phone call I heard with your terrible American accent. And then I also overheard you guys talking the other night while you were drinking that godawful peach wine. It wasn't exactly a tough case to crack.'

'You overhear a lot of things.'

'In my own house? Yes, I guess I do.' He gives another small smile and I can't quite tell if he's mocking me or being friendly. I smile back because I am very polite, even when intoxicated.

I lift my chin. 'I know you think soulmates aren't real, but I respectfully disagree.'

Brandon laughs out loud now. 'Oh, you do?'

I nod quickly and sit up straighter on the bench. 'When I was younger, my mum told me that one day I would find the person who was meant for me and that I would feel it like a bolt right through my body. That's what I felt when I saw Gary for the first time. I know it seems nuts, but—'

'You think Gary Montgomery will dump his model girlfriend for you?' Brandon interrupts.

'She's not a model.'

'She might as well be!'

'She is very beautiful, yes. But love is about more than looks. It's about a deep abiding connection. It's about *destiny*.'

Brandon shakes his head slowly, takes a sip of his beer

and turns a little more toward me on the bench. I can smell his soap. Something sweet. Almond, I think. 'You know...' he says. 'People like us... we don't get the Gary Montgomerys and Elsie Graingers of the world.'

'Who's Elsie Grainger?'

Brandon looks down at his knees. 'My ex. She's a human rights lawyer, and the most beautiful woman I've ever met. Probably will ever meet. Folks spot her on the street, they follow her sometimes. She's extraordinary. But she eventually realised that I was not in her league, cheated on me with some movie producer and now...' He mimes a bomb exploding out of his chest. His eyes water slightly.

'I'm sorry,' I say, meaning it. 'That sounds awful.'

'It was. *Is.*'

'Maybe you and Elsie just weren't meant to be... But Gary and I? I can feel it, right deep down and—'

'People like you and I don't get people like them, Nora...'

'What does that even mean *people like you and I?*'

He shrugs. 'Ordinary people. People who for the most part go unnoticed. Who don't get stopped on the street.'

My heart dips. I know I'm ordinary. And, over the last couple of years, I've gone more and more unnoticed, and that's been intentional. But to have someone say it so plainly, to outright tell me that I'm not good enough for someone else? He barely even knows me. I mean, *I* know that Gary is way out of my league – I'm not a complete idiot. But love is more than just the way people look or their station in life, right? It has to be.

The alcohol has blurred all of my edges, but the starkness of Brandon's words dart at my chest. Because the likelihood is that he is absolutely right.

Brandon pushes his shoulder into mine, playfully. 'Maybe people like us should stick together. Have a little fun while you're here instead of chasing after things that are never gonna happen the way you want them to. God knows you would save yourself a lot of pain. Trust me.' He leans slowly towards me and presses his thumb on my face just outside my eye.

Um, what is he doing?

'Your eye looks painful.'

'Oh. Yes. I got some bloody wind dirt in it. I should probably take out my contact lenses for a few days…'

'Mmmhmm.' Brandon's head moves towards mine and I see that up close he has a tiny scattering of freckles over his nose. Fuck. Is he going to try to kiss me?

He looks down at my lips and smiles slightly, his blue eyes flicking back up towards mine.

He *is*. Horrid Brandon is about to kiss me. I… thought he disliked me. I'm so confused.

I stand up before his lips reach mine.

'We can't do that,' I say firmly, placing my bottle down onto the porch table with a gentle clink.

'You're saving yourself for a *movie star*?' he asks in astonishment, half-laughing.

I know it sounds ridiculous. And Brandon is far better-looking than anyone I've ever been with before and for all I know he might be completely and utterly right about how much pain I have coming my way from this pursuit. But… Yes. I am saving myself for a movie star. For Gary.

'Yes. I am,' I say, after a hard swallow.

Brandon fully laughs this time and shrugs as a huge gust of wind whips around both of us, causing his hair to stick directly upright and mine to blow smack into my face, a chunk of it getting into my mouth.

He looks at me with a sad, sort of pitying smile. 'Goodnight, Nora.'

'Goodnight, Brandon.'

I wobble my way into my bedroom area and fall into the bed, the word 'ordinary' going round and round in my head.

CHAPTER TWENTY-EIGHT

Nora

I'm having an extremely weird dream, different than the ones I usually have. I'm dreaming that Gary is on Muscle Beach doing a naked workout and crowds of people are taking his photograph. I keep calling his name, but he doesn't hear me no matter how loudly I shout. Then Imogene is beside me with Roger Pepper and they start singing a duet. The melody is the same as one of the songs I planned to sing at my showcase gig, but instead of the words I wrote, Imogene and Roger Pepper are just singing "ha ha ha" over and over again. And then Gary morphs into Brandon and comes over and licks the side of my face. It feels quite nice at first and then I realise that his breath stinks a lot like the breath of...

'Winklepuff! Get off of her!'

I hear the giggling, sweet-toned voice of Kennedy and open my eyes to see, blurrily, that she is standing at the side of my bed with a glass of sludgy green stuff in one hand and my spectacles in the other.

I slip on my glasses and stare at the green sludge with a

frown. It looks disgusting. There are *bits* in it. What are those bits?

'What time is it?' I ask, knowing deep in the pit of my soul that whatever time it is, it is not a time that my body is supposed to be awake, especially when a person sleeps as terribly as I do.

I slowly sit up, immediately regretting it as my head starts to protest, big time. I get a flashback of singing last night and I can't quite believe I did that, even with all of that Dutch courage. And then I remember Brandon trying to kiss me. And him saying that I have zero chance with someone like Gary Montgomery. My shoulders sink.

'It's five thirty A.M.!' Kennedy announces chirpily, looking as bright-eyed and glowing as ever. 'Hangover brigade to the rescue!' She shoves the glass of green stuff into my hand.

'Hangovers are best cured by sleep,' I tell her, mashing my dry tongue against the roof of my mouth.

'Nonsense. Drink this.'

'What are all the bits?'

'A mix of hemp seed, flax seed and chia seeds.'

'Seedy.'

'Drink it up. Then put on your bathing suit and meet me in the living room, okay?'

'Bathing suit?' I goggle at her.

'A *swim* is actually the best hangover cure,' she says knowledgeably. 'And the ocean is looking incredible this morning. There's no one else out there and the winds aren't due to go crazy for another few hours at least!' She puts her hands on her hips and gestures to the window with an outstretched arm. Then smiles a wide, megawatt smile and says in a very exaggerated, chipper voice, 'It sure is another beautiful day in the City of Angels!'

I laugh at her weather-girl spiel and immediately regret it as the laugh turns into a dry heave.

'I can't go swimming!' I put a hand to my head. It is

very clammy. I did not have enough water while we were out, likely sweated in this heat all night and now I'm seriously dehydrated. 'I feel quite unwell.' I sigh. 'This was why I wanted to stay in. Plus, I have so much Gary-planning to do. I thought we were going to look at the forum to see if he is there under a fake name?'

'Oh, I've already done it,' Kennedy says merrily and I wonder if last night she was secretly knocking back water instead of tequila. Either that or she is some sort of android. 'I checked and triple-checked. He's not on there. I'm sorry. Come on, hurry!'

She flounces out of the bedroom area, Winklepuff trotting jauntily alongside her ankles.

My shoulders slump at the news that Gary isn't on the forums. Damn it. That would have been a real coup. I could have private-messaged him on there! Or maybe even gotten his address. Hmmm. Actually, showing up at his house would be treading a pretty fine line between trying to meet the person you think might be The One and stalking them.

I pull open one of the curtains behind me. Kennedy was right. The beach does look lovely and calm... I screw up my courage and take a tentative sip of the sludge. Ooh! It actually tastes quite nice – like lime and mint and apples and, well, seeds.

I gingerly step out of the bed and very very slowly get changed into my too-tight navy blue swimming costume, covering it up with one of my too-tight sundresses. I pop in my contact lenses and flinch as what I'm starting to think is a scratch from the wind dirt stings again. I shouldn't really be wearing them, but I can hardly swim in my glasses. I grab some of the soothing eye drops Billy Fever told me to use and it softens the niggle.

In the living room, I down a pint of water, while a bikini-clad Kennedy finishes whatever she's typing up and grabs a polka-dotted beach bag from the floor beside her. I think we're about to make it out of the house without running into Brandon when he comes down the stairs, dressed only in a white towel slung low on his hips.

Wow. Brandon works out. My eyes widen a little bit at his toned, tanned stomach.

He catches me looking and grins, runs a hand through his wet blonde hair, flexing his bicep a little as he does so.

I look away quickly, to find Kennedy giggling and rolling her eyes. 'TMI Brandon,' she says, miming a vomiting motion. 'Come on, Nora. Let's get out there.'

* * *

The ocean *is* an amazing cure for a hangover. As long as you take away the swimming part and focus on just lying there. I allow my body to get used to the slightly cool temperature before floating along, letting the gentle crystal-clear waves do all the work. My eyes squint from the glare of a sun that is bright and eager.

'You actually have to do some swimming!' Kennedy admonishes as she flips past me, her long blonde hair fanning out behind her and making her look like a Californian mermaid. 'Get those endorphins going. Endorphins bring joy!'

I internally roll my eyes and join her as she swims further out towards a bright yellow buoy. I'm usually more of a gentle stretch on the bedroom floor type, but I have to admit that it feels nice to push myself a little more.

After some more intense swimming, I feel a pleasant ache in my limbs. I stop and tread water, catching my breath and enjoying the taste of salt on my lips.

'So, did you and Brandon have a nice time chatting last night?' Kennedy asks, bobbing along beside me.

I narrow my eyes. What does she know? What do I say?

I clear my throat. 'Yes, it was nice,' I offer neutrally.

'He's great right?' she asks. 'He can be a little surly, sure, but he's a softie at heart…'

'He seemed pretty cut up about Elsie Grainger.'

Until he tried to kiss me, I don't add.

'Yeah, he fell pretty deep for that one. She was *not* good to him. He deserves something nice to happen. He's had a tough time, romantically.'

I nod slowly. 'He should get back out there. Find someone to distract him from feeling so sad and cynical.'

'That's exactly what I think!' Kennedy agrees, smiling a weirdly big smile before taking off into another speedy breaststroke.

I remain in the same spot and, squinting back at the beach, I can't help but sigh at how beautiful and peaceful it looks. The sky is a soft blush pink and streaked cerulean blue. The hazy light is almost dreamlike. I think of Mum and Dad and wish that I believed in heaven, because if I did, it would look like this beach and this sky and my parents would be there, as happy and in love as they ever were.

I dunk my head under the water in a bid to stop my sudden sadness in its tracks and when I bob back up, I catch sight of two men jogging down the beach. They're far away and the sun is in my eyes, but one of them stops to catch his breath, hands on his knees and looks out towards the water. I wonder if he can see me from all the way over there. I'm tempted to lift my arm and wave at the stranger, but I don't in case he thinks I'm signalling for help.

The other guy, yanks the man's arm as if to say 'Come on!' and they take off, running back down the beach.

I chuckle to myself. Running at this time in the morning is even weirder than swimming. And Imogene says I'm the crazy one.

I flip around onto my back again and watch a single wispy pink cloud float by. I stay there for a while and it occurs to me that the reason Kennedy is always so serene is because she gets to do this every day.

By the time we get back to the house, I am shattered, my whole body aching and tingling, but in a pleasant way. My hangover has completely gone, just as Kennedy said it would!

I dry myself off and sit down on my bed to do some work, which, while incredibly boring, is very simple and easy to whizz through. Afterwards, I grab my phone to check my daily Google Alerts on Gary's name. Oh, there's an article on Variety.com. I click it open and gasp as I read the words on the screen.

Here it is. Here is my chance!

I scurry into the living room. 'Gary is going to be doing the handprint ceremony at the Chinese Theatre!' I say to Kennedy.

Kennedy looks surprised at my excitable outburst. 'Really? I'm surprised he's doing that already. I didn't think he'd done enough movies…'

'It's obviously because they know how amazing he is,' I say, as if I know the man personally. 'He deserves all the success. The public can go to these things, can't they? I've seen pictures online.'

'They can,' Kennedy nods, pulling her bathrobe more tightly around her. 'It's a pretty open space, so I guess we can go see him do the ceremony. The celebrities usually sign autographs for the fans—'

'So I could meet him. I could actually meet him.' My skin springs into goosebumps at the thought of seeing Gary in real life again, and this time without being thwarted by stoopid Nicolas Cage and that horrid security guard from the set, John Alan. I feel slightly breathless with anticipation.

'When is it?' Kennedy asks. 'Will you still be here?'

'Yes! It's on Wednesday. At 2 p.m.'

'Oh! That's super soon.'

'Yes! Hurrah! I was starting to feel convinced that I really was as crazy as everyone thought, but after what happened at the beach – finding out about Gary's bookish tastes and meeting Tori – I know that I HAVE to do this.'

Kennedy nods thoughtfully, her eyes slightly narrowed.

'Okay…' she says slowly. 'Wednesday is three days away, right? So… how about, if you don't have to do any Gary-based sleuthing for the next few days, you use that time to joy seek in LA with me?' She points a thumb at herself to indicate. 'I mean, I have work and prep for my anchor audition, but there's plenty of time. It would be a real shame for you to miss out on this place, especially as you're on such a short trip.'

I consider her suggestion. The thought of doing lots of *activities* for the next few days sounds exhausting. But I did agree to try to find some joy. And hanging out with new people hasn't actually been as tough as I thought it would be…'

'That sounds great. But no more drinking! I have to keep a clear head.'

Kennedy holds her hand out to shake mine. 'Me too. Yay! Joy ahoy!'

Imogene's phone rings for half a ring before she picks up.

'Finally!' she breathes, her voice tight. 'I've been worried. You got kicked off a film set? Are you okay? Maybe you should come home. The last thing you need is to get arrested in a foreign country!'

Imogene's intensity would ordinarily have my shoulders up around my ears, but after the swim and all the great Gary progress, I am channelling Kennedy with my levels of serenity. 'I'm fine, silly.' I laugh. 'I've been texting you.'

'Yes, but it's not the same as hearing your voice. I can't tell if you're lying through a text, but I can from your voice.'

'I am fine, I promise,' I say. And for the first time in a long time, I think I might actually mean it. 'I am getting plenty of vitamin D, just like you wanted.'

'You wearing plenty of sun cream?'

'Yep.'

'Hmm. Tell me about what happened on the film set? What is your online friend like? Did you really meet Nicolas Cage? Are you feeling, you know, sane?'

I laugh, take a deep breath and regale Imogene with the tales of the last few days, leaving no stone unturned. When I'm finished, there's a pause on the other end of the phone. 'Imogene? Are you there? Have I been talking to a dead line?'

'I'm here,' Imogene says. 'You sound… different.'

'Good different or bad different?' I ask.

'Good. I think. You sound more, I don't know, awake. And this Kennedy? She sounds cool. I'm definitely less worried than I was.'

'That's good. And Kennedy is so, so great. You would really like her, I think.'

'Tell me more about this Brandon guy. He sounds hot.'

'Oh, he's all right. He's no Gary, of course. And he can be pretty damn grumpy.'

'Grumpy can be sexy, in the right light.'

'Nah, I'm not into it.'

'Are you sure? You like Mr Darcy and he was grumpy!'

'Grumpy is not hot in real life. It's just dickish. I'm here to meet Gary Montgomery! That's why you made me come here, Imogene!'

'And you still genuinely believe that he's your soulmate?'

I can hear her scepticism from all the way across the Atlantic.

'Even more than I did when I saw him at the pictures.' I say. 'I saw him across the movie lot and I felt this absolute buzz rush through my body! I'm so sure of how I feel. I've never felt so sure about anything.'

'Hmmm. Just… be careful, okay. I think what this Kennedy suggested about having a little fun for the next few days sounds like a great idea. And maybe you'll get to hang out with Hot Brandon some more.'

'You can't call him Hot Brandon! You've never even seen him… I mean, he *is* handsome, but in a very typical sort of way. Not like Gary. Gary's eyes are so dark they look black. Do you know how rare that is?'

Imogene sighs quietly. 'Listen,' she says in a serious voice. 'Please be prepared for the fact that this Gary Montgomery thing isn't likely to turn out how you want it to…'

'You don't know that, Imogene.'

'I sort of do, though… and I know I sent you out there, which may have been a major mistake. I couldn't live with myself if me trying to give you a much-needed dose of reality ended up with you coming back to Brigglesford way worse off than when you left…'

To my surprise, my stomach drops a little at the suggestion of being back in Brigglesford.

'How are you, anyway?' I ask quickly, changing the subject from Imogene's naysaying, which is totally confusing my newly unflustered mood. 'How's Ariana? How's Dan?'

'Oh, we're all fine!' Imogene says in a voice that sounds a little less buoyant than usual. 'Everything's fine! Same as usual, I suppose.'

'Are you sure? What have you been up to?'

'Working, mothering, wifing, going to the gym. Over

and over again for forever and ever! Ha ha! Everything's great.' Her voice slightly cracks.

'You don't sound great,' I say, feeling surprised and worried to hear Imogene sounding anything other than a woman who has her shit completely together. I sit back against my pillows. 'Want to talk about it? I know it's always you giving me advice, and admittedly I am not the wisest person around, but I can at least listen if you're feeling a bit shit?'

'I'm fine, honestly!' Imogene chirrups, faux cheerily. 'I'm just hormonal, I think! Listen, I have to go. Ariana's done a massive poo and it stinks. I have to go and change her, keep me updated with everything, okay? Everything!'

'Definitely. Love you, Im.'

'Love you, Sis.'

When the phone call ends, I stare at the wall for a bit, alarmed and saddened at Imogene's unusual flatness. I wonder what's going on with her? Was she hormonal or is it something more? Before I can think about it too much, though, Kennedy warns me that she's about to enter my area and swishes open the heavy curtain. She asks me to listen to a bunch of new, more serious, story ideas she has for her anchor audition. When Winklepuff joins her, jumping up onto the bed and frantically licking my face with his disgusting tongue, I laugh so much that all anxious thoughts about Imogene float out of my head.

CHAPTER TWENTY-NINE

Gary

Hey,

I am now being shadowed by my new *bodyguard* every second I'm at work. Yup. The studio also insist that John Alan escorts me to and from the set every day. I know this guy is only trying to look out for me, to protect me from this stalker woman, and I hate to be negative about people I don't know very well, but he's, well, he's kind of a dick. He has a gun, which I hate, and he acts like he's Bruce Willis in the *Die Hard* movies. Only with none of the coolness. He's shaped like a barrel on two sticks and he makes me stand behind him every time we're about to turn a corner. He puts a hand on his gun and hisses at me to RETREAT! It's getting embarrassing.

Just yesterday, I caught a couple of the crew snickering at me while John Alan smelled every single one of the blueberry muffins at craft services before he allowed me to have one. Nicolas Cage has taken to singing 'I Will Always Love You' from *The Bodyguard* when he sees me with John, which is nuts because that guy has more than his fair share of an entourage.

It wouldn't even be so bad if I got on with John Alan. I've tried making conversation with him, but his eyes are always darting from side to side, seeking out possible threats. I asked him what his favourite movie was and he said it was *The Next Karate Kid*. Not *Karate Kid One* or *Two* or *Three*. *The Next Karate Kid*. And, really, doesn't that tell me all I need to know about him?

I've promised the studio and Aileen that I won't leave my house without him, but I've been sneaking out early mornings to run with Seth. Which brings me to my three amazing things for today.

1. Seth is planning on asking Olive to marry him. He's going to do it back in New York at Gramercy Park, but he's already asked me to be his best man. I'm fucking psyched for him. I've never seen a couple more in love than those two… It makes me feel all kinds of romantic. Maybe I've been too hasty in putting off a proposal to Tori. I mean, it's inevitable, right? I'm a grown adult man and I'm happy with her. It makes total sense…

2. This morning, Seth and I went for a run on the beach, just after the sun came up. The sky was insane, all pink and blue streaks. It was like something out of a dream. The sky is the best thing about LA. I saw someone far out in the ocean, just treading water. I couldn't tell if it was a man or a woman, but I couldn't stop watching them. It made me eager to be back in the water, bobbing around and staring up at that sky.

3. I saw the dailies from the past two days of shooting and I'm feeling really proud of the work we're doing. The rest of the cast and crew

are cool and fun to be around and it just re-enforced to me that, despite the negatives, I'm lucky to be doing this. In fact, it's the best thing in my life right now and that's all thanks to Tori and Aileen. If I can get Aileen to read Olive's script and agree that it would be great for me—and John Alan to go away—things might actually start feeling better.

Gotta go. John Alan is waiting to take me home and he's staring impatiently at me with those weird shark eyes. Time to let him escort me through these dangerous streets and protect me from potential death by butter knife.

CHAPTER THIRTY

Nora

I don't think I have ever been this tired before. And I don't mean mentally tired in the way I usually feel at the end of a working week, or every time I think about my parents, or when Imogene tells me about the various attributes of Roger Pepper, but physically exhausted. Like I could fall asleep wherever I lay my head, which has never, ever happened in my life and especially not the past two years, when I've not had a single full night of sleep that I can recall.

Knowing just when Gary is going to be at the Chinese Theatre means that Kennedy and I've been able to spend the last three days acting like tourists. Zipping around a busy, glamorous, hot and windy city is not something I ever thought I'd enjoy doing. But, although I'm knackered, I'm feeling better than I have in quite a while. It's a feeling I didn't even realise I was missing.

Every quiet, before-bed moment I have is spent reading the newest *Harcourt Royals* book, because a) It is the very best of all the books, and b) Kennedy has read it and it's winding me up that she knows how it ends and I don't. And then every second not spent reading, sleeping, eating, walking Winklepuff or thinking about Gary Montgomery has been crammed with activity. I've barely had time to pee, let alone think constantly about how it's my fault that my parents are dead. I mean, the thought is still there, but it's a little quieter than usual and that, frankly, feels like a sweet relief.

Yesterday, after we went swimming, Kennedy drove me around on a tour of LA's best bookshops, including a gigantic one that was housed in an abandoned bank. In one of the bookshops, I found a whole set of signed *Harcourt Royals* books, which made me jump with joy until I realised that I am pretty damn skint and can't afford to buy stuff like that. But when we stopped off for lunch at a trendy and Insta-famous Taco Truck, Kennedy opened up a bag and revealed that she had secretly bought me the signed set while I was taking Winklepuff for a wee! And that made me cry because even before Mum and Dad, back when I had friends and a social life, I never met anyone who was so genuinely lovely and kind as Kennedy Jane Cooper.

In the afternoon, Kennedy had to work on her news story, so I took myself and Winklepuff back to the dog-friendly beach for another special rocky road ice cream. The Adonis who served me last time seemed very pleased to see me.

'You liked the product, huh?' he asked with a conspiratorial look, like we were in on some sort of secret.

'Yes,' I answered, a bit confused. Who wouldn't enjoy ice cream on the beach?

He then asked me if I wanted to try the special sundae, which was apparently even more special. Of course I said yes – and he was right! It was amazing and I spent the next hour on the beach wandering around and playing with Winklepuff, listening to a 'Get Pumped!' playlist on Spotify, feeling oddly confident and saying hi to strangers, not caring that very few of them seemed to hear me. I thought to myself that there must be something about ice cream that I find very soothing, maybe something to do with having it on happy family occasions as a kid...

When I eventually arrived back at the house, feeling very floaty, sun-soaked and ready for a snooze, Kennedy dragged me back out to a walking art tour in Downtown LA. Then today, after another early-morning swim, Kennedy went to work to do her weather report and then we met for lunch at a super-healthy place called Flower Child, where I saw actual Bette Midler eating a salad, which tickled me pink.

Brandon has shown up on our jaunts a couple of times, acting awkward and nervy around me, which has been a little bit annoying. He even joined us swimming this morning, although Kennedy swears she didn't tell him we were going. He kept swimming over to me and starting up conversations, which I then had to respond to because I am staying at his house for free. I suppose when he isn't telling me I'm ordinary or scoffing at my reasons for being in LA, he's actually not the worst person in the world. Close, though.

Now Kennedy, as part of her mission to help me to find joy, has brought me to the nearby Venice Beach boardwalk.

'This place looks very cool,' I say, looking around at the pop-up food huts and street performers and little market stalls selling delicate pieces of silver and turquoise necklaces and wooden beaded bracelets in all different colours. 'Are we going shopping?' I ask as Kennedy indicates that I keep following her down the boardwalk. We pass a little hut selling candy floss. 'We're getting candy floss? I love candy floss!'

'It's called cotton candy and, no, we are not eating that junk! Ew!'

Kennedy continues walking until the density of the crowds thins out and the smooth and dusty grey boardwalk stretches ahead of us, lined with the beach and the ocean on one side and shops and chunky palm trees on the other. Kennedy smiles with all of those perfect teeth and points at a little painted sign above a colourful wooden hut.

ROLLERBLADES FOR HIRE.

I feel the colour drain from my face, which cannot be easy considering how sun-reddened it is.

'We're going rollerblading!' Kennedy confirms, beaming. 'It's one of the funnest "corny LA" things to do and it's a *great* way to keep fit.'

I pull a face. 'But I already swam *and* walked today,' I grumble, looking down at my warm, comforting, round body that is used to being indoors and sitting down for lots of the time. 'I'm knackered! And I really don't think I'll like rollerblading.'

'You didn't think you'd like early-morning swimming and you're a natural,' Kennedy reasons. 'Even if you do spend half the time floating about and staring at the sky instead of actually swimming.'

She's right. Just a few days of swimming in a warm and peaceful ocean has improved my mood considerably. But skating is totally different. And my balance is terrible; I have been known to trip over thin air! I tell Kennedy this.

'You can do it. I believe in you, girl!'

'I really don't think so, Kennedy. Last time I skated on wheels, I was twelve and I roller-skated down a hill that was much steeper than I initially calculated – perspective is not my strong point. I went so fast, lost control of which direction I was supposed to go in and rolled right into a hedgerow full of stinging nettles.'

Kennedy looks like she's trying not to laugh at what, frankly, is a traumatising formative memory of mine. 'I had to soak myself in vinegar for over an hour to take out the sting. I stank like a chippy the whole next day.'

'A chippy? What the sweet hell is a chippy?'

'A fish and chip shop!' I roll my eyes. 'The kids at school kept asking me for pudding, chips and peas with pea wet. It was awful.'

Kennedy goggles. 'Pea? Wet?'

'You know? Pea soup. Pea juice,' I explain, exasperated. 'Anyway, the point is that I don't think I will be attaching wheels to the bottom of my already unstable feet. It's lovely of you to bring me here, but I think it's probably a no-go.'

Kennedy folds her arms across her chest and looks down at her tanned, sandalled feet. 'I told you I was going to help you to experience joy, so why won't you just let me? Why can't you just say ahoy to joy?'

The corner of my mouth lifts into a smile, but then I realise Kennedy isn't joking with the whole say ahoy to joy thing. I look hard at her. This virtual stranger who is being so generous with her time and her energy for someone who only last week she knew solely through the internet. The last time someone was this unreasonably kind to me it turned out to be my next-door-but-one neighbour Sleazy Bruce, who took my bins out for a month before revealing that I should join his pyramid scheme.

'Why are you doing all this for me?' I ask, a note of suspicion creeping into my voice. 'I don't understand.'

Kennedy puts her hands together in a prayer position. 'Because I am a very sweet person.'

I raise an eyebrow.

'I like you, okay!' she says, throwing her hands up in the air now. 'You're not like my other friends here. You're…'

'Much cooler?' I joke.

Kennedy pulls a face. 'Ha! You're easy-going, I

suppose. I feel relaxed around you.' She shrugs. 'Like I can be myself and totally nerd out… in fact…'

'What?'

Kennedy looks thoughtful for a moment before shaking her head slightly. 'Nothing. You know, I may have been tipsy on peach wine when I promised to help you find some joy. But I meant it. Seeing my new friend find joy outside of this whole, you know, "soulmate" mission will bring *me* joy. And don't you want me to have joy? After all the joy I am trying to bring to you? You would *deny* me joy? That is not joyful behaviour, Nora.'

I laugh at her faux manipulation, touched that Kennedy just referred to me as a friend and not just an online friend and the fact that, for some reason, she's trying to help me to become a happier person for the short time that I'm here.

'Okay, I'll try it,' I say tentatively.

'Yay!' Kennedy does a cheerleader-style fist pump into the air. 'It's so much easier than you think. I think you're really gonna love it…'

* * *

I hate rollerblading. HATE it. Rollerblading is *not* easier than I think. Rollerblading is very, very dangerous. Rollerblading SUCKS.

Kennedy just *glides* along the boardwalk in her jean shorts: tanned, toned legs moving seamlessly in time with her feet, like she was born wearing a pair of rollerblades. She receives admiring glances from passing strangers and another rollerblader calls out to her, 'Hey nice form!' to which Kennedy replies, 'Thanks, you too!'

I, on the other hand, am wobbling from left to right, my arms flung out to balance me, while simultaneously checking that a boob hasn't escaped from my sundress or that one of the buttons running down the front hasn't burst open, exposing my knickers for all to see, which, as it happens, are skaggy bed knickers because I need to do some laundry.

'Careful, careful, aaaaaargh,' I whisper to myself in fear. I stop occasionally and try to shuffle to somewhere I can put my hands on a building or a palm tree to get some balance, but all I end up doing is clogging up the increasingly busy boardwalk and have people yell at me.

I like my body very much, but it was not made to be supported only by wheels. Kennedy seems nonchalant to my struggle. She looks like something out of a Tampax advert, hair flying out behind her, high-fiving an occasional passer-by, a healthy modern woman, unencumbered by her menstrual tide.

Not only is rollerblading dangerous, but it's really really hard. My thighs are on fire, even worse than when I did a workout video called Squat Nation and had to apply muscle heat rub for a week afterwards and screamed every time I got in and out of a chair. Plus, my stomach muscles are all tight because I'm holding my breath with the dreaded anticipation of these possibly being my last moments on earth.

'Tell Gary I loved him,' I try to call to Kennedy, but she's way ahead of me and an older skinny man standing outside a store selling bongs narrows his eyes.

'Tell him yourself, Lady!' he calls as I zoom past him, my arms flapping in circles like a cartoon character.

I try hard to catch up with Kennedy and breathe a sigh of relief as I spot a gentle downward slope ahead of us. Good. Downward slopes mean I can just keep my legs still, the hill will do all the work for me and my poor thighs can get a few seconds of relief. I try to slow down, keeping an eye on Kennedy, who is already halfway down the slope ahead. Right at that moment, an enormous gust of wind gushes into my face, blowing something into my already sore eye.

'Argh!' I yelp, lifting my hand up to rub whatever the hell it is out of there. 'Please don't be an insect,' I cry, immediately getting a vision of some creepy-crawly making a home in my left eyeball.

Before I can get whatever it is out, the wind blasts again and a load of tiny sand grains from the beach splat across my face.

'Argh!' I yell again, this time more loudly, meaning the sand gets all on my tongue.

I squint open my one working eye and see that Kennedy is now way, way ahead of me. I attempt to bring myself to a stop, but this downward slope seems to have increased my speed much more than expected and I can't slow enough to pull a foot up onto the stopper of my boot. My heart thuds with panic as I realise that essentially I am skating down a hill with a gob-full of sand and no ability to see where the hell I'm going. Shit. I'm going to hit someone. Maybe even a child! Fuck what if I roll over a toddler causing serious injury? That would be horrible! What would Gary think? Oh my god.

I put my hands out in front of me as I speed along with my stinging eyes struggling to stay open and shout as loud as I can. 'Move out of the way, people! Move your toddlers away! This train is not stopping at the staa— Argh!'

FUCK!

I feel myself crash into something, though I don't know what it is because the sting has forced my eyes closed. Shit, I think it's another human. I put my hands out and have a feel around because every time I try to open my eyes it hurts like hell. It's a large human. Not a toddler, phew.

'Oof!' growls the other person. A man. A man with a solid body.

'I'm sorry!' I squeak, immediately stumbling onto the

ground and rubbing my eyes. 'I couldn't stop and I have crap in both of my eyes. Are you hurt? I'm so sorry.'

'I'm okay,' he says. 'Are you?'

I recognise that voice. It sounds exactly like…

'Brandon!' Kennedy shouts, panicked. 'Is she okay? Jeeez!'

Brandon?

What the hell is Brandon doing here?

'I'm all right!' I reassure them, my eyes still scrunched closed as I rub at them. 'Are you sure you're all right, Brandon?'

'I'm fine,' he says, although he doesn't sound it. I heard that 'Oof' and it sounded very much like the 'Oof' of a man in pain.

I eventually manage to get the grit out of my eyes and open them. Stoopid sand. Stoopid weird wind. I rub my eyes again and Kennedy and Brandon come into view. They're crouching down in front of me, expressions of concern on their perfect faces.

Brandon leans in close and peers into my squinting eyes. 'When the Santa Anas blow, all bets are off,' he says.

I frown. I've heard that phrase before… It's what Jack Black says in *The Holiday*. Once of my favourite romantic films.

'I love that film,' I say.

'Me too,' Brandon replies with a half-smile.

Kennedy is watching us with a weird grin on her face.

'Let's take these off,' Brandon says, untying the laces on my rollerblades.

'God, yes please,' I respond gratefully. I fiddle with my fingers awkwardly as Brandon unties the boots. I feel my face turn red at the strange intimacy of it. 'I'm not made to be on wheels!'

'Understatement,' Brandon grins, his eyes ever so slightly flicking up towards my thick thighs.

'I'm sorry,' Kennedy says, holding a hand out to help

me to my feet. 'You did tell me about your bad balance. I thought you were exaggerating. I should never have forced you! Shit, I thought it would be joyful for you.'

'It's okay! I'm okay!' I reassure her.

She nods slowly, looking from me to Brandon and back again. 'Okay. Good. Um... So, yeah, I just remembered I need to shoot off... Get more work done, y'know? Brandon's here now, so he can walk you back, right? Yeah. I'll see the two of you back at home! Bye!'

What?!

Before I can protest, Kennedy gives me a brief hug, then spins on her skates and speeds off super quickly, as if she can't wait to get away. Shit. I must have really embarrassed her, making such a massive ungainly scene in the middle of the boardwalk.

I glance uneasily at Brandon and together, we walk, me now in bare feet, along the beach and back towards the skates rental hut.

Neither of us speaks for a few minutes, just the sound of the neighbouring people, the wind and the gentle waves of the ocean our soundtrack.

'How did you know we were here?' I say eventually when the silence gets too awkward even for me.

'Kennedy invited me to meet you guys here,' Brandon answers, looking past me towards the sea. 'I didn't think I'd make it, but I finished work early so finally managed to track you down. Thank god I did! That was super dangerous. Like you said, you're not built to be on wheels!'

'I said I wasn't *made* to be on wheels, not *built*,' I say spikily, although they're pretty much the same thing.

'Kennedy can be very persuasive,' Brandon says with a grin, ignoring my spikiness. He is trying to be nice. 'She loves a project.'

'What do you mean, a project?' I ask.

Brandon shrugs and looks down at me, his eyes twinkling. 'She likes to fix things, make herself useful to whomever she's with. She's been doing it since we were kids. It stems from many years spent seeking the approval of our affection-withholding mother.' He laughs darkly to himself. 'You know, Kennedy once asked our parents to adopt a stray mangy cat we found on a family hike. It was the ugliest thing I'd ever seen. Had this weird twitch in its eyes and this one pointy snaggletooth. Kennedy begged, wanted to build the cat an activity hut, put a bow in its hair, rescue it and make it happy. Of course, Mom and Dad said no. But as soon as she got her own place after college, she adopted Winklepuff from a shelter. When you, a total stranger from the internet, needed a free place to say, she said yes, no questions asked! She's a good person, but, like I say, she loves to rescue things and she can be quite bossy about it!'

I turn to him with a frown. 'I hardly think I'm a mangy cat Kennedy's taking pity on.'

'That's not what I meant at all. I'm just saying that LA is full of perfect people, or at least pretending to be perfect. You are...'

'A mangy cat.'

'That's not what I said.'

'You implied it.'

'Well, you are a little *odd* and Kennedy clearly wants to help you. Just don't let her boss you about too much, okay?'

'Odd? Ordinary? Which is it?' I say, spiky once more. Something about this guy puts me right on the back foot. He is definitely a bit of turd. But also sometimes nice. Ugh.

Brandon rolls his eyes. 'You're a very sensitive person, huh? You should relax!'

Am I sensitive? I've never ever been described as sensitive before. Quiet, shy, weird, yes, always, but not sensitive. Yet everything Brandon does seem to elicit a sharp response from me.

I shrug and look out at the sea, thinking back to the vision I had at home after I first saw Gary in *Justice of The Peace*. Me, floating in a warm, sparkling ocean, laughing with Gary, feeling happier than I've ever felt. The thought immediately makes me feel better.

'I'm sorry,' Brandon says, leaning his elbow into mine as we walk. 'My ex Elsie always said I had no tact. I should just learn to keep my mouth shut!'

I don't tell him otherwise and we walk on in silence, him occasionally leaning into me and bumping my shoulder playfully and smiling at me like he doesn't think I'm ordinary at all.

Brandon is a very confusing person indeed.

CHAPTER THIRTY-ONE

Nora

Today is the day!

The ceremony is at 2 p.m.

Kennedy got back from work twenty minutes ago and is meticulously curling my hair while chatting about how Erin has asked her to get together for a drink tonight and wondering whether that drink would be a date, or just a way for Erin to psych her out before her anchor audition tomorrow.

I'm ordinarily not a cynical person, but I wouldn't trust Erin after the way she behaved the other night, even if she did say I had hair like Penelope Cruz. I tell Kennedy this and she hmms and aaaahs, before agreeing that she should probably say no. She's feeling confident about the story she's decided to go with – she's prepared a report on three women under thirty who are making strides as indie movie directors in Hollywood, which sounds awesome.

As we chat, Kennedy finishes my hair and adds some bronzer and lip gloss to my face. Both eyes are red and sore from my various altercations with wind and dust, so I have to wear my glasses instead of my contacts. But the glasses, at least, are really cool. Large, winged and gold-framed, inspired by the ones that Esme is described as wearing in *Harcourt Royals*. The whole time I'm getting ready, my heart pounds with nerves and excitement for what the day is about to bring.

I dress in jeans and Kennedy's white T-shirt that I wore for the night out at the karaoke bar. Looking into the full-length mirror in the living room, I take a deep breath. My hair looks glossy and flowing and much more glamorous than it ever has. I finger a curl tentatively, my throat dry, my insides feeling like a washing machine on a speed spin.

'You sure you want to do this?' Kennedy asks, peering at me in the mirror. 'It's a pretty public place to try to meet Gary for the first time…'

I put all of the things that could go wrong out of my head. Remember, fate loves the fearless. I am doing the right thing… Right?

'It's the best chance I'm going to get,' I eventually say, giving our reflections in the mirror a firm and confident nod. 'And anyway, it's not like it could be any more disastrous than my attempt to meet Gary at the film lot, right…?'

* * *

'This is *crazy*.' Kennedy breathes as the Lyft drops us off and we make our way through the crowd of people outside Grauman's Chinese Theatre on Hollywood Boulevard. The sun is beating down fervently onto the forecourt and beads of sweat prickle the back of my neck.

'It's so busy!' I grumble. Standing on my tiptoes, I can just about see the red-carpeted podium Gary will be speaking at. From what I've seen online, there will be a large box of cement laid out for him to stick his hands into, but there's too many people here for me to get a clear view. 'Why are there so many people?'

'I don't know,' Kennedy replies drily. 'Maybe they all think they're Gary Montgomery's one true love.'

I tut at her, but as I look around, I realise, to my dismay, that she might be right. All around me are women and men looking moonily towards the podium outside the theatre, as if waiting for their long-lost love to return from war. A few of the younger women are holding placards like teenage fans do at pop concerts. I crane my neck to read what they say: 'Gary, I love you!' and another one that says, 'I love you, Gary!' I respect the economy of the sentiment.

I'm not like these women, am I? A desperate fan, wanting to touch fame and talent because it is so far out of my reach? That's what Imogene said… that I think Gary Montgomery is my soulmate because he is so unreachable that there's no risk involved. Except I'm here to prove that little theory wrong. Because I have never felt the way I did when I saw Gary on the screen and then in real life at the movie lot. But… what if all of these fans around me think the same? That *they* are supposed to spend the rest of their lives with Gary Montgomery, if only they could meet him just one time…

Stop it, Nora. Now is not the time to doubt yourself, not when you've come this far. Think of the vision you keep having of you and Gary in the ocean together, the fact that he reads CJ West's *Harcourt Royals* books, that he loves cheese toasties just like you do, that the dog you are looking after is in love with his dog, think of that thunderbolt right through the belly, exactly EXACTLY like Mum said it would feel.

I take a deep breath and try to calm my jittery heart.

'We've got to get further forward,' I say decisively to Kennedy.

'I don't see how we can!' she calls back over the excitable crowd. 'It's pretty crammed.'

'Follow me!' I square my shoulders and start elbowing as gently and politely as I can through the crowd.

'Hey!' a very tall woman growls as I push through. 'Watch it!'

'I'm sorry.' My eyes widen as the very tall woman looms over me, snarling slightly. 'My, uh, my friend is um heavily pregnant and we're trying to get to the front where there is more room for the baby to, er, breathe…'

It is a stupid lie. I knew it as I was saying it. Babies in bellies don't need *room to breathe*. Plus, Kennedy's stomach is so flat it's almost concave.

The woman looks Kennedy up and down, her mouth pursed to one side. 'She sure don't look pregnant to me.'

'It's a phenomenon,' Kennedy says, patting her stomach and not missing a beat. 'I have a backward-tilting uterus. Thank god I got a test, otherwise I would never have known I was with child. Can you even imagine!'

A backward-tilting uterus?

The woman nods slowly. 'Oh yeah… I saw something about that on the TV last week.'

'On *Good Morning Los Angeles*? I saw it too. *That's* what made me get tested!'

Wow! Kennedy is an *excellent* liar.

The woman looks at Kennedy earnestly. 'My god. We gotta get you through to the front!'

And then, to my delight, the very tall woman goes ahead of us elbowing people out of the way on our behalf, much less politely than I was doing.

'Move aside! Pregnant lady comin' through!'

'Backward tilting uterus!' I add, much to Kennedy's amusement.

When we reach the front of the crowd, we thank the very tall woman and invite her to stay at the front and hang out with us.

She shakes her head. 'I'm so tall I can see everything from the back without blockin' anyone's view,' she says proudly. 'Good luck with the baby!'

Kennedy rubs her stomach indulgently and we thank the woman again as she heads back onto the scramble of people behind us. I feel a bit guilty, but I can't let good manners get in the way of destiny, not when I've come this far!

I look around. Wow. We are right behind the rope barrier and just a few feet from the podium and cement box placed upon the red carpet. Gary will immortalise his handprints right there before the stone is set and taken to the pavement. I side-eye Kennedy and we grab each other's hands in glee.

'You are a surprisingly good liar,' I laugh, narrowing my eyes. 'Backward-tilting uterus?'

'Hey, you started it, I just took the baton.'

'Well, I'm glad you did. Look at how close we are! I'll definitely be able to call Gary over to us after the ceremony. Shit! This is actually going to happen. I'm going to get to meet him today!'

I look up onto the podium, my insides aching with the thought that I'm going to get to see him again in real life so soon. I wonder if his eyes will meet mine. Will he know? Will he feel what I feel?

As I'm considering all of the things that could happen, I suddenly see something that I did not expect to see today at all. It's that horrible security guy from the movie set! The Australian guy with the stupid name – John Alan. He's striding across the front of the podium, talking speedily into a walkie-talkie and directing other security guys where they should stand. What is he doing here? I thought he only worked at the movie lot? Shit.

I nudge Kennedy. 'That's the security guy who chucked me off the set,' I hiss, trying not to be too obvious with my pointing.

'Who? Where?'

'That ship-sized man over there…'

'The one who looks like he's been pathologically avoiding Leg Day at the gym?'

'Yes, exactly!'

Kennedy gasps and quickly hands me the large floppy white sun hat she's wearing before standing slightly in front of me. With my newly curly hair and the fact that I'm wearing my glasses today, I look pretty different than I did the day of my encounter with John Alan… I hope. Nevertheless, I dip my chin, my heart hammering as John Alan gets down on his knees and starts inspecting beneath the podium, wiping his finger on the carpet and giving it a sniff. What the hell is he doing? Why is he being so fastidious? Does Gary have an actual dangerous stalker? Or do they always have these security people at these events?

Down the left side of the red carpet, there are at least fifty photographers, with massive professional cameras. Directly above the podium, a big projector screen plays clips from *Justice of The Peace*, as well as various press interviews Gary has done.

Kennedy follows my gaze to the projector screen. 'Like I said, he's no Joseph Gordon-Levitt, but he *is* sexy…' she says as if admitting something previously unknown. 'In a sort of dark and brooding unconventional kinda way.'

'He is the most beautiful person I've ever seen and will ever see,' I whisper, peering up at the screen and trying my best to shield my face with the big hat. 'God, can you believe he reads the *Harcourt Royals* books, Kennedy? Maybe we should email CJ West and let her know. Those books barely sell and surely that kind of publicity would send them into the stratosphere where they belong!'

'Look! Something's happening,' Kennedy interrupts, waving over towards the doors of the theatre.

My heart squeezes as someone comes out of the front doors of the theatre. But it's not Gary. It's a smart, older-looking woman with wild silver curls and lots of elaborate gold jewellery. She steps up the podium and taps the microphone twice.

'Welcome to Grauman's Chinese Theatre,' she says confidently. Her voice is scratchy and loud... and I recognise it...Specifically, I recognise it telling me to stay the hell away from Gary Montgomery. That woman on the stage is Gary's manager, Aileen Gould!

'My name is Aileen Gould,' she announces with a wide, perfect-toothed smile. 'And it is my great pleasure to present this wonderful man for such an incredible honour today. He is a true star, the likes of which we haven't seen in this generation, and a magnificent, thoughtful actor who is at the beginning of what is set to be a very illustrious career indeed. We could not be prouder of our own Texan Cowboy, who, despite his speedy rise to stardom, remains one of the sweetest and most humble people I have ever worked with. And I should know... the man is dating my daughter!'

The crowd laughs and I wriggle uncomfortably, pushing the nagging thought of Tori Gould out of my head.

'Ladies, gentleman and children,' Aileen continues, pointing at a toddler and his mum standing in front of me and Kennedy. The pair of them are holding balloons with pictures of Gary's face looking warped and stretched over the rubber. 'I am beyond pleased and very proud to introduce the one and only... Gary Montgomery!'

The crowd around me erupts into cheers. Kennedy gives a polite clap and I just stand still and stare, my breath caught in anticipation of resting my eyes on his face once more.

John Alan opens up the door to the theatre, one hand on his gun holster.

Gary walks out. He's dressed in a sharp navy blue suit with a crisp white shirt, collar unbuttoned. His usually chin-length flop of hair is slicked back neatly away from his face. He looks even more tanned and gleaming and otherworldly. Now, less than five metres away, I can see his full face rather than just the profile I saw outside of his trailer. My hands tremble, my stomach flip-flops and I'm afraid to blink in case I miss a second of his image on my retinas.

Gary beams and waves at the screaming crowd. It's different than the smile I saw him do at his phone on the movie lot. This smile is bigger, toothier, not quite as soft around the eyes.

I want to run up to the podium immediately, to point at myself and yell, 'I'm here! It's me!' But that would be psychotic, so I refrain and continue to smile up in his direction, my whole chest filled with pride for him, even though we have never spoken. This must be such a big, weird moment in his career.

Then, to my dismay, Tori Gould steps out onto the stage, grabbing onto Gary's hand and waving, not at the crowd of fans, but at the photographers. She looks incredible in an almost fully sheer white dress and towering heels. Holding her phone in the air, she takes a selfie in front of the crowd, before pulling a reluctant-looking Gary into one too. Gary's face relaxes as he points and waves to the far left of the crowd, right near the bank of photographers. I follow his wave to see a young man and woman, hugging each other and waving back at him madly.

When the cheering ends, Gary taps the microphone lightly and squints into the crowd.

'Wow. Hey, everyone,' he says in the smooth, deep voice I've heard on screen, but which here, now, in real life sends a tingle of electricity right through my whole body. I have never wanted anyone more in my life. 'Thanks for the intro, Aileen. I'm so lucky to have you.'

Aileen presses a hand to her chest, and then waves him away with an indulgent grin.

'I'm truly honoured to be here today,' Gary goes on, his voice continuing to send mad, thumping sparks of desire right into my swimsuit area. 'I didn't expect this at all, let alone so soon in my career... But, of course, I'm absolutely thrilled and so very thankful to...'

I don't hear what comes next because a couple behind me seem to be arguing, their voices escalating snippily.

'Stop sighing like that! I know you're bored, but I had to see him! This is my only chance!' says the female voice.

I spin around to see a very pretty forty-something woman frowning at a beefcake of a man who I assume she is attached to, considering the way he is talking about Gary.

'You're married to *me* babe,' the beefcake grumbles. 'I don't like the way you're lookin' at him!'

'It's no different to how you look at Angelina Jolie!' she snaps.

'But I don't trick you into coming out to see her do a fuckin' handprint ceremony! I thought we were comin' here for a tour! I wanna leave, Rhonda.'

'No! You said we could stay a little while if I put out tonight! We made a deal.'

I can't hear a word Gary is saying.

'Shsssssh!' I say firmly to the bickering couple. 'I can't hear him.'

The woman's pretty face contorts. 'Don't you talk to my husband that way!' she says. 'Who do you think you are?'

'Yeah,' the guy says, putting his arm around the woman as if they hadn't just been rowing.

I roll my eyes at Kennedy and turn back to Gary, but within a few seconds the couple have started up again.

'You wanna blow him, doncha? I can tell by the way you're lookin' at him,' says the beefcake.

'I don't! I promise. I only wanna blow you!'

'Why can't you just be honest with me? I won't be

angry. Just say it. You wanna blow Gary Montgomery more than you wanna blow me.'

How rude are these people! The rest of the surrounding crowd around me seem to agree and I hear a few of them calling out angrily at the couple.

I'm trying my best to block out the distraction and focus on Gary when I hear the boorish couple get into an altercation with someone else in the crowd. I'm about to turn around and ask calmly for them to all please be more respectful when there's some sudden jostling. And then I feel a massive bump into my back and before I can even gather what is happening, I have been pushed forward towards the rope barrier. The strength of the push means that my body knocks over the small metal rope holders and… No no no! Oh god. No! I am flying forward and I cannot stop it.

I will time to stop and rewind because my already shitty balance and massive boobs mean that what is about to happen is both inevitable and utterly horrifying. Oh my god. I am toppling over, head first, into the box of cement. Aaaaargh!

The entire left side of my face plunges into the wet paste. It's all cold and squelchy and thick. Ewwww. My hands, thankfully, are on the red carpet and I brace myself to release my face from the gunge, but before I can, I feel a pair of strong hands around my waist, yanking me out.

I have so much goop all over my face and smeared over my eyes that I can barely see anything. I squint one eye open to see only blurry shapes, tinged with cement grey. Shit. Where are my glasses?

From the stage area, I hear Tori shout, 'Oh my god, is that fat girl trying to get to Gary?'

From behind me, Kennedy shouts, 'Get off my friend!' to whomever has grabbed me.

I struggle to get away from the grasp, but the person is

strong, and before I know it, they have picked me up and marched me inside the theatre.

As the door closes behind us, I hear the microphone feeding into the speakers around the theatre lobby.

Gary clears his throat and it echoes around me as I am carried down a corridor to god knows where. 'Anyway… where was I?' he quips, getting a relieved-sounding laugh from the crowd outside.

Oh my god. I was only trying to get those idiots to pipe down and instead I've ruined Gary's big day. Shit. How on earth will I face him now? Shit, Nora. SHIT.

The man carrying me plops me down outside a bathroom. I spin around… Of course. It's John Alan. He looks a little blurry without my glasses, but I recognise the general bald redness of his head and his barrel-sized chest.

'I've lost my glasses!' I say immediately. 'Can you get them for me? Fuck. They're probably in the cement!'

'I knew you'd be back,' John Alan says wearily, ignoring my request. 'I can always spot the repeat offenders. Go and wash your face and arms and get back out here. Don't even think of trying to escape. I have security waiting on the other side of that bathroom window.'

I'm too shocked and horrified to answer back, to even process what has just happened. I go into the bathroom and head for the sinks.

With trembling hands, I run the warm tap, grab some paper towels and start cleaning myself up. Rubbing at my face leaves it sore and red.

'Hurry up, lady,' John Alan calls from outside of the bathroom.

I step back outside, my head down as John Alan leads me to a small side room, filled with cleaning supplies. He points at a plastic chair and indicates for me to sit. We can still hear the ceremony going on outside. The voice of some producer or other droning in through the speakers inside the theatre.

'You're staying there until the end of the ceremony,' John Alan says, leaning back against a shelf filled with rolls of toilet paper, one hand still on his gun. 'Until Mr Montgomery decides if he wants to press charges.'

'Press charges?' I gasp. 'Why? It was a bloody accident! I was pushed!'

Before John Alan can respond, Aileen's distinctive scratchy voice sounds out through the speakers.

'Well done, Gary!' she says. I assume, he's now putting his hands in the cement which was no doubt smoothed over as soon as John carried me off. 'We are so proud of you on this special day. And I am even more proud to have the greater honour to now exclusively announce... the engagement of Gary Montgomery and my daughter Tori Gould! I have never seen two people more deeply, blissfully in love. I swear they are deliriously joyful over one another! I know they will be beyond happy together for the rest of their lives.'

Through the speakers, I hear the whooping and applause of the crowd and the whir of a million camera clicks. And there, in a storage cupboard, a million miles from my home and everything I know, my heart cracks.

'I thought that maybe if he just saw me...' I mumble, tears springing to my eyes.

John Alan looks me up and down and sighs, his eyes full of pity. 'Mr Montgomery saw you at the movie lot. He said, and I quote, "Keep that weirdo Plain Jane stalker away from me." Look, miss. You've just gotta face facts. It's never gonna happen... I've met my fair share of stalkers and it never works out well.'

Bile rushes into my mouth, my face draining of all blood.

Gary's right. I'm nothing more than a stalker. An unhinged weirdo Plain Jane Stalker.

Oh my god. What have I done?

CHAPTER THIRTY-TWO

Nora

There is one reason I am not sitting in a jail cell right now: Gary Montgomery apparently decided he didn't want to press charges against me for my 'attempted attack'. Kennedy and I then had to convince John Alan that I would never even google Gary Montgomery's name again and he only relaxed once I logged into my email to show him that I had a return flight to the UK already booked. We then had to wait around in the janitor's closet until the end of the ceremony so that 'Gary could leave safely'.

I asked for my glasses back, but no one could find them in the hardening cement or around the theatre in general.

Kennedy, with a look of pity that I couldn't bear, asked me to come back home, but I just wanted to be alone. So I've come to the beach where they sell the ice cream that always makes me feel better. I'm sitting on a faded wooden bench, eating a special rocky road sundae and staring out at the windy, foaming sea. Everything is a little blurry because I don't have my glasses, and rather than making me feel happy and giddy like it usually does, the sundae is just enhancing the bone tiredness that has blanketed my entire body.

I realise that I'm crying, the tears drying almost instantly as the warm wind blows on my face. I need my sister. I pull out my phone and press her number with trembling hands.

She answers after three rings, her voice sleepy and confused. Shit. It's 2 a.m. there. I forgot. Am I the worst? I think I might be the worst.

'Hey, Im,' I say, trying to disguise the shaky-breathed crying. 'I butt-dialled you by accident. Go back to sleep and I'll ring tomorrow.'

'What's wrong?' Imogene asks, clearing her throat. 'I was awake anyway,' she lies. 'I can chat!' Then I hear a fumble on the phone and Imogene hissing at Dan to fuck off, which makes my hand fly to my mouth in surprise. I've never heard Imogene mad at Dan before. 'I've come downstairs,' Imogene says eventually. 'Talk to me.'

I open my mouth to say something, anything, but all that comes out is a howl of bawling.

'So-ho-horry,' I manage to get out through the sobs. 'Give me a se-heh-heh-cond...'

And then I bawl again. It's coming right from my core and I can't seem to stop it. Not ideal that this is happening on a public beach, albeit a currently quiet one.

'Go for it,' Imogene says softly. 'Sounds like it really needs to come out...'

I nod, even though she can't see me.

She stays on the phone while I clutch my stomach and cry until there are no tears left.

'Right,' she says firmly when the wails have settled down into pathetic little whimpers. 'Tell me what happened?' The calmness in her voice gives me cause to suspect that Imogene's been expecting this call. That this, right now, is the dose of reality she said I needed. The reason she told me to come here and do this.

I take a deep breath and tell Imogene about my day, about falling in the cement, about John Alan almost arresting me and saying that Gary called me a weirdo Plain Jane stalker, I find myself telling her about Brandon saying I was odd and ordinary, how people like me don't get to be happy. I tell her about Mum and Dad, although of course she already knows, and I tell her how forceful I was about them coming to my showcase gig. Dad had said he was feeling under the weather and I stropped, told him he *had* to come because I needed to show them that I could make a career in music. I wanted attention.

'It was my fault,' I say shakily. 'It genuinely was my fault, Imogene. I'm so sorry. I mess things up. It's what I do and I just can't seem to help it. What's wrong with me? I thought if I could find my soulmate, if I could have what Mum and Dad held so dear, that I... I don't know... I'd feel closer to them somehow? That I finally did something that they believed in. Shit, I don't even know what I'm talking about. It's all muddled. There's so much in my head. Gary is engaged now. He is deeply and blissfully in love with Tori Gould. How could I have been so stupid?'

Imogene pauses for a moment. 'It. Wasn't. Your. Fault,' she says very slowly. 'Shit, Nora. You could say it was Mum and Dad's fault for giving birth to you. Or it was the record company's fault for giving you a showcase gig. Or it was my fault for telling Dad, six years ago, that I thought he should definitely buy a blue BMW, or it was the bloody tyre designer's fault for making one single faulty tyre that just happened to be on Mum and Dad's car. You can't look at it as being anyone's *fault*.'

I nod again and take a deep breath. 'Why do I feel so guilty then? It's just there in my stomach. All of the time.'

'Because you *were* being selfish that night. It doesn't mean you caused the accident, though. It was an *accident*.'

'That's the last impression they had of me. Selfish, attention-needing Nora.'

'Are you kidding me? They were so proud of you. Yes, they were worried that making a career in music would be hard on you, but they were excited about it. They loved you, they loved us both so, so much. You know I heard Mum singing one of your songs about a week before...'

'Really?' I gasp, sitting up straighter. 'Which one?'

'Something about a whisper of moonlight on a lake?'

'Eek, that was a terrible song.'

'I agree, and Mum couldn't sing for shit. But she loved it. Said it made her feel all lovey-dovey.'

I smile for the first time that afternoon.

'She *always* felt lovey-dovey.'

Imogene laughs. 'She really did. Her and Dad, it actually got a bit annoying sometimes. They were so... perfect.'

'They were, right?' I laugh. 'A bit smug, really.'

Imogene chuckles and we sink into our memories for a moment.

'I'm sorry it didn't work out with Gary,' Imogene says at last.

My skin crawls with humiliation. I never even got the chance to meet him. Of course I didn't. I was never going to. Imogene knew that.

'Have I messed you up even more?' she says in a small voice. 'I was trying to be cruel to be kind. It seemed like a desperate situation.'

'No.' I run my hands through my now bedraggled and cement-spattered curls. 'I think you were right. I've been depressed. I didn't want to admit it, but... I feel sad about Mum and Dad all of the time. You were right about the whole counselling thing. I mean, I genuinely, genuinely thought he was my soulmate. I really really did. I *felt* it. And to him I'm just some crazy plain girl who tried to ruin a big moment in his career. Which is, you know, essentially true.' I squeeze my eyes shut so that I don't start howling again. 'I clearly need some help.'

'Firstly, you are not plain. You are beautiful inside and out. Except when you're on your period and you get a spotty chin. Secondly, I'm proud of you for being brave enough to go out there. To go do something so bonkers for love. Even if it's not really love and just a symptom of wayward mental health. Thirdly, I'm going to book you a flight for tomorrow. It's time to come home now.'

'It's only a week until my scheduled flight…' I say. 'I can wait, I don't want you to spend any more money. Dan will go mad.'

'Oh, who cares? I work hard. I have savings. I can spend my money how I like, right? I'm booking you in for therapy. Come back tomorrow. It's time to sort you out.'

I sigh. She's right. It's time to get help.

It's time to leave LA.

CHAPTER THIRTY-THREE

Gary

Hey,

I don't think I've been this angry in my life. It's unbearable. My chest feels tight and full, my skin is prickly and my muscles are knotted up. I mean it was already a weird day to begin with and then it just all got fucking bizarre.

Christ! I'm not making sense. Breathe, Gary. Breeeeeeathe.

Okay. So... I'm engaged.

Did I pop the question? No.

Did I know anything about it? No.

Was I completely fucking blindsided. Yes!

It was the handprint ceremony today, which was frankly a bit of a strange thing to be happening considering my relatively short career. I was giving my speech, there was a crowd, everyone was happy and then my—and just to reiterate that I cannot believe I am writing this—my *stalker* tried to attack me.

At least according to John Alan. Seth and Olive thought this woman got jostled by some altercation in the crowd, but John Alan confirmed it was the same woman who came to the set with the butter knife. I didn't even notice what was going on until someone was face down in the cement. And it was weird – just like the time at the movie lot, the shape of her was super familiar. She must have been following me for a while and I've spotted her out of the corner of my eye. It's the only way I can explain the feeling of recognition.

Anyway, John Alan carried the woman away and the ceremony continued. And then, and this is the bit that I am feeling extremely angry about, Aileen announced to the crowd, and the fucking press, that Tori and I were getting married. What. The. Fuck? We hadn't even discussed it and I certainly don't remember proposing. I could hardly deny it on the stage because there were a million damn journalists and photographers there, but Jesus Christ.

As soon as we got back to my place, I asked Aileen and Tori what the hell was going on. Aileen said that the stalker trying to attack me and Tori shouting that she was fat (which I didn't hear) was incredibly problematic *optically* and that she immediately needed to change the story into something big and positive. So she made an executive decision to announce an engagement. For my career. For Tori's career.

Fucking hell.

I asked a very quiet Tori what she had to say about her mother doing shit like this and she started crying and apologizing over and over. Which made me feel like an asshole for getting mad, especially after everything she's done for me. After we slept together for the first time, she made me promise that I'd never make her cry. Well, today I almost broke that promise. Tori said we were going to get engaged soon anyway, and she's right. I have been thinking about proposing. But now it's all been tainted. Made into some business decision. I'm not naïve. I know that Aileen's only trying to look out for us. But still. I'm so fucking angry!

Before we came home, I asked John Alan if I could meet this woman. Show her that I was just a normal schmuck when it came down to it and that I really wasn't worth following around. But he said that would only encourage her and that to meet her face to face would just be a cruelty. It was so strange though. I was curious to see her face. You know, not covered in cement. Tori said she was fat. I mean, she didn't look like most of the woman in Los Angeles, but something about her looked pretty fucking sexy to me... Argh. What is going on with me? I'm engaged to someone I didn't propose to and now I'm wondering if I am sexually attracted to some random woman whose face I have never seen and who wants to maybe kill me with a blunt knife. I'm going mad.

I found what I think were the stalker's glasses on the sidewalk after everyone had gone home. They're in my bag right now. I'm not quite sure why I picked them up. I should probably give them to John Alan – glasses are expensive and I think he took down her address. I'll do it tomorrow. Fuck. What a horrible, irrational, damn stupid day.

I can't write three amazing things today. I'm feeling that shitty overwhelmed feeling again and I can't stand it. Plus I'm missing my mom these last few days, which feels ridiculous because I never even met her. But not having her here, never having had her here, feels like I've just got this stomach ache that's always there. That's always going to be there, no matter how happy or successful I am. There's just always going to be this mild, gnawing pain that pops up every now and then without invitation.

Fuck. I should probably call Ira for an in-person appointment...

Seth's knocking on my door. Gotta go.

CHAPTER THIRTY-FOUR

Nora

I'm sitting on Kennedy and Brandon's porch, snuggling Winklepuff and looking out at this view that I've become so happily accustomed to. Winklepuff gazes up at me, peeved at the fact that my tears are falling onto his head. I bury my face in his fur and apologise. At least I've done one thing right since I've been here and it's successfully take care of this guy. Yes, it was through nefarious means and the fact that I'm feeding him secret ham in order to get him to respect me is not ideal. And he did make love to another dog under my care, but apart from that I've done a pretty good job, considering I lied to Kennedy about my experience in dog caretaking. The warm weight of him is incredibly soothing. He pushes his head into my neck as if he's trying to comfort me.

'You're a good boy,' I sniffle. 'I'm really going to miss you. Even with your halitosis issues.'

Winklepuff responds with another death breath yawn and snuggles further into me, giving a happy, content snort.

I try to memorise the floury softness of the rippled

sand on the beach, the swell of the shimmering indigo ocean, and the warm bloom in my chest that happens whenever I'm floating about in there early morning. I wish I could take that feeling back home with me. The soft hazy pastel colours here are making the prospect of grey, smoky-skied Brigglesford, Sheffield, a little less appealing than perhaps it should be, considering I've lived there my whole life. But like Imogene said, it's time to go home, to figure out why on earth I thought that a man I saw on the screen at the pictures might be my one and only true love.

I think, again, of what Aileen said at the ceremony. How she'd never seen two people as deeply and happily in love as Gary and Tori. I had just assumed that they weren't meant to be. Convinced myself they were 'just dating' so I didn't have to feel like a monster about my intentions. But deliriously joyful over each other? That sounds like how Mum and Dad were. And imagine if some grieving randomer had come along and tried to ruin that? I can't be that person. If I love him as much as I, rightly or wrongly, believe I do, then I want him to be deeply and happily in love. I want him to be deliriously joyful. Even if it's not with me.

I take a deep breath and as Winklepuff scrambles off my lap, now fucked off with the shower of tears I am continuing to rain over him, something happens to me. A melody pops into my head. It's out-of-focus, tentative, but it's there.

With shaking hands, I slowly take my phone out of my pocket, open the notes app and start to type out phrases that fit the shape of the melody playing in my head. I softly start to hum, my voice croaky, my throat dry from the crying. When I look up again, thirty minutes have passed and I think I've just written my first song in two years.

I run my thumb over the phone screen, over the words

I just wrote, and a little spark of something positive ignites in my chest.

'Thought you could do with this.' Kennedy comes out onto the porch and hands me a mug that says, 'I'm Rootin Tootin Gluten Free!' on the front of it in a navy blue cursive script.

I smile gratefully and take the mug, giving it a sniff. It smells rank.

'It's fennel and cumin tea. It will lift your spirits, I think.'

'Thanks,' I say, warming my hands with the mug even though it's already boiling hot outside.

'Taste it,' Kennedy urges, sitting beside me and staring at me.

I reluctantly taste it. It is rank.

'It has chamomile in too, so it will soothe you.'

I smile at her, touched by her thoughtfulness.

The pair of us just sit there staring at the ocean for a while, the Santa Ana winds occasionally smacking into our faces and lifting our hair up from our heads.

'Don't leave tomorrow,' Kennedy says eventually, breaking the silence.

'I have to,' I say. 'Imogene's booking me a flight. There's not really anything else to stay for…'

'You're feeling terrible right now, but you have another week here. Surely better to spend that time swimming and sunbathing and doing nice things with Brandon and I rather than going home alone. You can put it off, right?'

'I'm too humiliated to stay. Imogene says I need to get back ASAP and start working on getting over my grief, fixing all of my *issues*.'

Kennedy nods. 'She sounds really smart. But… a few days won't make any difference. And, in a really selfish way, I don't want you to go!'

'Really?'

'Really. You're not an intellectual snob like everyone I

usually hang out with and everyone at work and it honestly feels like a relief. I feel more like myself around you. I'd love you to stay just a little bit longer…'

I squint at her. 'Haven't I majorly embarrassed you? Don't you think I'm crazy?'

'No,' Kennedy says firmly. 'You just have a crush. Infatuations can make us do dumb things. Trust me, I know…'

I'm about to respond with my line about how this is more than a crush, but she's right. That is obviously all it is. How embarrassing.

'Did you ever think I had a chance with him?' I ask, biting my lip.

Kennedy looks down at her knees and fiddles with the edge of her vest top. She scratches the back of her neck. 'Honestly? No. Not that you couldn't get someone like him. You are funny and beautiful and, now that the shyness is fading, really fun to be around. But no. He has a girlfriend.'

'Fiancée.'

'Yes. And he's a movie star… ya' know?'

I frown. 'Why did you encourage me then? Help me with everything? Make the Creepy As Fuck Soulmate Procurement Wall with me?'

She shrugs. 'I figured that you were working through something. Something that you believed in. I also figured you had enough people telling you were out of your mind. I wanted to be your friend.'

'You were. Are.'

'And you may not have gotten Gary Montgomery, but you've gotten a little bit of joy back, right? Joy ahoy! More time spent doing that would be awesome…'

That's true. I have done more this last week than I have done in the past two years. I had forgotten how amazing it feels to have your face in the sun, to feel the anticipation of what might happen next, how real, vivid, moving life outside of my cosy house is so much more powerful than I remembered. I mean, I'm never going to be an extrovert gallivanting at parties, but maybe, when I get back to Brigglesford, I'll leave the house a little more, try to remake a place for myself in the real world...

But still, I can't stay. 'I told Imogene I'd be back tomorrow. She's booking a flight!'

Kennedy sighs and folds her arms across her chest. 'So tell her not to book it. To be honest, Nora... I expected you to be here another week and I haven't found another morning dog-sitter for this guy.' She ruffles Winklepuff's soft head. 'You would be leaving me in the lurch. You want to leave me in the lurch? It's my interview tomorrow! You know how hard I've worked for it. My mom will be so upset if I don't get the job! You want to put this stress on me? After I invited you into my home? Let you borrow my white T-shirt? Used my wildly impressive journalistic skills nefariously in order to help you with your outrageous capers? You would do that to me? Wow. I am shook. I thought we were becoming real friends. My god, Nora. I let you use my Olaplex hair conditioner and that shit is *expensive!* This is how you repay me?'

I tut. 'You are massively guilt-tripping me!'

Kennedy leans in closer and peers at my face through narrow eyes. 'Is it working?'

I laugh in spite of the sad, sorry feeling I'm wrapped up in, at this beautiful, nerdy, sunny, kind-hearted stranger who offered me a place to stay and pledged, albeit drunkenly, to help me to rediscover some joy in my life. Why? Because she is a good person. That's it. She thinks I deserve happiness. I can't leave her in the lurch, no matter how gut-punched I'm feeling. That *would* be really shitty of me. I've already been selfish enough.

'Well, I did promise to look after Winklepuff,' I say. 'And you *did* let me use your Olaplex... Okay, I'll text

Imogene and tell her to expect me back on the original return date.'

'That's settled then,' Kennedy says, standing up from the porch so quickly that it makes Winklepuff jump a little. 'We will go out tonight!' she announces. 'Things may not have worked out with Gary, but you can still seek joy for yourself in other ways. We could go out for plant-based tacos! It's no use staying in and moping around. You need a distraction.'

I'm not sure plant-based tacos are the key to my own personal joy.

'I thought it was your big anchor interview tomorrow,' I say. Don't you have to work?'

'It is and I do and I'm fully prepared! But, I mean, I have to *eat*, right? We can just head out for a little while.'

I imagine going out somewhere with sweet alcoholic drinks and good music. It sounds like a lovely relief from the way I'm feeling right now.

'Deal. But not plant-based tacos. At least not for me. Do you know anywhere that does a good cheese toastie in this city?'

* * *

I send a text to Imogene telling her to hold off booking flights as I'll just stick to the original plan. Then, after a couple of hours of work and a short nap, I shower and start to get ready for the evening. My will to not stay in bed crying for the whole evening is revived only by the thought of a lovely, soothing cheese toastie.

I inspect myself in the mirror and even though I can't seem to stop the tears of sadness and humiliation and guilt that are pretty much all-consuming, and my eyes are still red from wind dust and cement and having to wear contact lenses again because I lost my glasses, I notice that I actually look better than I have in years. It's more than shiny hair. I have colour in my face. Rosy, slightly pink cheeks and a scattering of freckles across my nose. I think back to Imogene saying on the phone that I sounded more awake the other day. I *feel* more awake.

Heading back into the room, I am faced with the Creepy As Fuck Soulmate Procurement Wall. The pictures of Gary and Tori, the maps and addresses, the screenshots from forums. It looks properly fucking crazy. I gawk at the poster of Gary that Kennedy put up and I try to tell myself that the cosmic prickle that shimmers all over my skin when I look at his face is just my mind playing tricks on me. I think of him and Tori in bed at home, having sex and laughing about me, about what a weirdo I am.

Don't start crying again.

I want to rip the whole Creepy As Fuck Soulmate Procurement Wall down, but I'm already running late. I'll do it when I get back in a bit. I speedily brush some super-sensitive mascara through my lashes, add a little pink balm onto my lips and slip in the tiny crystal earrings Kennedy lent me. I dress in a palest blue sundress, which, with its gravity-defying cleavage abilities is a little more appropriate for evening time than day. I grab a thin gossamer silver shawl and wrap it around my shoulders. There. Ready.

I swish open the curtain of my sleeping area and head into the living room to see that Kennedy is not ready for our outing but sprawled on the sofa in the yoga pants and vest top she was wearing before, her laptop resting on her belly.

'You're not ready yet?' I ask, glancing up at the wall clock with a frown. She definitely said to be ready for seven thirty.

She sits up quickly and pulls a face of distress. 'I'm so sorry, but I'm gonna have to bow out. I have more prep to do for my audition tomorrow.'

'Oh!' I say, feeling a little deflated. The idea of being

distracted from this horrible feeling for at least a little while was appealing.

'Yeah, I know. It's so terrible. There's been an… unexpected twist in the story… I need to research a little more before the audition. I'm so sorry! My mom has called me three times today already to check I'm prepared. I can't let her down.'

I wave her away. 'Don't worry about it. I guess I'll just…' I thumb back in the direction of my bedroom area when Brandon comes down the stairs dressed in a black shirt and khaki pants.

He rolls his eyes at Kennedy. 'Why are you not ready? You said seven thirty?'

'I didn't know you'd invited Brandon out with us,' I frown. The last thing I need right now is Brandon 'told you so-ing' me.

'I thought it was a siblings-only evening,' he says to Kennedy with narrowed eyes.

Kennedy widens her own eyes innocently. 'I thought it would be nice for us all to get out. You're both heartbroken and I was *so* looking forward to cheering you both up. But this unexpected extra work, huh? There's nothing that can be done. You'll just have to go without me! You may as well. I reserved a table at Jama's on Washington Boulevard. Nora, they do a great grilled cheese there. Not that I've ever tried it, but I've heard amazing things!'

I get the distinct feeling that we've been set up. Why on earth would Kennedy do this? Can't she see that Brandon and I aren't exactly best buds? That there is a *weirdness* between us. I'm about to say a polite no thank you very much when Brandon shrugs and says, 'I suppose we could…'

He gives me a small hopeful smile and I see something in his face that I recognise. Heartbreak. He's hurting too.

'Maybe for a couple of drinks…' I say eventually with a resigned sigh. Misery loves company, I suppose.

'Just a couple,' he agrees, shoving his hands into his pockets.

'Perfect!' Kennedy says, getting up from the sofa and almost pushing us out of the door. 'Look at that! Your Lyft is here! Have fun, you guys!

'We'll be back pretty soon, probably,' I tell her as she waves at us from the porch.

'Probably won't be gone for long at all,' Brandon agrees.

'Definitely,' I say. 'Back soon.'

CHAPTER THIRTY-FIVE

Nora

Brandon and I are sitting at a corner table in this small, quiet bistro/bar. It's an open-mic night, which has given us somewhere to look during the many uncomfortable silences that have occurred thus far.

After eating a massive, disappointingly bland cheese toastie and watching Brandon chow down a big bloody steak, we start to drink in earnest. It's taken a beer and a vodka Martini for us to develop some semblance of rapport and after a lot of half-baked starts and interruptions and starting to talk at the same time before insisting that the other person go first, we've finally settled into a conversation. Brandon is telling me about his work in set design and, against my better judgement, I'm finding it quite interesting and far more complex than I ever would have thought. He heads up a small company that designs sets for movie studios on a freelance basis, although they generally do most of their work for 20th Century Studios. He tells me about his love for writing and, while he's pretty secretive about what exactly he's working on, his passion for it is something I recognise keenly in myself.

When he explains that he worked as an intern on the set of the Meryl Streep and Alec Baldwin movie *It's Complicated*, I gasp with delight.

'I love that movie!'

'Well, it was certainly a more realistic representation of relationships than all those other sappy romantic hooey movies out there.' He laughs. 'I'm more of an indie horror fan myself.'

'I love that sappy romantic "hooey", as you call it. It's uplifting and magical! I love it when two people overcome all the odds to be together because they are simply meant to be.'

'Like with you and Gary?' Brandon rolls his eyes ever so slightly. He doesn't say it in a mean way, but it stabs me in the chest, nonetheless.

I shrug, my cheeks turning red. 'Yeah, well, I guess I've watched too many of those sappy romcoms,' I say quietly.

Brandon clears his throat and takes a sip of his drink. 'I mean, they're not all bad! I get the appeal. But they *are* selling something that's not real. The promise of one perfect person. If you go out thinking that's a real thing, you're just setting yourself up for disappointment.'

I see the flash of pain in his eyes. He lifts his hand to order two more Martinis to our table.

'So she was a human rights lawyer?' I ask with a sympathetic smile, keen to change the subject.

'And she looked like a model. Can you imagine? A smart model! The jackpot, pretty much.'

'I'm sure plenty of models are smart, Brandon,' I say, prickling. I take a large gulp of my drink and try not to ruin what is turning out to be quite a pleasant chat.

'She told me I was her soulmate. We were together for three years. I was going to propose. And then she met a big-time producer and I was toast. Out of nowhere.'

I see a slight glisten in his blue eyes and my heart goes out to him. Elsie Grainger clearly did a real number on

Brandon and it's obviously still a sore point. I change the subject.

'I appreciate you not saying "I told you so" about Gary. I genuinely feel like… *felt* like it was real. That he might actually be the person I've waited my whole life to find.' I sigh, long and low. 'So weird.'

'Here's to weird,' Brandon pulls a silly face and holds up his glass.

I clink it with mine.

By the time we've finished a couple more drinks and I'm starting to feel pleasantly, numbly drunk.

'Hey, you should get up there,' Brandon suggests, pointing at the little stage where a variety of amateur open-mic acts, hosted by a man who calls himself Santa Monica Homeboy, have been performing for the now almost-empty room.

I shake my head. 'Oh, I suffer from terrible stage fright,' I say. 'It's kind of my thing. I haven't been on a stage in two years.'

'But you got up at the karaoke?'

'True,' I say, nodding. 'But I was *very* drunk then.'

'And now you're sober?' He laughs.

He's right. I'm drunk now too. I squint at the stage and around at the few people left sitting at the tables.

'There's hardly anyone here,' Brandon adds. 'Surely if you were gonna face this fear, now would be a great time to do it. A small stage, barely any audience, a city that you'll be leaving in a few days…'

He makes a good point. Everything has gone completely wrong. I literally have nothing left to lose. Not even my dignity. And it did feel good finding my voice at the karaoke.

I neck the rest of my drink and the rest of Brandon's and when Santa Monica Homeboy is finished singing a My Chemical Romance cover, I shuffle up to the stage, really no longer giving a shit about anything.

I ask if I can borrow Santa Monica Homeboy's guitar. He shrugs and hands it over. I don't put the strap across me on account of my gigantic bosom getting in the way, but I pull up a little chair and sit on it, resting the guitar on my knees.

I think of the song I came up with this afternoon when I got back from the ceremony. The melody would go well over a C to E to G chord structure, I think. I haven't played the guitar in such a long time and my hands begin to shake, despite the fact that the vodka has dulled my nerves. I squint out into the lights and the room beyond that consists of Brandon, smiling encouragingly and slightly drunkenly, Santa Monica Homeboy and a group of three glamorous-looking older ladies who look like they've accidentally stumbled into the wrong venue.

I take a deep breath, close my eyes and start to sing the first song I've written since my parents died.

I saw a way out of the grey
A golden light peeking through a foggy day
When I loved you
When I loved you

My every mistake disappeared
No longer a fuck-up, so selfish, so weird
When I loved you
When I loved you

I thought that your eyes would catch mine
And you'd know like you know your own name
That this was a definite sign
That nothing would ever again be the same

A person can get things so wrong
But she'll bundle it up, hide it in a song
And every day all her life long

She'll think about
Those hazy Californian days
Those crazy, batshit, brand new days
When she loved you
When she loved you

When I've finished singing, I open my eyes and my stomach plunges when I realise there is no applause, not even a tiny scattering. I look at the few people in the room, and two new people who must have come in while I was singing. They're all staring at me with their eyes wide and their mouths open.

Shit. I thought I had been doing pretty well, once I'd gotten into it. Was it really that bad? I look down at my dress to see if I've popped a button and that's why everyone is gawking at me strangely. And then the three older women rise to their feet and start clapping slowly as if completely stunned. Santa Monica Homeboy also gets to his feet and shouts, 'Sing, girl!' to me. Brandon just looks at me, shaking his head, and raises his glass.

My face breaks into a wide smile as I realise that these people enjoyed my song. I feel my cheeks flush red with a mixture of pride and embarrassment, my heart thumping in my ribcage.

I step down from the stage and head over to Brandon, a massive grin on my face and then, before I can say or do anything, he stands up, puts one hand on each side of my face and kisses me.

My instinct is to pull away, because I did not ask for this kiss and also this is Brandon who I'm not interested in and who definitely is not my soulmate. But his mouth is warm and tender, and while my knees aren't exactly knocking with desire, this is very pleasant indeed. And, honestly, after the day I've had, it feels so fucking nice to feel desired. To be touched, to have someone weave their hands into my hair, to grab my bottom.

When we pull away from each other, I can't look him in the eye. Brandon calls over to the waiter for the bill.

'Oh, are we going now?' I ask.

Brandon's eyes dance with amusement. 'I'd like to keep on kissing you, but I'm not quite as keen on the audience, you know?' He tilts his head slightly in the direction of the three glamorous ladies, one of whom is looking at us as if she would like to join us in a throuple and the other two looking slightly repulsed at our very horny display of affection.

I hiccup and cover my mouth with a giggle. I suppose I wouldn't mind a little more kissing... And I certainly don't need any more to drink.

'Come on then,' I say, leading the way. 'Let's get out of here.'

* * *

We are silent the whole Lyft ride home and when Brandon tries to grab my hand on the way I don't let him because, while kissing is fine, holding hands seems just a little too sweetly romantic for me right now. And sweetly romantic is not what I want tonight. At least not with Brandon. All I want is to forget how I feel. To not feel humiliated and sick and heartbroken for a little longer.

Brandon unlocks the front door and Winklepuff scooches over to us, spinning in circles of joy at seeing us. There's no sign of Kennedy. She must be in bed. I squint at the clock. It's after midnight.

I sit on the sofa and Winklepuff jumps up onto my knees. I scratch behind his ear in his favourite spot and he rewards me with a little kiss on my hand.

Brandon grabs a couple of beers from the fridge and puts them onto the driftwood coffee table before plucking Winklepuff off my knees and plopping him gently onto the floor.

'So, Nora. Where were we?' he asks, tilting his head to the side and leaning in to kiss me again.

I pull back and squint at his face. He is very handsome. Definitely a more traditional-looking romantic lead. I run my hands over his muscled arms and feel a flicker of desire deep inside.

'You want to come to my room?' he asks.

I hesitate, Gary's face flashing through my head, the vision of being in the ocean with him, laughing and splashing each other, my whole body feeling light with joy. And then I think of him being deliriously happy with Tori. How he thinks I'm a Plain Jane Stalker Weirdo.

Ouch.

'Yes,' I say firmly. 'Yes I do.'

Brandon scoops me up like some sort of caveman, laughing and audibly grunting with effort as he does, and carries me upstairs to his bedroom.

The curtains are closed in his room so I can't really see the décor, although I can see that the room is lined with shelves full of books and his desk is piled high with papers and scribbled notes like my old desk used to be, back when I couldn't get enough of writing songs. I take a deep breath. It smells lovely and fresh in here. Like sea kelp and almonds.

Things move quickly and after a millisecond's more kissing, we drunkenly remove each other's clothes, dramatically flinging them to various corners of the room, the pair of us panting hard and fast.

When I am naked, Brandon runs his hand across my belly.

'I've never seen one like this before,' he smiles, poking it slightly. 'It's soft. Hmmm. I like it.'

'I like it too,' I say, lifting my chin.

I peer at his perfectly sculpted belly. That's nice too. I run my hands down it. He groans. I look into his eyes.

They look horny and very blue and slightly sad. I expect mine look pretty similar.

I just want to forget this whole day. To escape my heart and my head and just be in my body.

'I think you should take off your trousers,' I say.

He agrees.

CHAPTER THIRTY-SIX

Gary

Hey,

I felt so bad about getting so angry at Tori (even though it was Aileen who announced our 'engagement') that when she asked if she could organize an official engagement party, I said yes. It would have happened eventually anyway, right? I mean, it didn't help that Tori got down on her knees and begged me, sobbing and pleading. What the fuck is a person supposed to do when someone they love is on their knees and begging?

Ira says I agree to things like this because I need everyone to be happy all of the time. Probably something to do with my dad being in a state of grief my whole life. It can't be as simple as that, can it? Either way, I now have an engagement party in the works. Tori and Aileen want to invite press and possible sponsor partners for Tori's Instagram page, which sounds fucking gross and, for some reason, I'm going along with it. Of course I was going to propose to Tori in my own time, but now it's all become some sort of PR exercise.

Aileen has always done right by me and I owe Tori

everything. I have to suck it up. Seth reckons I need to shut the whole thing down, do things the way I think they ought to be done, but I don't even know what that is? With this and the stalker, the unending attention from *Justice of The Peace*, the whole bodyguard thing and the pressure to do a good job on *Nightcar*, I just don't want to cause any more shit for myself.

I spoke to Pops about it and he said that as long I was happy, then he was happy. Am I happy? Can you be happy if you're not sure you're happy? I love Tori. She's good for me. She's smart and sexy, and isn't this ambition, this tenacity of hers, one of the things I fell for when we met? Maybe I just need to fucking relax about things for once.

Anyway, I snuck out to surf this morning, which didn't clear my head at all but made me feel awesome about the progress I'm making. After that I slipped on my cap and sunglasses because John Alan says I should not leave the house without them and I took the stalker's glasses back to the Chinese Theater in case she needed them. They were really cool glasses too, like the ones that Esme wears in *Harcourt Royals*. I handed them in to the theater manager, who then took me to look at my now dried handprints.

When I reached the cement, I looked real close and, right there, on the edge of the stone, was the slightly blurry imprint of a surprised-looking face. I could barely make it out, but it was there. The ridiculousness of it made me laugh so hard that tears came to my eyes. I can't remember the last time I laughed like that. The theater manager kept apologizing and saying they could organize to have the stone recast. I said no fucking way. I think every time I want to laugh harder than I ever have done before, all I have to do is walk down to Hollywood Boulevard and spot that odd little face imprint in the cement.

Aside from the surprisingly cheering faceprint I'm still feeling pretty shitty about the past couple of days, but as

Ira says, one can always find three amazing things to be happy for. So here goes.

1. That surprised-looking face print in my handprint flagstone. It will make me laugh *forever*.

2. Tori wants live music at the engagement garden party she's planning so I emailed that awesome Adam Levine tribute singer I met in the Lyft to sing a couple songs. Tori didn't seem too keen, but kept quiet considering I'm agreeing to every other thing she wants. The singer—Billy Fever—messaged me straight back and said that he would be delighted to perform for us. He was so happy that I had remembered him and said I was his number one fan—in joint place with some other person.

3. I'm having a late brunch with Seth and Olive today. Olive keeps telling us about some British food called black pudding, which sounds truly fucking gross. I'm seeing Ira afterwards, so it will be great to talk things through with him. Writing in the journal is helping, but not enough.

CHAPTER THIRTY-SEVEN

Nora

Text from Imogene *I thought we agreed that you were coming home? Nora! I'm worried about you. Please don't try to meet Gary Montgomery again. I don't want you to get into trouble… Ring me! Im.*

I wake up after a terrible and fitful sleep. I open one eye to look at the clock on the wall: 10.30 a.m. Shit. Kennedy is off having her big audition and interview and I didn't even get up in time to wish her good luck! Damn it. I send a psychic message of good luck across the universe and hope that it reaches her, although, frankly, my belief in the cosmos has been massively eroded over the last twenty-four hours. Stoopid, lying cosmos.

I sit up, grab a warm bottle of water from the bedside table, down it and thank god that Brandon and I agreed I should go back to my own bed before daybreak. I can't even begin to imagine the awkwardness of waking up beside him this morning.

The sex was good. Surprisingly good, actually.

Brandon certainly knew what he was doing. It successfully distracted me from the way I feel, at least for a little while and hopefully it did the same for him. But hung-over pillow talk with a one-night stand? A one night stand? No, thank you.

I pull on my dressing gown and mooch out into the living room, apologising to Winklepuff as I do for getting up so late and leaving him without an early-morning walk.

As I enter the kitchen to make a cup of tea, I shriek in fright as I bump into a tiny red-haired woman rummaging through the drawers.

'Erin!' I gasp, pressing my hand to my chest. 'I didn't know you were here!'

'Oh hey,' Kennedy's work nemesis/ex-hook-up jumps back from the drawer and smiles widely as if she couldn't be more thrilled to see me. 'I was just looking for a teaspoon. It's Nora, right? Kennedy's little internet friend?'

'Yep.' I nod, reaching over to pluck a teaspoon from the cutlery caddy on the worktop. I hand it to Erin, who uses it to stir a cup of tea. 'Though less of the *little*. It was a real effort to grow this belly.' I pat my tummy and Erin laughs out loud, her head thrown back. Huh. It's been a while since I've been brave enough to be myself around strangers, to say what pops into my head without worrying it's the wrong thing. I think my time in LA has whittled the nerves away without me even realising. I laugh with Erin, noticing as I do that she's dressed in Kennedy's blue stripy nightshirt. Well well well. Did she stay over? I thought Kennedy was working on her audition last night? 'Is Kennedy at the news station already?' I ask.

'Oh, yeah, she left super early to get a blow-out beforehand. Her mom booked her an appointment with some stylist on Rodeo Drive. Anyway, she said I could help myself to tea before I left. I've got my audition this afternoon! Wish me luck.'

'Good luck but… I obviously want Kennedy to get the job!'

'Ha, yes… right! Of course you do.'

Erin stands there in the doorway of the kitchen as if this is her house and she's waiting for me to leave. Something about her is definitely a little off…

'Oooookay then,' I say after it's clear there is no more small talk to be had. 'I'm going to get a shower. You can let yourself out, right?'

'Oh yeah, yeah…' Erin grins, taking a sip of her tea and leaning against the kitchen counter. 'I'll see you around, I guess.'

'I'm actually leaving in a few days.'

'Hmmm, that's good.'

'Good? What do you mean?'

'Oh nothing! Ignore me. I'm still half-asleep.' She closes her eyes and does a little snore before laughing that over-the-top laugh again, although I'm not sure what's funny. Shrugging, I head to the shower. By the time I get out, Erin has left.

After getting dressed in jean shorts and the loosest vest top I've packed, a yellow cotton thing that still stretches obscenely across my chest, I smother on a ton of factor 50 sun cream, take some Advil, down a pint of water and pull on my comfy trainers. I head out with Winklepuff and catch the bus down to Marina Del Ray, which Kennedy recommended as one of his favourite places to pee. I've brought my notebook and pen because my heart is aching and my brain is jumbled with thoughts, worries and emotions. After yesterday I know that one of the best ways to process it all is to write it down.

By the time we've reached the marina and Winklepuff has done his business, my shower-wet hair has air dried. I twist the long locks and pull them over one shoulder. Then, heading into a dog-friendly café, I order a pot of extra strong coffee and am absolutely delighted to find a full English breakfast with actual black pudding on the menu, rather than all the usual chia seed pudding and egg-white omelettes that are all over Venice Beach.

After texting back Imogene, reassuring her that I'm okay and that a few more days here won't make a difference, I eat my breakfast, sharing the bacon and sausage with Winklepuff, who looks like he's going to shit himself with excitement at these new forbidden flavours. When we're finished, he licks my knee for three straight minutes as a sloppy, smelly thank you. I am disgusted, but touched. I think I finally get what all the fuss about dogs is. They are super cool.

Feeling buoyed up by the breakfast and the extra strong coffee, I pop Winklepuff onto my knees, where he curls up for a post-meat snooze, open up my laptop and do a solid hour of prioritised virtual admin tasks, almost bashing my head in with boredom multiple times throughout. When I'm done, I open up my notebook and tentatively start to sketch out more of the lyrics that have been racing non-stop around my head.

When I've finished the first verse of another melancholic song about lost love, I tie Winklepuff's lead around my wooden chair and head to the loo, my bladder full to the brim with coffee. Once I've finished *my* business, I head out of the cubicle towards a shiny tiled mirror bank, framed with little light bulbs like in an old Hollywood movie. Another woman stands beside me, trying her best to gather her wild curls into a mustard-coloured scrunchy that does not want to hold them. She smiles at me. Her rosy cheeks and amused eyes look slightly familiar.

'My god, it's so hot,' she says, fanning her hands in front of her face. 'I need to put my sweaty hair in a bobble, but there's too much of it! For Fleperty's sake!'

'Oh! You're British!' I exclaim. 'Me too. You're the first Brit I've met out here.'

'Hey, wow! You're northern, right? Where are you from?'

'A little village outside of Sheffield,' I say.

'A little village outside of Manchester!' she counters happily.

'I'm Nora,' I say, slightly waving at her.

'I'm Olive. Olive Brewster.' She waves back, giving up with the bobble and shoving it in the pink bumbag slung around her waist. 'I've been here in the US for two years, usually in New York, but I've come to visit a friend in LA with my boyfriend. Was gagging for an English breakfast, which is why we came here. I properly miss England.'

'That was a fine breakfast, right?' I say. 'I had a hangover and that black pudding fixed me.'

'Same here! The guys I'm here with think the whole concept of black pudding is disgusting,' she tilts her head towards the door. 'But they're just dumb Americans who know nothing.'

I laugh and re-twist my hair over my shoulder in the mirror.

'I saw you scribbling away out there with your dog,' Olive continues. 'Do you want to join our gang? We're having a little hair of the dog. Would be brill to have another Brit at the table, even things out a bit.'

Ordinarily I would decline an invitation from a complete stranger to dine with her and her 'gang', much preferring to be on my own, but as I noted this morning, my usual nerves with new people have softened considerably since I've been in LA. In fact, I might even be starting to enjoy it.

'Yes please,' I grin. 'Thank you!'

'Hoorah! We're sitting on the other side of the place from you,' she tells me as we leave the bathroom.

I untie Winklepuff from the table leg, grab my stuff and follow Olive over to a table where two men are sitting next to each other wearing baseball caps and sunglasses.

Oh. These guys look like a pair of chumps. Olive seemed so cool too! Who even wears sunglasses inside?

'Hey, you two turds!' Olive says to the two guys. 'I found another Brit in the loos. She's from a village not too far away from me and I like her. So she is going to join us for Bloody Marys.' She turns to me. 'Nora, this is Seth, love of my life, and Gary. Guys, this is Nora.'

'Hey! Welcome,' Seth says warmly, taking off his sunglasses and looking much less of a douchebag for doing so. He flashes Olive the smile of a man completely obsessed by her. She gazes back at him with total heart eyes. That's how Mum and Dad used to look at each other. I get a pang in my chest and look away.

The other guy takes off his sunglasses, giving me a friendly wave and a warm smile. It takes me about five whole chaotic seconds to realise that the man smiling at me is *Gary Montgomery*.

Oh my god.

He tells me to take a seat.

Oh my god.

My mouth opens and closes a few times before I plonk myself down in the booth next to Olive. Does Gary not recognise me from yesterday at the Chinese Theatre? He *is* giving me a curious look as if maybe he recognises me, but it doesn't seem to be angry in any way. I wait for him to point at me and declare 'You're the Plain Jane stalker who's been trying to attack me!'

He doesn't, though. He doesn't seem to have a clue who I am.

Olive catches me staring and bounces her hand at her forehead. 'Shit. I keep forgetting you're super famous,' she says to Gary. She turns to me and laughs. 'Sorry! I should have warned you in the toilets. It's always a shock for people to see him in real life. I remember when beloved pop icon Beyoncé was the musical guest on our show – I work at *Sunday Night Live* with Seth – and I almost vommed on her shoes, I was so taken aback. These two are total goons, so no need to feel weird or shy.'

I look closer at Seth and recognise him from YouTube clips of the legendary New York comedy show.

'Wow,' is about all I can get out. My eyes cautiously flick back to Gary and I'm pretty sure my face has gone bright red. I can feel my cheeks buzzing. My breath feels so heavy that I'm sure everyone in the café can hear me panting. This is how I felt the first time I saw him at the cinema. But I was in a dark room then. I could disguise it. Holy shit!

'You all right?' Olive giggles, pouring Bloody Mary from a jug into a glass and sliding it over to me.

I nod quickly. 'Mmhhhm,' I say because my brain doesn't seem to want to form full sentences.

'A few years ago, I saw Robert De Niro in Zabar's,' Seth says. 'I approached him and before I could stop myself, I found myself inviting him out for a drink. He said, polite as can be, "No thanks, pal." I was mortified. I don't know what possessed me.'

'Who's this fella?' Gary asks me, bending down to tickle Winklepuff's head, who returns the affection with a single lick of Gary's hand.

'T-th-this…' I clear my throat, willing myself to pull my shit together and not completely freak out. 'This is Winklepuff. I'm staying with friends for a couple of weeks and helping to look after him.'

'He's nice,' Gary says casually as if he isn't Gary Montgomery and this is all completely normal. 'He's a cool dog, I can tell.'

The urge to stroke Gary's face, to tell him what I feel about him, to ask if we could just leave here and spoon each other for the rest of the night is strong. Dangerously strong. Shit. I know now that this is just a weird infatuation that I'm going to have to figure out in therapy when I get home, but, my god, it feels *so* real.

I realise that everyone is waiting for me to say something else, because that's how conversation works between normal people. But my brain seems to be malfunctioning. I don't know what to say. *Say something, Nora!*

'Winklepuff likes ham and pee-ing,' is what comes out of my mouth. Shit. Why did I say that?

'Hey, just like me!' Olive cuts in cheerfully, which makes everyone laugh.

My eyes meet Gary's again and up close they're even darker and sexier and cleverer than I would ever have thought. They do not, however, look like the eyes of someone who believes I am his soulmate. They look polite and distanced and more than a little weary. I want to take his hand and tell him that things are going to be just fine.

Okay. Get a grip Nora. Gary is deliriously happy with Tori Gould. You have a crush. He is engaged. However much you didn't intend to be his stalker you kind of *are* his stalker. You almost got arrested. Twice. You could get arrested again if he figures out who you are. Be cool. Please, for the love of god, BE COOL.

'I didn't know this place was dog-friendly,' Gary muses, scratching behind Winklepuff's ear. 'I would have brought my girl.'

'That's no way to talk about Tori,' Seth quips daftly, although Gary seems to prickle a bit at the comment.

I feel a sharp surge of relief that Gary did not bring Janet today – imagine if Winklepuff, reunited with *his* one true love, got over-amorous again? That would have been too horrifying to contemplate.

I take a sip of my Bloody Mary, and then another one.

And then another one.

'Are you an actress?' Gary asks, a slight frown creasing his forehead. 'You look kinda familiar.'

'Um, no, not at all,' I say, finding it hard to meet his eyes. 'Just, uh, a virtual assistant from Sheffield. And a singer songwriter, well, amateur.'

Gary nods and smiles and my heart flips over. I can't help but smile back. I try my very best to keep it a normal, polite smile and not a mooning, drooling grin. I'm not sure I manage it.

'You should probably put your sunglasses back on,' Seth says, nudging Gary with his elbow. 'He's got a *stalker*,' he tells me, pulling a faux-terrified face. 'His bodyguard goes everywhere with him now and, when he's not with him, he insists Gary wears a baseball cap and sunglasses. I'm doing the same in solidarity, so now, of course, we look like a pair of—'

'Dickheads?' I volunteer, before my brain can reach my mouth.

Olive and Seth laugh out loud.

'I like her,' Olive announces.

Gary doesn't laugh but his eyes glint with curiosity. Shit. Is he remembering my face?

'A stalker?' I say in a surprised voice as if it is the most bonkers, out-of-the blue thing that could ever happen. 'Blimey! Gosh!'

'Yep,' Olive says. 'It's properly weird.'

'Gary found her glasses and he *kept them*,' Seth adds. '*That's* the weirdest thing.'

He has my glasses? Why? Is he collecting evidence for the police? Shit. I need my glasses back! Putting contacts in wind-attacked eyes cannot be ophthalmologically wise.

Gary chuckles. 'I dropped them off at the theatre this morning.'

It is very difficult to display any emotion other than polite interest at this news.

'They found a butter knife at the movie lot when they caught her there,' Seth continues. 'I mean, a butter knife! I'd love to know what she was intending to do with it.'

'She wanted to butter you up, obviously,' Olive says.

'And he didn't even give her a chance,' Seth laughs. 'How dairy!'

I swiftly realise that they're talking about the knife I took to the lot, the one I wanted to use to make the cheese toastie for Gary, which, now I think about it, was a really stupid, bonkers idea. My god. What is wrong with me? I splutter so much that I almost spit out my Bloody Mary.

'Hey,' Gary says, leaning over and patting me firmly on the back. 'You okay there?'

I nod quickly and catch my breath. He leaves his hand on my back for a moment and my whole body switches on. Like I've been asleep my whole life and someone just plugged me in. Oh wow. I swallow hard and peek up at Gary, because surely, *surely*, he feels that too? But his face is just concerned about my spluttering fit. Of course. Because I have a stupid crush and he is not my soulmate.

'I'm okay now. Thanks,' I say with an embarrassed smile.

Gary narrows his eyes at me for a moment and then removes his hand from my back. He recoils a little. Is he repulsed by me?

I clear my throat again and take a sip of water from the filled glasses on the table. I should go. I should go before I make this whole embarrassing trip even worse. This is exactly why Imogene wanted me to get a flight today. I can't help but end up embroiled in shit like this.

I go to stand up, but my body doesn't want to move. It just sits there. And then it says, 'I… I read somewhere that you just got engaged? Congratulations!'

Why am I still talking to him? I need to leave. But I don't want to leave. Not ever.

'I am,' he says with a big toothy smile. 'And thanks. I'm really looking forward to it.'

I notice an odd look pass between Olive and Seth. Gary also catches the look and rolls his eyes. What is that about?

'So what are you in LA for, Nora?' Olive asks. 'Do you like it? Don't you think it's too hot?' She lifts her wild curls up from her neck and once more tries and fails to secure them in a scrunchy. 'Should have brought Anders with us,' she mutters to herself.

'Anders?' I ask.

'My best friend back in NY. He's a hairstylist. He'd have found a way to control these bad boys, but the heat is making then expand. They breed like Gremlins.'

I laugh, seeing exactly why she works on a comedy TV show. Seth is gazing at her with admiration, like he sees it too.

'I'm in LA to visit a friend,' I tell them, sidestepping the truth, of course. 'She's helping me to rediscover the joy in my life.'

'How's that working out?' Gary asks.

I shrug one shoulder and try to hold myself together. My voice comes out a little shaky. 'Well, one pretty big part of the plan fell through, but I've been writing songs again, which I'd not done in a couple of years. I tried rollerblading and even though the Santa Ana winds blew sand into my eyes and I almost broke my neck, I was pleased I tried it. Oh, and I've been catching the LA sunrises and swimming in the ocean – that's pretty damn magical.'

'It really is,' Gary murmurs, smiling almost to himself.

'I prefer a nice clean, safe pool,' Olive declares. 'The wind is mad here. It's scary out there!'

'Fish creep me out,' Seth adds.

'Me too,' I say. 'But Kennedy – that's my friend – forced me out there and the water here is so warm and the fish pretty much stay out of your way. If you swim on your back when the sky is painted with pink and purple streaks and there's no one else around and you just look up and let the water hold you, it's like being in some sort of lucid dream. It's heavenly. Maybe the nicest thing I've ever done.'

I notice the three of them looking at me oddly. Shit, I garbled a bit then.

'I'm sorry. No one asked for a monologue, ha ha! Too much Bloody Mary!'

Gary stands up from the chair quickly. 'We should go,' he says curtly. 'I have an appointment. And John Alan is coming by to do another house safety check.'

A house safety check? I've really upended things for him. Shame creeps up my neck. I am an idiot.

Olive rolls her eyes slightly. 'Blummin' John Alan. I wish he'd bugger off.'

Gary nods. 'Agreed, and John Alan is such a dumb name. I don't know why, but it kinda bugs me.'

I laugh out loud. 'Yes! That's what *I*—' I cut myself off sharpish, because I was about to say 'That's what I thought!' which would reveal me to have some form of intel on John Alan.

Gary, Olive and Seth look at me curiously.

'What were you going to say?' Seth asks. 'That's what you…?'

'What?… Uh… that's what I… will call my… first-born son. It's a good name. John Alan.'

Nora, you dick. Why are you the way you are?

Olive and Seth laugh weakly, both of them holding their hands out to me to shake, saying that it was lovely to meet me. Olive pulls me into a warm hug and tells me it was brilliant to hear another northern voice.

I wait for Gary to also hold out his hand for me to shake. But he barely even looks at me, just gives a half-hearted wave before leaving and heading to the counter to pay the bill and head off back to a glamorous life that could never include someone like me.

Then, with Olive and Seth in his wake, Gary leaves the café and doesn't look back.

CHAPTER THIRTY-EIGHT

Gary

Hey,

I'm sitting in the waiting room at Ira's clinic and I needed to get this out, so I'm writing it in my Notes app.

I just had the *weirdest* brunch. Like truly, confusingly strange. I was hanging out with Seth and Olive at this café in Marina Del Ray and Olive brought this round-faced dark-haired British woman out from the bathroom. She was called Nora and Olive thought it would be nice for her to have a drink with us for some reason. When I saw her face, my heart started thumping really hard. What the fuck? I thought I was having some bizarre anxiety attack, but, well, it didn't feel awful like anxiety usually does. It felt, I dunno, *exciting*. Like the heart pounding I get when I'm surfing.

I managed to keep myself together for the majority of the conversation, but then this woman had a coughing fit, so I patted her back to help her. And, fuck, when I touched her... Maybe it was one of those electric shock things that sometimes happen? But I felt this current run through me and this warm desperation in my chest. Like I never wanted to take my hand away. The whole room went quiet and I just wanted to grab her hand, take her away from everyone else and hold her, kiss her, *fuck* her. I had to do some very good acting to keep my cool and not humiliate myself or just pull this stranger's body into mine. What the fuck, Gary?

And her face, my god. Her face was so open and bright and… familiar. Her lips were red and plump and the way she scraped her front teeth over them after she had spoken… Her eyes were kind of painful-looking actually, she said she'd gotten sand in them somehow? But they were big and warm and thoughtful, a little like a cow's eyes, but, you know… not. Maybe like a sexy cow. What am I even saying? What is wrong with me? Is this a reaction to the whole sudden Tori engagement? I'm feeling overly attracted to strangers now? First the stalker and now this random brit?

I had to get out of the café before I said or did something completely creepy and inappropriate like kiss a total stranger. Jeez, I hope Ira has some intel into why I just felt so completely irrational in the presence of someone I've never met before and will never meet again. Jesus Christ.

On the drive home, Olive and Seth asked why I was being so quiet. Seth reiterated that I didn't have to marry Tori if I didn't want to. But that's the thing. I *do* want to. I mean, I would have preferred to give it a few more years, but it's happened how it's happened and it's a waste of time to keep on feeling pissed off about it, especially when I'm in the middle of a shoot. Tori is a *great* girlfriend. Solid and supportive and beautiful and, like Aileen says, we're a perfect match. I would never, ever want to hurt her. I promised her I never would. I owe her absolutely everything. We may not fall over ourselves in laughing fits all the time like Seth and Olive or stay up late chatting endlessly into the night, but there's respect and rapport and partnership. There's attraction and ease and steadiness. That's good. That's enough. And I love her. I do.

Anyway, three amazing things that happened today.

1. ~~Her face~~
2. ~~Her voice~~
3. ~~Her~~

Cut it out, Gary. You're just having a strange few days and feeling a whole lotta fucking pressure. You read way too much *Harcourt Royals* last night and it's clearly made you mushy. It's not like you'll ever see this woman again anyway. She doesn't even live in this country.

She wasn't even your type, you dumb dork.

CHAPTER THIRTY-NINE

Nora

After getting a car to Grauman's Chinese Theatre to pick up my glasses, I get dropped off about half a mile from Kennedy's house so that Winklepuff and I can walk the rest of the way back. I'm in a complete daze, my emotions more wayward than they have ever been. I'm aching with longing after being up close to Gary, relieved that he didn't seem to recognise me and that I didn't completely lose my shit, perturbed by the coincidence of actually running into him, gutted that he clearly didn't feel any sort of connection with me and embarrassed that I ever thought he would. I mean, look at me. I catch sight of myself in the reflective surface of a nearby building. My face looks pale, and my air-dried hair looks totally messy. Plus, my eyes are all squinty and gammy.

The wind blasts my hair into my face as if to mock me. I spit it out of my mouth and ask the wind why it won't just bugger off. That's one thing I will not miss about this place – these stupid devil winds.

I think of Gary's tall, relaxed stature, and that undeniable, enigmatic charisma that's even more blinding in real life. *Of course* he isn't attracted to me. I almost laugh to myself. It seems so ridiculous that I thought he might be. Shit. I really am as delusional as Imogene said I was. The laugh turns into a half sob and I shake my head at my own reflection.

'You know there are people in there who can see you?'

I turn around to find a teenage girl, watching me watch my own reflection in the mirrored window.

'What?'

'Yeah,' she says, tapping on her phone as she speaks. 'It looks like a mirror from the outside, but inside it's an office full of people. They're probably laughing at you. I used to intern there and we found it hilarious, the faces people pull when they're looking at their own reflection.'

Shit. Well, that's embarrassing. It's just one thing after the other at this point.

'Oh, thanks for that,' I say to the girl, before sticking my tongue out at the window and stalking away with Winklepuff.

* * *

I'm so stuck in my own head, feeling absolutely stunned about what has just happened, replaying the moment that Gary touched my back, that I barely realise I've already reached Kennedy's house. I notice that Brandon is sitting on the front porch, typing speedily into his laptop. Shit. Fuck. With everything that's happened this morning, I almost forgot that last night I had drunken sex with Brandon. I get a memory of him poking my belly, kissing my neck, turning me over onto all fours and pulling on my hair.

Fuck. I stop short, not sure what to do. I really don't want to talk to him right now in the cold and sober light of day. I wouldn't even know what to say to him... Will he want to have sex again? Will he want to *not* have sex again?

I'm not sure how I feel about either of those possibilities. My brain is already jumbled enough having just had brunch with *Gary Montgomery.*

I'm pondering whether I should just leg it back down the street when Brandon must sense me staring, because he looks up and gives me a wide, knowing grin. I'm about to reluctantly head over to him when a car beeps its horn behind me. I spin around to find Kennedy in her car, the convertible top down, 'Mmm Bop' by Hanson blasting conspicuously out of the speakers.

'Hey, girl!' she yells, dipping her sunglasses down her nose. 'Hop in. Let's go get some dairy-free ice cream!'

'What? Now? What about Winklepuff? Him too?'

'Of course. Come on. Time's a wastin'!'

I shrug at Brandon and, glad to have a ready-made excuse to put off talking to him, I scoop Winklepuff up and climb into the car.

I look over at Kennedy and stifle a giggle. Her hair is big, stiff and curled under at the ends and she has so much thick make-up on she looks like she's just about to enter a beauty pageant. She's wearing a stiff white blouse and a tight navy blue skirt. Her high heels are kicked off on the car floor in front of me and she's driving in a pair of raggedy white sneakers.

'My audition was amazing!' she yells over the music before I can ask her where we're going.

'That's bloody brilliant,' I reply, feeling guilty that the world's most unexpected brunch means I had also forgotten about Kennedy's big anchor interview. 'Tell me stuff! Do you think you got it?'

Kennedy nods once as she turns the corner, heading towards the motorway. 'It went super well. They *loved* my story and, you know, I gave it my all. I'm just glad it's done, to be honest. Maybe my mom will stop texting me every second to make sure my tone of voice is exactly the right mix of warm and smart without being stuck up or to make sure I'm wearing enough mascara so my eyes "pop" on the screen.'

I grin at Kennedy's heavily mascaraed spider lashes. 'Definitely enough mascara.'

'Right? I hate wearing all this junk on my face. But Mom's right. It does make my eyes pop.' Kennedy sighs. 'Erin's auditioning this afternoon, so I should know pretty soon whether I got it or not.'

'I saw Erin this morning,' I say tentatively... 'dressed in one of your shirts... I thought you were working last night?'

Kennedy grins, a cheeky glint in her eyes. 'I was working! Erin showed up because I said no to going for a drink with her. She said she came by to wish me luck.'

'Oh?'

'She wished me luck. And then we fucked, obviously.'

'Kennedy! I thought you hated her!'

She rolls her eyes. 'I do. She's the worst. But she's also so very, very hot.'

'Are you sure she wasn't trying to psych you out? Distract you from your work?' I say, thinking back to Erin's odd behaviour this morning.

Kennedy shrugs as we slow to a crawl on the traffic-packed road. 'Probably. But she was wearing this flippy red Alaïa dress and I'd had a glass of wine with my dinner and that movie was on TV – *500 Days of Summer*. Zooey Deschanel *and* Joseph Gordon-Levitt were in it, so I was already feeling frisky when she showed up. And, you know... I got carried away.'

'I do know,' I mumble, thinking to last night and my own getting carried away with Brandon.

Kennedy smacks her forehead, as we turn onto a narrower road stacked with tall trees on each side. 'Oh yes! I had completely forgotten! You fucked my brother! This is the famous Mulholland Drive by the way...'

My eyes widen at her bluntness and the fact that she's

being so nonchalant. Also, they really do tell each other *everything*.

'Um. Sorry. Yes. I was so drunk. I didn't mean for it to happen. It just… did.'

Kennedy pulls up onto a dirt road and turns off the engine. 'Oh, I knew it was going to happen. The chemistry between you two!'

'Um, what? The chemistry? No. We actually don't seem to get along very well. We'd both had so much to drink.'

'Are you kidding me? Not getting on well is total foreplay. I should know – I'm a…' Kennedy trails off, her cheeks pinkening beneath the layers of foundation.

'You're a what?'

'A, um, person who is weirdly discussing my brother's sex life. Gross. But my point is that you both needed a distraction from your heartbreak.'

I think of Gary barely looking at me as he left the café this morning. She's right. It was a pretty out-there notion. Completely bonkers, in fact. Tears spring to my eyes again. I will them away.

'Hey,' Kennedy says thoughtfully. 'You know… maybe fate had it aligned so that you would come here and meet *Brandon* and not Gary. The universe works in mysterious ways!' She puts on a deep cheesy voice like the guy who does the trailer voiceovers for movies. 'HE'S a heartbroken and surly American set designer slash writer, SHE'S a beautiful English book nerd with a romantic heart, both of them on the lookout for that special something. Will they find it in the City of Angels? Nobody ever said the path of true love would run smooth! With help from a hot, creative and much smarter than she looks weather girl and the best, cutest dog in California, who knows what will happen!'

I can't help but laugh at her silliness. I screw up my face. Could she be right? I think of last night and how fun it was to escape with Brandon. And how sweet he was when I fell over on the rollerblades. Then I think of how he was so rude when I first met him. How he said I was ordinary.

'No,' I say to Kennedy. 'It was definitely a one-off. Plus I'm going home, so...'

Kennedy puts on the trailer man voice again. 'Can true love blossom an ocean apart? With an open mind and help from a hot blonde very smart weather girl, maybe it could! It is possible!'

I shake my head and nudge her in the ribs.

She bends down, rifles under her car seat, and pulls out two still-icy bottles of water. 'Here y'go. Come on!'

She gets out of the car and I follow her lead, placing Winklepuff onto the dusty ground.

'Where are we going?' I ask.

Kennedy opens up the car boot and rummages around in a gym bag, pulling out some leggings and a T-shirt, which she discreetly changes into. 'For a hike!' she says brightly, pulling out a wet wipe and rubbing it all over her face, before spraying on a ton of sun cream.

'What? A hike? Noooo!' I grumble. 'You said we were going for ice cream!'

'You wouldn't have come if I'd told you the truth. When we were drunk on peach wine, I told you how much I like to hike and you said that you couldn't imagine anything more boring than hiking and that you'd rather be on hold to a company that sold radiators.'

'I did say that. So why did you bring me here?'

Kennedy ruffles her hair out of its big stiff blow-dry and pulls it up into a bobble. 'Because Mission Joy Ahoy is still very much in play and after yesterday at the ceremony, I think it will do you some good. Come on. It's not long and the view is just... well, you'll see.'

'Sorry, Winklepuff,' I say as we start to walk up a

gently sloped trail, the blazing sun beating right down upon us. 'I guess we have joy to find.'

He looks up at me and I'm pretty sure he's thinking that there better be a hock of ham at the end of this trail or else he will lose his shit.

Kennedy links her arm through mine. 'So, what did you get up to this morning?'

I think of Gary. How when he touched me, my whole body lit up. How I ached to just sit and look at him for as long as I could. How I wanted to tell him about my vision of us laughing in the ocean, how he found my glasses, how when he smiled I wanted to touch his face, how my already fractured heart shattered a little more when he left, barely even saying goodbye, how it reiterated my delusion and what a mess I am at the moment.

But it just all feels like too much to put into words, especially since Kennedy has admitted that she, like Imogene, thinks this attempt to meet Gary was more than a little ridiculous. That *I* am pretty damn ridiculous.

'Ah, nothing much!' I say, taking a big gulp of my cold water and deciding it would be easier to just direct the conversation away from me. 'Hey, tell me more about your audition. Were you scared? How long did it take? Why the hell did you have such big hair?'

CHAPTER FORTY

Nora

When we finally get home a couple of hours later, I am truly worn out. Kennedy was right about the view, though. It was one of the most beautiful things I have ever seen. We walked up through San Vicente Mountain Park from Mulholland Drive. At the top, there was a 360-degree view of the entire city, all hazy beneath a perfect cornflower blue sky. My favourite spot was the view down over the beautiful blue-green Encino Reservoir, which was framed in the distance by the most gorgeous mountain horizon.

We stayed there, just staring for around forty minutes and I felt a rush of hope come over me. I may not have found my soulmate and I may legitimately be smack bang in the middle of some sort of grief-related breakdown, but I've found something here. I've rediscovered how miraculous it is to be in the world, to be living in my body rather than just my head. I've found songwriting again. And, best of all, I've found Kennedy, a bona fide friend. As we looked out over the vista, she grabbed my hand and told me she'd miss me when I was gone. I squeezed her hand

and told her I'd miss her too. I knew that as soon as I reached Leeds and Bradford airport and travelled back to the grey, sensible skies of Brigglesford, this whole trip would feel like nothing more than some hazy-skied, ridiculously warm, joyful, heart-breaking fever dream. And while I'll always be obsessed with romance novels and movies with dreamy happy ever afters and soulmates and the hope of one day being as happy as Mum and Dad were, I know that there is joy to be had from just me. Nora. And all I need to do to find it is step outside of my warm safe cocoon every now and again.

After a much-needed snooze, I wake up to find the sky darkening, the twinkle light wrapped palm trees on the beach glittering and the scent of a nearby food truck wafting in through the window. Stretching my arms above my head, I smile at Winklepuff, who joined me for the nap and seems to have no intention of getting up just yet. My eye catches the many pictures of Gary on the Creepy As Fuck Soulmate Procurement Wall. I really should take them down. I yawn. I'll do it later.

I head into the kitchen to grab a glass of water and gulp it down so thirstily that it dribbles onto my chin. Leaving the kitchen, I walk right into Brandon's large chest.

Shit. Argh! This man has seen the face I do when I have an orgasm. I immediately start to sweat.

'Shit. Sorry.'

'No problem,' he grins, reaching forward and using his thumb to wipe away the water droplets from my chin as if this isn't a very very awkward moment.

'Oh! Thanks.'

I zip past him and head into the living room. 'Um, is Kennedy about?' I ask.

'She's gone to a SoulCycle class, I think?'

I perch down on the sofa. 'Really? She's nuts. We *just* went on a hike!'

Brandon chuckles and comes to sit down beside me. His thigh is touching mine. 'SoulCycle is actually really great. You should try it.'

'I've done enough exercise this week to last me a lifetime!' I laugh, scooching a little further down the sofa so that our thighs are no longer pressed up against each other's.

Brandon's eyes flick down towards my stomach, his eyebrows raising. We sit there for an excruciatingly silent few seconds. Then Brandon smiles at me, his eyes shining cheekily. He reaches his hand out, tucking my hair behind my ear. 'Hello,' he says. 'How are ya?'

As he leans forward to kiss me, I suddenly know with a deep and true certainty that I don't want to kiss him again. There's just no point. He is hot and last night was an amazing, fun distraction, but I was super drunk and super heartbroken. I'm still super heartbroken, but I know, despite what I feel about Gary and despite what Kennedy said about our 'chemistry', that the universe did not send me here to find Brandon. I have no clue what it sent me here for, but it was not... *this.* There's no thunderbolt through the belly. And that's what I want. It's what I really want.

I move away and smile at him. 'Listen,' I say, shuffling uncomfortably. 'I think last night was... maybe a one-off? I mean, it was great. Really great. But... you know...' I trail off because I have no clue what to say.

Brandon blinks, his chin tucking into his neck with surprise. His cheeks turn slightly red. 'You're kidding right? '

'Um... no?'

'Wow. I mean, I'm not trying to have a relationship with you, Nora!' he scoffs. 'You're here for a few more nights... I just thought. Last night was nice, right?'

I nod. 'It really was,' I say, admiring the way his big tanned arms look in his tight white T-shirt. 'I just… My head's all over the place and I…' It's my turn to flush red. 'I'm… in love with someone else.'

Brandon laughs out loud. 'Gary Montgomery, huh?'

I shrug and give a little laugh. 'Of course I know now that I'll never have someone like that, but it doesn't mean I don't feel the way I feel. It's weird, I know.'

Brandon's mouth twists. 'Understatement.'

He reaches into his jeans pocket and pulls out his phone. He taps onto the screen and hands it over to me. It's a YouTube clip. My whole body burns as I see the title: 'EPIC FAIL!! Creepy Girl Tries to Attack Gary Montgomery!!!'

With a trembling finger, I press play. It's a mobile phone video of me from the back, taken right after I was pushed, although of course, you can't actually tell that I've been pushed. It looks like I'm running towards the podium before falling into the cement box. The way I wobble forward before tripping does look a little as if I'm trying to rush desperately towards Gary. I feel a sweep of relief that the video doesn't show my face and then another spike of humiliation as I watch John Alan pushing past everyone, grabbing me around the waist and carrying me away. The phone camera zooms into Gary's face. He looks completely alarmed. The video ends freeze-framed on his horrified expression.

'Read the comments,' Brandon says.

I know that I shouldn't. I know that the comment sections are never a good place to end up. Nevertheless, I scroll down.

Poor Gary M! Psycho alert!

. . .

Obeeeeeeeese.

She looked like she got pushed forward by the crowd

A future millionaire will like this comment.

She's trying to kill him! She could sit on him and he would full dead of suffocated.

Tori Gould is SO ELEGANT WE HAVE NO CHOICE BUT TO WORSHIP HER

I Have Watched This 10 timezzzz, When She Falls. LOLOLOLOL.

What a dumb fat bitch

I click off the screen quickly, bile rising into my throat.

'I didn't need to see that,' I say quietly to Brandon, dropping his phone as if it has burned my hands.

He shrugs. 'Maybe you did…' He puts his hand on my shoulder and rubs it as if to comfort me, his finger trailing along my back. Is… is he coming onto me again? Right now? After he just made me read my own hate comments?

'What is wrong with you?' I cry, standing up from the sofa, fury burning in my chest, at him and at myself. 'I don't want to sleep with you again, Brandon. Jeez!'

He stands up too. 'Wow... I thought I was helping you out! I... I thought you'd be grateful.'

'Helping me out? What?'

'I mean... look at you. I thought we could distract each other is all. You're a lovely girl, but you're not exactly model material, Nora...' His eyes travel over my body.

And it suddenly becomes clear to me. This isn't chemistry. Brandon's grumpiness isn't sexy or hot or Mr Darcy-ish. His heartbreak isn't the only reason for his odd and moody behaviour, for his ability to make me feel shit about myself. He's just... a bit of a dickhead.

Tears of frustration spring to my eyes. I take a shaky breath and lift my chin. 'I get it,' I say quietly. 'I don't look like the other women in this city. But, you know, I like my thighs. And I like my belly.' I poke my belly like he did last night. 'And I like that I was brave enough to do something so outlandish because I believed that maybe I could experience the magical, once-in-a-lifetime love that my parents had. And yeah, I may not be model material, but I'm not someone to be pitied either.'

Brandon holds his phone up in the air. 'I think we both know that's not true... Everyone is laughing at you.'

I stare at him for a few seconds. He may be more attractive than me. And more successful than me. But he's not a better person than me. I am Nora Tucker. I'm a good human who believes in true love and kind people. My mum and dad loved me. My sister loves me. I don't need anyone to make me feel like I should be grateful for their attention.

'I might have done some really very embarrassing stuff,' I say, looking directly into Brandon's blue eyes and holding their gaze. 'And I'm probably a little bit delusional, true. And you were right... Someone like me will probably never get someone like Gary Montgomery... but thanks for helping me to realise that I'll also never allow myself to settle for someone like you.'

Brandon's mouth opens and closes.

I swallow down the sob in my throat, turn on my heel and return to my area, hiding under the covers until I hear the gentle thud of Brandon's feet heading upstairs to his bedroom.

CHAPTER FORTY-ONE

Nora

I find myself waking up naturally at 5 a.m. after a long and dreamless sleep. I spent the rest of last night hiding out in my room. Kennedy came in when she got back from SoulCycle. She'd obviously spoken to Brandon, but I just pretended to be asleep. All I can think about is those horrible YouTube comments and how quickly Brandon's true colours shone through when he was rejected by someone he thinks of as 'lesser' than him. Yikes.

With bleary eyes, I creep out of the bed, pull on my swimming costume, scrape my hair into a bun, put in my soothing eye drops and, leaving Winklepuff curled up in his bed basket, head outside to the beach. The sky is that amazing bluey pink and the sun is bright, but it's a little chillier than it has been over the past few days. The Santa Anas are still hanging about.

As I walk across the sand towards the ocean, I feel a touch of trepidation at the size of some of the waves further down the beach; they're pretty aggressive-looking. I head to my favourite spot and wade in, sucking in my breath sharply as the cooler-than usual water hits my legs, then my waist and finally my neck. I gather up the courage to duck my head under and then I start to swim, feeling my muscles stretch and warm in a way that they never really got to do back in Brigglesford. I spot a man on a surfboard further down the beach, taking the waves cautiously. I lie on my back and do my favourite thing, staring at the blooming sky and this magical fuzzy light that I'm going to miss so much. Nothing I could conjure up in my fantasies could be as beautiful and enchanted as this sky.

I'm thinking about the fact that Imogene must be pissed off with me because she hasn't texted since I told her I was staying here a little longer – when I hear a short shout of distress from down the beach. I flip over from my back quickly and notice the man further down the beach is nowhere to be seen, his surfboard bouncing violently on an aggressive wave. Oh shit!

Without thinking about it, I immediately start to swim over to where he was, but outside of my gentle and shallow patch of water, the large waves are too much to deal with. I'm not strong enough to tackle them and a swathe of water flops right over my head, getting in my ears and up my nose. When my head pops up and I manage to get my bearings, I notice that the man's head has also popped up and, without grabbing his board, which seems to have gone off on its own journey, he swims to shore. He strides out onto the beach, holding his arm to his chest. His hunched stature shows that he's hurt himself.

'No!' I whisper, swimming back to the beach and running over to him as quickly as I can, not even caring that running is not my natural state and that my gigantic boobs keep hitting the bottom of my chin.

I reach the man, who is looking down confusedly at the gash on his forearm. It's bleeding quite heavily, the blood dripping onto his toes.

'Shit, are you okay?' I ask, rubbing the salt water out of my eyes.

'Um, I think so, I got a little cocky out there and this happened.' The guy holds up his arm before lifting his head.

I inhale sharply as my eyes meet his.

Oh god…

What is Gary Montgomery doing on the beach outside Kennedy's house?

He stumbles back a little.

'It's you,' he says, frowning in recognition.

'You sure you're okay?' I ask, noticing how pale his face looks and worrying that he might pass out.

'Feeling a *little* woozy. Very masculine,' he says, pulling a silly face, although he is clearly in pain.

My usual awkward shyness fades away as Gary's injury propels me into action. 'Come on,' I say, the mandatory first-aid training we did at high school coming straight back to me. 'My place is just there. We need to clean the wound and stop it bleeding. See what we're working with.'

Leaving our towels on the beach, we hurry to Kennedy's house. Inside, Winklepuff starts jumping up at Gary and licking his knees, making little yelps of joy.

'Ham!' I say firmly.

Winklepuff thankfully settles obediently onto his bottom. I make a silent vow to repay him with some premium Parma as soon as I can. I grab some fresh towels and the first-aid kit from the downstairs bathroom and bring them through to where Gary Montgomery is standing in the living room, looking way too pale and dazed for my liking. I wrap the towel around his arm to stem the bleeding.

'Sit down,' I command, pushing him down onto the sofa and trying to ignore the fact that my hand on his shoulder is making me far hornier than it should, given that this man is bleeding right in front of me. Removing the towel, I grab a little bottle of antiseptic and wipe it over the wound.

Gary breathes in abruptly.

'Sorry,' I say, feeling his pain in the pit of my stomach.

I take out some wound adhesive and place five strips over the cut, grab a bandage, rip off the plastic packaging and wrap the wound, as carefully and neatly as I can, securing it with a tiny gold safety pin.

'I don't think it needs stitches, but you should probably go to the hospital to check... Did you hit your head? Is anything else hurt?'

He shakes his head no. 'I think I just caught my arm on a rock when I went under.'

'Right.'

He looks incredibly confused. Is he in shock? It must have been so scary getting dragged under those waves. 'Do you want a brew or anything?' I say. 'It might help with the shock? You know, the sugar.'

'A brew?' he asks, eyebrow raised.

'Tea. A cup of tea.'

'Oh. Sure.'

'Good.'

'Thanks'

'No problem!'

As I stand up from the sofa, I realise that I'm still dripping wet and wearing my too small swimming costume. Jeez. I get a flash of what Brandon said last night and cross my arms over my belly, trying not to look down at my crotch to check whether I am revealing more than is appropriate.

Gary's eyes travel briefly down my body before he turns his head quickly away and peers out of the window.

I grab the other towel and wrap it around me. It's a small towel so it barely covers anything. Argh.

'I thought I heard voices,' a messy-haired Kennedy says, padding down the stairs in her dressing gown. Then she looks, almost in slow motion, at the blood on the floor and then up to Gary Montgomery sitting right there on her sofa in nothing but a pair of navy swimming shorts. She presses both hands to her chest. 'Holy fuck that's actual Gary Montgomery,' she breathes. Then, eyes wide, their expression turning from surprise to confusion to horror. 'Oh god, Nora,' she whispers. 'No! What have you done to him? This has gone too fa—'

'Actual Gary Montgomery was surfing and injured his arm. I was swimming and I helped him. *That's all.*'

'Thank god! I thought that…' She stops herself and takes a steadying breath, thankfully realising that she's half-asleep and not in full control of her faculties.

I give her a pointed look, silently begging her not to say anything that might reveal my true identity.

She glances over at Gary again, who is looking as uncomfortable as someone who has run into a vague Facebook friend in the supermarket and has to pass them in every aisle thereafter. 'This is so weird,' she says, rubbing her eyes and flattening her bed hair. 'Actual Gary Montgomery in my house.'

'It's just Gary,' Gary tells us, a wry expression crossing his face. 'I mean, my father did like the name Actual, but my mum insisted on Gary before she… well yes. Gary it was— Is.'

'Tea,' I say with a firm nod. 'I'm going to make tea now.'

I head towards the kitchen when Kennedy suddenly makes a weird noise and flies down the rest of the stairs at great speed. She dives past me, and yanks the curtain to my sleeping area closed with a yelp.

Oh my god. The Creepy As Fuck Soulmate Procurement Wall. Holy shit. Thank god she remembered. Imagine if Gary had seen that! He'd have for sure thought he was in some type of *Misery* situation right now and I would one hundred percent be getting arrested today.

'Thanks,' I hiss under my breath to Kennedy.

'Should I leave you alone?' she whispers back, looking around as if she is somehow still asleep and this is all a weird dream.

'Yes,' I mumble out of the side of my mouth. 'Yes, please.'

Kennedy tells Gary it was a great honour and privilege to meet him and that she hopes he feels better soon before slowly heading back up the stairs to her bedroom, not without looking back at us in confusion at least three times.

When she's gone, I make tea for the two of us as quickly as possible and take it out to find Gary is staring with wide eyes at my copy of the latest *Harcourt Royals* book on the coffee table, his mouth slightly ajar.

'Oh, hey I have that book!' he says.

'I know!' I say without thinking. *Shit, Nora. Control yourself!*

'You know?'

'Oh, no. I mean. Hasn't everyone read that book?'

'I've never met a single other person who has read that series. Is it your room-mate's?'

'No, this one's mine,' I say, handing him the mug, which looks tiny in his large hands. 'Although we're both pretty obsessed with it, it's actually how we met. On the online fan group?'

'There's a fan group?' Gary laughs out loud, his eyes sparkling with the kind of excitement that only a true book geek would get at discovering there is a group of people out there who are as specifically nerdy as you. He catches himself, flushing a little red in the cheeks, which is the most adorable thing I've ever seen. This big hunk of a man blushing over his nerdy love for a book series about a powerful and sexy princess and an eco-warrior stripper.

I laugh at his reaction and sit down onto the sofa beside him, being careful to keep a respectful distance between us.

'I had a very similar reaction when I discovered the forum. Are you on Facebook? There's a group on there too!'

Gary nods, using the towel to wipe over his face. I wish I could tell him to leave the water droplets on his eyelashes because they look perfect, but that would be super creepy.

'I have a secret account, under a fake name.'

'Ah, right.' I nod. *Do not ask what the secret name is, Nora. Do not ask that...* 'What's the secret name?' I immediately ask, before clamping my hands over my mouth. Why am I such a fool? I clear my throat. 'Not that I want to know. You don't need to tell me. I mean, not that I would tell anyone, but yeah, sorry, just ignore me.'

Gary laughs, his eyes narrowed curiously. 'You wanna know what the secret name is?'

'Yes!' I put my hands over my face.

'It's Preston Peabody,' Gary says.

'Oh! Why?'

'Well, it's my dad's middle name and my mom's maiden name.'

I pull a face. 'That's a bit obvious, if you're wanting to hide from rabid fans,' I say lightly, as if I am not one of them.

Gary chuckles again, his dark eyes glinting. 'Well, no one has discovered it so far.'

He's right. I didn't think of it, and god knows I've searched for a secret Facebook account.

'Well, the forum and the Facebook fan group both go by the name The Crown Kissers, if you're interested.'

'The Crown Kissers?' Gary purses his lips, barely suppressing a smile.

Now it's my turn to go red because it dawns on me. How have I not noticed that Crown Kissers sounds exactly like a euphemism for blow jobs. I gasp. Considering the tongue-in-cheek nature of the books, I'm pretty sure CJ

West knew exactly what she was doing. 'I didn't come up with it!' I protest.

Gary nods slowly. 'As soon as I get home, I'll find the group. I think I'd like to become a Crown Kisser.'

He is teasing. Gary Montgomery is making a joke. With me.

'The Crown Kissing Life is a fine life,' I say. 'It's lovely to bond with other passionate Crown Kissers.'

'I always felt like a Crown Kisser in my heart, so it sure will be great to find my tribe, at last,' Gary shoots back.

The pair of us crumple into laughter, and for a moment I forget that this is Gary Montgomery of mega fame, the object of all of my attention since the night I saw him at the pictures. Right now he's just a semi-naked guy on the sofa who I really really like.

We stop laughing and Gary looks at me for a long moment. It makes the hairs on my body spring to attention. Then he sort of shakes his head a little and coughs.

'So, um, have you read the bit at the Winter Gala yet?' he asks politely.

'What?' I say, trying not to stare too much at his naked torso.

'In the book?' Gary says, pointing at the book on the table.

'Oh! Oh my god, yes!' I say. 'I *just* read that bit! I cannot believe that fake journalist fucked everything up for Bastian! He was so excited about her expert fish knowledge too.'

I can't believe I'm talking about *Harcourt Royals* with Gary Montgomery right now. And the conversation is going well. I don't feel shy or scared any of the bad things I usually feel when I talk to people I don't know.

'Oh, well, I won't spoiler you,' Gary says. 'But trust me it gets even better!'

'Eek. I cannot wait. Maybe you should bugger off, so I can get back to it.'

Gary smiles at me, knowing immediately that I am joking. 'Oh, well, I'm sorry my near-death experience took you away from Esme and Bastian.'

'I forgive you,' I say nobly.

A silence settles over us. It isn't awkward, but it's definitely something. I'm not quite sure what it is. This is all so weird.

'Okay!' Gary says, extra loudly, standing up from the sofa. 'I should probably get outta here.'

'Oh yes, of course!' I say equally as loudly. 'Is your arm feeling better?'

'My what? Oh! Yeah. My arm.' He looks down at the bandage as if he'd completely forgotten it existed. 'Yeah it is. Thanks for the rescue, Nora.'

I feel a lump in my throat. 'Any time, Gary.'

I follow him as he makes his way to the door.

He's going to leave. I should say something. Now is the time. Now is my chance. I should tell him that I came here for him. That I'm certain he's my soulmate and doesn't he feel it too?

I open my mouth, my heart thudding through my chest. I'm about to say his name when he speaks first.

'I should hurry. I have a suit fitting for my engagement garden party tomorrow night and I promised my fiancée I'd be on time for once.'

I clamp my mouth shut. His fiancée. Tori. An actual human being who Gary is deliriously in love with. Who he asked to marry him. Who is not me.

I take a deep breath and nod casually. 'Of course.'

Gary formally holds out his hand for me to shake. I touch it and almost jump as electricity shoots right up my arm. He slightly jumps too, though I'm pretty sure it's because I jumped first, like some sort of skittish kitten. Then

Gary's eyes travel across my body once more and I'm pretty sure I see a glint of something in his eyes. Attraction? Shit. I know that look. That is definitely attraction. Oh my god.

We stare at each other for a few more seconds and then eventually Gary gives the same distracted half-wave he gave at the café, turns around and, without looking back, leaves.

As soon as the door clicks shut, I hear Kennedy's bedroom door burst open and she clatters down the stairs, now fully dressed in a cream floaty dress, her hair in a messy bun on top of her head.

'Holy fuck!' she says.

'Holy fuck,' I say back, starting to pace very quickly around the room.

'That was weird…'

'It was.' My knees sort of buckle and I plop myself down onto the sofa, feeling a little dizzy. I'm about to tell Kennedy about what I thought I saw in Gary's eyes, that ever so brief glimpse of desire, how we both jumped when we touched each other. But I stop when I realise she is frowning at me a little bit. 'I thought you had, like, kidnapped him or something.'

'You didn't think that!' I say. 'Not really.'

'I sort of did.' She pulls a face. 'And I shouldn't have jumped to that conclusion, you know?'

I nod. She thinks I'm as crazy as Brandon and Imogene do. I button my lips. There's no point in telling her what I thought I saw. Considering all the ridiculous calls I've made since I've been here, it is super possible that my imagination is still playing tricks on me.

Kennedy grabs my hands. 'You do know that seeing him on the beach was just a coincidence, right?' she says gently.

I nod, although I can't help the little thought, right there at the back of my mind, that wonders whether fate is intervening. I mean, I've just bumped into him two days in a row. That's a pretty massive coincidence.

I shake my head and try to push the notion away. I've already gotten myself into enough shit. And Gary very clearly said he was going for a suit fitting for his engagement party. I need to pay attention to the facts. He is engaged to someone else. He loves someone else.

'Just try to keep focused on reality,' Kennedy says. 'Speaking of which, what the hell happened between you and Brandon? He was in a real sulk last night. Lovers' tiff?'

I'm about to tell her, as tactically as I can, that her brother is a bit of a prick, when there's a frantic knock on the front door. My first ridiculous hope is that it's Gary, coming back to kiss me, to tell me that he felt that spark too.

I hold my breath, pull open the door and receive the second enormous shock of the morning when I see Imogene standing there, her clothes crumpled, her eyes tired and her usually perfect hair in a wild halo around her head.

'Imogene?'

Kennedy pops her head over my shoulder. 'Your sister!'

Imogene gives me her sternest look. 'I made you come here. Now I'm going to bring you home.'

CHAPTER FORTY-TWO

Gary

What the hell was that?
    Fuck.

CHAPTER FORTY-THREE

Nora

I grab hold of my sister and pull her into a hug. She drops her suitcase onto the floor and wraps her arms around me. The emotion of this whole trip and the fact that Imogene and I never really hug makes me burst into tears.

Kennedy ushers Imogene in, offering to make us both chamomile tea, like the absolute angel she is.

Imogene and I sit on the sofa. She leans back and inspects my crying face.

'Stop crying,' she says. And, because she's my big sister and she says it so firmly, I do, leaving behind the odd sniffle here and there. 'You look different,' she adds suspiciously. 'Like, a lot different... Did you get Botox out here?' As Kennedy returns with the tea Imogene wrinkles her nose. 'You let her get Botox? When she's in such a fragile mental state?'

I frown a huge frown, proving that I have had no Botox. 'Course I've not, you turd,' I say. 'And I am not fragile. Stupid, yes, but not fragile.'

Kennedy sits down in the armchair opposite us. 'For the record, Botox is a very useful tool for subtly delaying the signs of ageing. But Nora's fresh face is nothing more than a by-product of joy.'

Imogene screws her face up and I notice there are dark shadows under her eyes. 'Joy?'

Kennedy beams. 'We have been seeking joy. It's really helped her with the whole "thinking Gary Montgomery is her soulmate" thing. She's actually discovered some magic of her own out here.'

Imogene smiles, seeming to warm quickly to Kennedy. 'That's good. I love her, but can you imagine what I thought when she told me this big famous actor was her one true love?'

'I can't imagine. I mean, I went along with it for a while because I thought it was the kindest thing to do, but after the whole handprint ceremony mess? I knew it had to stop.'

'Exactly.' Imogene rolls her eyes. 'And when she said she was staying here for longer after she'd *just* agreed to come home, I didn't trust that she wouldn't try to get to him again and get herself into major trouble.'

I look between them, my mouth open. 'I'm right here!'

'Well,' Kennedy says, ignoring me and smiling conspiratorially at Imogene like they're new BFFs, 'I made sure to distract her by setting her up with my brother Brandon. I've been pushing them together the whole time and a couple of nights ago they...' Kennedy wiggles her eyebrows.

'Hot Brandon!' Imogene says. 'I knew it.'

'Oi!' I shout at the pair of them. 'Stop having a rapport! Stop talking about me like I'm not here.' I stand up and put my hands on my hips. 'I cannot believe you've been "pushing us together", Kennedy!'. I turn to Imogene. 'Brandon and I are *not* a thing. He's mean and I don't think he really likes me at all. I certainly don't like him.' I side-eye Kennedy. 'No offence.'

Kennedy waves me away. 'He's a grump right now, but

he's heartbroken. You just need to let him warm up. He's a good guy. Esme and Bastian didn't get on at first and look at them now!'

I sigh. 'I know he's your brother and you love him, Kennedy, and he is clearly going through some shit, and obviously I am too, but it's really not going to happen. I… I'm in love with Gary.'

'Christ,' Imogene says and buries her head in her hands.

'I know it's never going to happen,' I say, sitting back down. 'But I can't help how I feel, especially now I've met him! It's going to take me some time to get over…' I look at my feet. 'Probably my whole life.'

'You actually *met* him!' Imogene asks. '*What?*'

'He actually just left, right before you got here!' I tell her.

Imogene sits up straighter in her seat and instinctively pats down her hair as if Gary could return at any moment and she needs to look her best for him.

'He injured himself on the beach.' I explain. 'I helped him. I *rescued* him and bandaged his arm. I know I was wrong about him being my cosmic partner, but he *did* keep looking at my boobs. That… might be something?'

'No!' Kennedy and Imogene shout at the same time. 'It's not.'

'Of course he was looking at your boobs,' Imogene adds. 'They're massive.'

Kennedy frowns. 'You know,' she says thoughtfully. 'I really believed I was being an amazing matchmaker with you and Brandon… I usually get romantic relationships so spot on.' She looks genuinely peeved.

I go over and give her a hug. 'Not this time, I'm afraid. Thank you for trying, though. You are the loveliest, sweetest person I've ever met.'

Kennedy hugs me back as Brandon himself heads downstairs wearing nothing but a towel on his lower half.

Does he strut around like this on purpose, to show off his crazy abs? Ugh.

Imogene's jaw drops. She looks at me as if to say 'You are truly an idiot for turning that down.'

Brandon picks Winklepuff up from where he's jumping at his legs, eyes Imogene and scowls. 'Oh great. Another one of you,' he says before disappearing into the kitchen and clattering around loudly. 'She's not staying here too, Kennedy!' he shouts back. 'So don't even ask.'

Kennedy goes red. 'Sorry,' she says to Imogene. 'He's...'

'A bit of a dickhead?' Imogene cuts in, blunt as ever.

Kennedy does a gloomy smile. 'Maybe at the moment, yes. He's going through a lot, you know? He has a good heart underneath it all.'

Imogene stands up and rubs at her weary eyes. 'Listen,' she says to me, 'I'm staying at the Chalk Sands B&B a mile down the road. Nora, why don't you walk me there?' She blows the air out from her cheeks.

I frown at her. She looks super frazzled and unlike her usually pristine self. But then I guess she has just been on a flight for eleven hours so she can save her wayward sister from herself.

'I'm so jet-lagged I can't think straight until I've gotten some sleep,' she continues. 'It's beyond time for you to get back home, so I've booked us flights back for tomorrow night. You might want to start packing your things. I'll just use the loo before we go...'

Kennedy's mouth drops open as she points Imogene in the direction of the downstairs bathroom.

'She's a bit of a grump too,' Kennedy huffs and then presses a finger to her chin. 'Oooh, maybe I should set *her* up with Brandon...'

'Kennedy! She's married!' I elbow her, unable to help the laugh that escapes me.

I stop giggling and sigh at the thought of going back

to Brigglesford. I know that Imogene is right. It *is* beyond time for me to go home, get back to real life, start to do the things I promised Imogene I'd do if this whole experiment didn't work out. But knowing this doesn't stop the swirling ache of longing that, despite my new, practical knowledge of the situation, hasn't left my heart. Not one tiny bit.

* * *

I walk Imogene back to the hotel and, along the way she barely notices the beautiful scenery. Instead she tuts and sighs and just generally acts down in the dumps. I ask her if she's okay and she tells me she's just tired, that she had a fight with Dan before she left because he didn't want to look after Ariana alone for a couple of days. I apologise to her for causing all this bloody trouble. I want to make her feel better, so I tell her how keen I am to start grief therapy – which isn't exactly a lie – and that I'll even go on a date with Roger Pepper – which kind of is a lie.

Imogene laughs and tells me that she will allow me to choose my own romantic partners from now on, as long as they live within a five-mile radius from where I live and are not famous or engaged to be married. When we reach her B&B, she faces me and puts her hands on my shoulders.

'I've missed you,' she says.

'I've missed you too.'

'No, I mean… *you're* back. I've not seen you this animated since before Mum and Dad… And if this escapade has made that happen, then I did the right thing telling you to come here. I know you're hurting. I can see it… but I'm proud of you.'

A lump shuffles into my throat. 'I wrote a song the other night.'

Imogene smiles widely, her eyes shining with unshed

tears. 'I hope it's better than that moon on a lake crap Mum was always singing.' The pair of us burst out laughing and I think of how nice it is to have my sister here. If we've only got one day left in the City of Angels, we need to make the most of it.

After making plans for Imogene, Kennedy and I to have dinner out later on so that Imogene can experience a little of this amazing place before we leave, I amble along the bustling beach back to Kennedy's, trying my best to imprint the salty, suncream-y smells, the happy, energetic sounds and the hazy, colourful sights onto my brain.

* * *

I spend the rest of the day walking Winklepuff about and treating him to Santa Monica's finest Parma ham as promised, finishing off the swim I missed this morning, writing some rough lyrics to a new song idea that I can't get out of my head and steadfastly avoiding Brandon. Bit by bit, I take down the Creepy As Fuck Soulmate Procurement Wall and stuff the papers and pictures into the paper recycling bin. As I pull the poster of Gary off the wall, I try not to notice how the photograph doesn't even begin to capture the magnificence of him in real life. I'm tearing up the poster when I hear a squeal from the living room. Kennedy is shouting, 'Oh my god, oh my god!' over and over again.

I yank open the curtain, tripping over my suitcase as I do, and fall into the living room.

'WHAT IS IT? WHAT'S WRONG?' I yell, panicked.

But from the look on Kennedy's face, nothing is wrong. She is smiling, her perfect white teeth on full display. She points down to her phone. 'I fucking got it,' she says. 'I got the junior anchor position!'

'Oh my god, oh my god!' I echo. 'That is incredible!'

I grab her hands and the pair of us start to dance

around the living room. Winklepuff jumps about too, barking frantically.

Kennedy laughs. 'My mom is going to be so excited! This is all she's ever wanted for me!'

'She's going to be super happy,' I agree. 'And this is all you've ever wanted for yourself, right?'

Kennedy nods, her eyes wide. 'Oh yes. Definitely!' Her smile falters the teeniest tiniest amount before beaming back up to full wattage. 'I'm going to go and call my mom. I should probably call Erin too. I bet she's way bummed out.'

'She'll be fine,' I say, feeling pretty sure that Erin is the sort of person who will somehow always land on her feet.

Kennedy twirls around, her arms in the air. 'Call your grumpy sister. That quiet dinner we were gonna have has been upgraded! We're celebrating!'

I'm not sure Imogene will be too pleased about that and I'm feeling both physically and emotionally exhausted. But Kennedy has achieved something amazing and she deserves to have an incredible night.

'We *are* fucking celebrating!' I call back.

CHAPTER FORTY-FOUR

Nora

Once she'd had a nap, Imogene was much more receptive to the idea of a proper night out than I expected and turned up at Kennedy's house with her hair fully set into huge rollers, wearing a T-shirt and jeans because, of course, she didn't bring anything fancy with her as 'she was only coming to drag my arse back to Brigglesford'.

Kennedy, who is around the same size as Imogene, has lent her a gorgeous silver dress and a pair of gold strappy heels. And so, to a soundtrack of Kennedy's favourite early 90s pop, we get ready to go out.

While I comb out Imogene's hair, Kennedy keeps checking her phone. 'Erin still hasn't answered,' she says worriedly. 'I hope she's okay...'

'Honestly, I bet she'll be fine,' I reassure her, getting up to pour her another glass of white wine from the bottle we've opened. 'Like you said, she's probably just bummed out she didn't get the job. She was pretty confident she would...'

Kennedy nods thoughtfully, shakes her shoulders and takes a deep decisive breath. 'You're right.' She puts her phone back in her pocket and takes another sip of wine. 'I'm so excited for us to go out! One more round of Joy Ahoy before you leave.'

'Where are we actually going?' I ask.

'It's a surprise.'

I twist my lips. 'The last time you surprised me I ended up almost breaking my neck on rollerblades.'

'You went rollerblading?!' Imogene laughs out loud. She assesses Kennedy through narrowed eyes. 'You're good. I could barely even get her to leave the house back in Brigglesford. Rollerblading. Wow.'

Kennedy shrugs proudly. 'All of my other friends are so uptight, so perfectly put together and Nora is…'

'A complete mess?' I finish, pulling a face.

Kennedy comes over and lays her head on my shoulder. 'I was going to say interesting. You're really interesting. So it's been fun getting you out of your head. My other friends might have their "shit together" on paper but… they're… I don't know. Not like me.'

I think back to the night when we met up with Kennedy's work colleagues at the bar. They looked like her, but they were a completely different sort of people to her. And she acted so oddly around them. All uptight and overtly intellectual, like she was trying hard to disguise her floaty, geeky vibe.

'Maybe you should see if there are any other Angelenos in the *Harcourt Royals* groups?' I suggest. 'Meet some other people with shared interests other than journalism and stuff? Some other book geeks?'

Kennedy nods and narrows her eyes. 'Maybe I should… I do love that group of nerds…'

'Oh hey,' I say. 'Did you realise that Crown Kissers is a euphemism for blow jobs?'

Imogene sputters out her wine. 'Crown Kissers? What the hell are Crown Kissers?'

Kennedy bursts into laughter. 'It's the *Harcourt Royals*

fandom name. And of course I knew it was a blow job euphemism! How did you not?'

'I just didn't think. That's hilarious! I love CJ West. I wish she wasn't so reclusive online. I'd love to meet her.'

'Me too,' Kennedy says wistfully. 'She seems like the kind of woman who knows exactly who she is.'

'We should email her and ask her to please please do some sort of meet and greet! How amazing would that be?'

Before Kennedy can reply, Brandon stalks down the stairs again and into the kitchen, emerging a few seconds later with a bottle of beer and a scowl. He scoops Winklepuff off the sofa and heads back up the stairs without saying a word.

'I take it your brother isn't coming out with us?' Imogene pulls a face.

Kennedy shakes her head. 'He's been writing away in his room all day and I expect he'll be there most of the night.'

Brandon's probably finishing the screenplay Kennedy said he was writing. Hmmm. I wonder if it's the story of an introverted chubby English girl who had the audacity to reject a muscled, successful American writer/set designer. I feel guilty for a second about hurting him, before remembering that he took great pleasure in showing me those comments on YouTube. Ugh. I don't want to think about Horrid Brandon. It's my last night in LA. It's Imogene's *only* night in LA. And Kennedy's big celebration. This has to be a night to remember.

When the three of us have finished getting ready, we crowd in front of the full-length mirror in the downstairs bathroom and admire ourselves. We look awesome. Imogene's now curled hair sits in a big 70's-style halo around her head and with the silver dress she's borrowed from Kennedy she looks like she belongs in Studio 54. I'm wearing Kennedy's freshly washed white sparkly top again with my jeans, because it's the only sort of dressy thing I can wear and the only thing of Kennedy's that fits me. I've gathered my hair up into a ponytail on top of my head. My eyes need a major rest from the contacts, so I'm wearing my beloved glasses, the gold edges looking awesome next to the lovely orangey red gloss on my lips. Kennedy is wearing a red dress with a flared skirt that stops mid-thigh. Her hair is also tied up into a chignon and over her ear she's wearing a little pink flower.

We're all three of us smiling. I look at these two women. One of whom I've known since I was born, the other who I met IRL less than two weeks ago. Both of them the closest friends I could ever hope to have. I may not be leaving LA with my soulmate tomorrow, but I will leave knowing that there is joy out there in the world for me. Joy that doesn't come solely from living my life through movies and books and fantasies. I will leave knowing that I'm capable of so much more than I ever thought possible. That I might be hurt and wayward and struggling with grief and guilt, but I'm also brave and hopeful and open-hearted. And there's more out there in the world for me. I know that now. I know it thanks to these two incredible women.

I'm so lucky.

CHAPTER FORTY-FIVE

Nora

All the nice things I thought about Kennedy and Imogene at the start of the night: I take it back. I take it all back. They are pains in my arse. The pair of them.

While I've chosen to abstain from drinking on account of the eleven hour flight to get through tomorrow (and also because I don't want to ever smudge the memory of how Gary may or may not have looked at me this morning), Imogene and Kennedy have decided upon what is known in Brigglesford as 'A Mad Fucking Bender'. The two of them are knocking back margaritas and twirling each other around on the dance floor of this Culver City salsa club. I'm about as good at dancing as I am at rollerblading, so I stand by the bar and watch my sister and my new best friend making absolute tits of themselves.

I laugh at Imogene as she does a sort of spinny motion hula, her cheeks red and her halo of hair now significantly flatter than it was two hours ago. It's actually really lovely to see her kicking back and not giving a shit. Her life is so responsible, always go go go, always taking care of everyone. It strikes me that I'm not the only one who's forgotten how to find joy since Mum and Dad died.

Kennedy is actually pretty pissed. She's now wiggling her bum in Imogene's direction as the live band play a funky mambo number.

The two of them spot me watching and chuckling, and drag me over to the dance floor to join in.

'Noooooooo!' I protest. I surely have had enough humiliation to last a lifetime.

'Come on, sis,' Imogene yells over the music. 'It feels so fun! I love to salsa!'

'I love to salsa too!' Kennedy cries happily.

Their silliness is infectious and I start to move in time with the music, albeit a little stiffly.

'You gotta loosen your ass!' Kennedy giggles drunkenly, doing a little wiggle.

'You mean my hips?' I call back, laughing at her.

'No! Your asssssss.'

'Yeah.' Imogene joins in. 'Salsa is all about having a loose arse.'

The pair of them point at me and chant at me to 'Loosen my ass! Loosen my ass!', very much enjoying winding me up.

I try to do a more fluid motion and I close my eyes to get more into it. I think I might be doing an excellent job, but when I open my eyes again, they're both laughing at me, Imogene taking a video on her phone.

'Oi!' I yell, laughing. 'Stop that!'

I feel a tap on my shoulder and when I spin around, I see the handsome face of the Adam-Levine-singing Lyft driver. He is wearing maroon-coloured leather pants and a tight white T-shirt that shows off his jacked muscles. His hair is slicked back off his face with sweat and he is wiggling his narrow waist from side to side. 'My number one fan!' he yells happily. 'You are here! Your eyes are looking much better now! I am very happy.'

'Billy Fever!' I call back, pulling him into a sweaty hug as if we are long lost friends rather than a taxi driver and his customer.

'Actually, you are my number two fan now!' he says. 'My number one fan hired me to sing at his engagement garden party so that makes him my number one fan!'

'Oh wow. Congratulations!'

'I am here with my friends to celebrate! They are somewhere around. Would you like to dance with me in celebration of my big gig?'

I shake my head, indicating my clear inability to salsa. 'I can't dance very well.'

'When you are feeling unconfident do what I do and pretend you are Adam Levine – the most impressive and confident person in the world!'

'Um, what?'

Billy doesn't answer my important question and instead takes me by the hand and starts spinning and twirling me this way and that. The way he holds my waist means that I don't have to think too much about what I'm doing and I pretty quickly find myself falling into step with him. I start to laugh as he spins me around and dips me down. My whole body loosens, even my ass.

I notice Imogene and Kennedy watching us, laughing out loud and clapping with glee. When the song is over, Billy Fever kisses my hand.

'Wow,' I say. 'I didn't know I could do that! Thank you!'

Billy beams at me. 'You cannot let the fear stop you from finding out what you can do! Fate loves the fearless!'

'Wh-what did you just say?'

I know it's probably a well-known quote, but I've never heard anyone say it except for Mum and Dad.

'Huh? It is so loud in here. I have to go find my friends!' Billy says, pulling a handkerchief from his leather pants pocket and using it to dab at his forehead. 'They will be missing me by now. Be ready for my next newsletter. It will be packed with bonus Adam Levine trivia!'

And then, in a whirl of wiggling hips, he melts back into the crowd.

* * *

On the way home, Imogene and Kennedy have our car stop at a In-N-Out Burger drive-through, where Imogene drunkenly orders everything on the menu and Kennedy orders an avocado salad.

We sit on the porch outside the house and gobble up our food before I walk Imogene back to the B&B down the road.

When we reach the front door, Imogene turns to me, her eyes trying to focus on my eyes and not quite managing it. She takes a deep breath. 'Dan and I have been having problems,' she says with a hiccup.

'What?' My eyebrows shoot up, not least because Imogene admitting that there is anything at all wrong with Dan has never happened, although there has been plenty of reason for it to. 'What's gone on?'

Imogene hugs her arms across her chest and leans to the side. I put my arm out so she doesn't topple over. 'He's been… shirking for a while. I have to take care of everything: the childcare, the bills, the household. It's exhausting. We've been arguing way more than we ever have before.'

'What are you going to do?' I ask.

Imogene shrugs. 'I don't know. I love him. I love our family, but… I don't know.'

'I'm sorry. That sounds shit. And here I've been piling all of my issues on to you. What a tit.'

The corner of Imogene's mouth lifts in a sad smile. 'Don't be daft. Seeing the difference in you today. Seeing you so alive like you used to be. It's just cemented to me that I've been depressed too and I think that maybe I've been ignoring it even more than you have. I thought that if I carried on as normal, keeping busy, avoiding Dan's recent shitness, throwing myself into Ariana, and work and, I don't know, micromanaging you, that I could somehow outrun it…'

'Oh Imogene.' I say, taking hold of her hands and squeezing them. I'm shocked. She always seems so together.

'What are we like?' she sighs, half laughing.

I do a stupid smile. 'You know, maybe we should go for counselling together. It could be a whole thing. A weekly date! The therapy sisters, kicking ass and making serious positive changes to their mental health!'

Imogene snorts with laughter.

'Hey, maybe you should date Roger Pepper,' I joke again.

Imogene doesn't laugh this time though. Instead she turns red and covers her face with her hands.

'You've already thought about it!' I gasp.

'He does have excellent banter,' Imogene grins.

'And his bidet, don't forget the bidet.'

'A bidet! Imagine that!'

We crumple into laughter and as I drop my drunken big sister off at her room, she pulls me to her in a hug that lasts for a full five minutes.

'I love Dan so much, though. And Ariana. And you.'

She goes quiet and I feel a swell of emotion in my chest as we continue to hold each other. Then I realise that Imogene has gone quiet because she has, in fact, fallen asleep on my shoulder.

Rolling my eyes, I manoeuvre her into the room, sit her down on the bed, pull off her heels, tuck her beneath the covers and kiss her forehead.

'Night, Nora,' she says sleepily. 'Love you all the world.'

'Night, Im,' I reply. 'Love you all the world too.'

* * *

Back at Kennedy's, Winklepuff barks with excitement as soon as I enter the door. Kennedy and Brandon must be in bed. He's going to wake them up! Eek.

'Shhhhh,' I say. 'Be quiet, man!' But he ignores me and tries to scramble up my leg, yelping and barking with unadulterated excitement.

I hurry into the kitchen and, right at the back of the fridge, behind the microgreens and the organic tahini and the huge blocks of tofu, I pull out a little packet that says 'fizzy sour neon strawberry laces'. I take off the little peg I put on the top and pull out a piece of the ham I hid in there, safe in the knowledge that the last thing Kennedy would ever open was a food stuff that describes itself as neon. I dangle the piece of ham from my finger and thumb and head into the living room.

'I got the good stuff!' I hiss but stop in my tracks when I realise that Kennedy is not asleep but approaching the bottom of the stairs and staring at me, her jaw dangling down.

She sways from side to side, even more drunk than Imogene. 'I knew it!' she says, pointing an accusing finger at me. 'You've been radicalising Winklepuff!'

'Um... I didn't... um...'

Winklepuff leaps up and takes the ham from me, gobbling it up with a satisfied smack of the lips, completely oblivious to the fact that he's just proven my guilt.

'You big liar!' Kennedy smirks.

I narrow my eyes. Oh... she doesn't seem as mad as I thought she would be. 'You're... not super angry at me?'

Kennedy wobbles over to the sofa and sort of belly

flops into it. 'Brandon's been doing it for years. He's got a secret stash of pastrami in his mini fridge.'

'You knew? And you're not super angry at *him*?'

She shrugs one shoulder and says, 'It took him a long time to bond with Winklepuff. I expect the meat helped their relationship along!'

'Why didn't you say anything to Brandon?'

Kennedy chuckles and pulls a sly face. 'I like having something to hold over him, should I need it…'

'I'm sorry for lying,' I say, my cheeks turning red. 'It's just… he really really likes ham.'

'If an expert dog handler thinks that a little meat is good for Winklepuff every now and again, who am I to argue?'

I peer at her. Her lips are pursed, holding back a laugh.

'You know I have no experience with dogs?' I ask, burying my head in my hands.

'I knew it the minute you arrived! When you kept saying "Heel, boy," you looked like you were going to pass out with panic.'

She leans back against the sofa sleepily and giggles at my horrified reaction.

'I'm so embarrassed,' I say, fully cringing. 'I don't know why I even said it. It just came out.'

'Oh sweetie, you're not the only one who's been lying,' she says, her eyes crossing as she looks at me in what I suspect is an attempted earnest way. 'I've been lying too.'

'Why? What have you been lying about?'

Kennedy looks at me for a few seconds and bites her bottom lip nervously before giving her head a little shake. 'I… I told you that I think Joseph Gordon-Levitt is the sexiest man in America. Well, I actually think he's the sexiest *person* in the whole *world*.'

I press my hand to my chest and gasp. 'How could

you? How could you keep this big life-changing secret from me? You call yourself a friend?'

Standing up, I hold my hand out to Kennedy and then help her upstairs, tucking her into bed like I did with Imogene.

Downstairs, I quietly pack the rest of my clothes into my suitcase, trying my best to ignore the aching feeling in my chest. I'm really really going to miss it here.

As I climb into bed I allow myself to picture Gary's face as we locked eyes this morning. I smile. There was that moment, at least. There will always be that.

CHAPTER FORTY-SIX

Gary

It's three o clock in the morning and I can't stop thinking about her. I have to see her again.

CHAPTER FORTY-SEVEN

Nora

I can't quite believe it's my last day in Los Angeles. I wake up with the sun and, leaving Kennedy to sleep off the inevitable hangover, I put in my contacts, pull my costume on and head to the beach for one last swim.

The sun is already blazing and it makes the boundless water sparkle like diamonds. I wade into the ocean and swim about for a little while before flipping onto my back and gazing dreamily at the blissful peach and pink skies. I try to burn the image into my memory. I get the feeling I'm going to need to access it a fair amount back in drizzly Brigglesford.

I'm about to swim back to the shore when I spot a distant figure at the edge of the water. Somehow I don't feel surprised to realise that it's him. He's wearing the same navy blue swimming shorts as yesterday and carrying a large gym bag. When he holds his still bandaged arm up in a tentative wave, I mirror the action.

My breath catches in my throat as he puts down his bag, strides into the ocean and begins to swim towards me.

I rub my eyes, unsure if I'm still asleep and this is some sort of extra pleasant dream.

I scan the rest of the beach, worried that he's brought John Alan with him, or the police. Maybe he saw the serial killer board yesterday and decided to make his escape but then return this morning with backup. But no. The beach is quiet. It's just Gary Montgomery. And me.

I squint at him as he stops about a metre away and starts to tread water. My heart begins to thump so loudly that I'm pretty sure it's making my boobs jump with the force of it. I swallow hard, my mouth fully dry now.

'Hey,' he says brightly, as if him being here in the fucking sea with me right now is normal.

'Hi,' I say back, dumbly.

'I live just down there.' He points in the direction of some of the bigger houses further down the beach. 'About a fifteen-minute walk away.'

He's been that close the whole time? Fifteen minutes away?

I hold my hand up to my forehead so that I can see his face without the sun in my eyes.

'You forgot your surfboard...' I say.

'I actually came to see you. I was about to knock on your door when I looked out here and saw you.'

I bite my lip. 'Why... why did you come to find me?'

Gary looks slightly confused. 'I... don't fully know.' He gives an awkward laugh and runs his hand across his stubble. 'I, um, wanted to say thank you for helping me yesterday, I guess.'

'Oh, you're welcome,' I say politely as if this a normal situation. 'Did you go to the hospital?'

'Yeah. You were right, I didn't need stitches. They did a much better job with the bandage, though.' He holds his arm up to show me, mirth flickering in those penetrating eyes.

'Hey! I learned that technique on a first-aid course.'

'When?'

'Um, when I was sixteen.'

'Might be time for a refresher.'

'Oi!' I go to splash a little water in his direction and I only mean to do it a tiny bit, but I misjudge the strength of my hand and end up aggressively splattering a load of water right splat into his face. 'Oh fuck! Sorry! I actually didn't mean to do that!'

Gary wipes the water away from his eyes, his mouth dropping open in shock. And then he dips both of his hands in the water and splashes me back, even harder than I splashed him.

'Please no!' I yell, my voice wobbling.

When I clear the water from my eyes, I see that Gary is watching me and properly laughing.

'Please no?' He laughs even harder. 'That was dramatic.'

'I know! I didn't mean it to come out all wobbly like that,' I laugh back. It's not even that funny, but the pair of us are laughing out loud like this suddenly seems like the most hilarious moment that has ever happened.

And then I stop laughing just as quickly as I started because the biggest sense of déjà vu blankets my brain. I remember. This is it. This is the weirdly vivid vision I had before I came here. Me and Gary laughing in the ocean. I touch my hands to my lips tasting the saltiness, I squint up at the pink sky. It is exactly as I saw it. What is happening? My heart rate ramps right back up.

'Hey… are you okay?' Gary asks, swimming a little closer to me, eyebrows furrowed.

'I…' I trail off. I can hardly tell the truth, can I? Oh I'm fine, just realising that I had a premonition of this most magical of moments, no big deal. 'Yeah.' I nod quickly. 'Just a bit of water up my nose.'

Oh, very sexy, Nora.

'Right.' The corner of Gary's mouth lifts in amusement.

'I'm going back to the UK tonight,' I blurt.

'I have an engagement garden party at twilight,' he replies, frowning.

'Yes. You mentioned yesterday.'

He nods, his onyx eyes scanning over my face, towards my lips and then up to my hair. He rubs his hand over his chin. 'Listen, um. I have a day off shooting today. Would you... maybe like to go for a walk?'

'Yes,' I say immediately, not even thinking about what this turn of events means or caring what tomorrow will bring.

Gary smiles widely now, a slightly dazed look in his eyes.

'Good,' he says. 'That's good.'

* * *

I ask Gary to wait outside while I head back to Kennedy's. If he comes inside, Winklepuff will start barking and then the whole household will be up and I'm not ready to share this just yet, especially since I'm barely processing it myself.

Quickly drying myself off, I rummage through my packed suitcase for something to wear. In lieu of anything else, I grab one of the too tight sundresses, shove on my flip-flops and meet Gary back outside. He is stuffing a green towel back into his gym bag, having put on sunglasses, a grey T-shirt and some sneakers in addition to his swim shorts. He looks perfect.

'Okay!' I say brightly, like this is not the weirdest, most exciting, most unlikely thing that has ever ever ever happened to me. 'Let's go.'

CHAPTER FORTY-EIGHT

Nora

Text to Imogene and Kennedy: *Hi both, I have a couple of errands to run. Will be back soon, turning phone off, don't worry. :D Nora x*

When Gary suggests we grab something to eat, I, in a bid to seem cool and laid-back and like I'm not completely freaked out by what is happening right now, tell him I know a great place to get some ice cream.

Gary does me the favour of not reacting to my weird suggestion of having ice cream for breakfast and tells me instead to lead the way, apologising for wearing his cap and sunglasses on account of advice from his security. I flush red because the only reason he has to do that is because of me. Shit, would he be terrified if he knew who I actually was?

I think probably.

I keep my mouth shut and we barely say a word to each other as we walk to the dog-friendly beach where Bud's Ice Cream truck is located. I can see the Bill and

Ted-voiced Adonis lifting up the shutters. Thanks god it's open.

I point to the truck. 'The best ice cream I've ever had,' I say.

Gary, surprisingly, bursts into laughter. 'You... want to get stoned with me?' he asks. 'At this time in the morning? I gotta say, I did not expect that...'

'Huh? Stoned? No. I've never smoked weed in my life,' I say. 'I took Rescue Remedy once and that was pretty nice, but no. Not weed! Why would you think—'

Gary points up at the ice cream truck. 'Bud's Ice cream...' he says as we reach the counter.

'Yes?' I goggle at him.

'It's pot ice cream,' he laughs.

I blink. What? Pot ice cream? No. No, I would have known if I'd been getting stoned every time I'd been here. Of course it's not pot ice cream!

Adonis guy recognises me and his eyes sparkle knowingly. 'It's you again.' He looks to Gary. 'This chick loves the product, dude. The special rocky road in particular. You want some more?'

'The product?' I gasp, realisation slowly dawning. 'This *is* weed ice cream?'

Adonis laughs. 'Bro, you didn't know that? You've been here, like, five times?'

'You didn't, you know, feel it?' Gary asks in disbelief.

I blink and think back to all the times I've had this ice cream while I've been here. 'It made me feel happy and giddy and a little dazed, but, well I thought that was just, like, the joy of ice cream!'

Gary crumples over into laughter. 'The joy of ice cream!' he repeats. 'Oh, man.'

Adonis starts laughing too. 'I told you it was special, bro!'

I send him daggers. 'I thought you just meant it tasted really special. I thought you were just really proud of it!'

'Nah, man. *Special.* That's, like, the code here. Everyone knows it.'

'Not me!' I protest. 'I can't believe it. I've been licking weed ice cream this whole time! I'm a pothead.'

'Accidental ganja fiend,' Gary adds, clutching his stomach with laughter, tears creeping to his eyes. 'Nora, it's called Bud's Ice cream. BUD!' Seeing him laugh so hard brings a swell of joy to my chest that is so big that I can't help but laugh too. The pair of us just stand there laughing until tears squirt out of my eyes. My belly hurts with it. And, all at once, my nerves about Gary – who he is, what he does, and what the fuck is happening right now – evaporate. He's not Gary Montgomery the movie star. He is just a guy. A guy I'm laughing with. A guy who is laughing with me.

Adonis looks from me to Gary and then back again. 'I guess you two don't need any of my shit this morning…'

'I think maybe grilled cheese might be a more appropriate breakfast,' Gary says, wiping the tears from his eyes.

'I think you're right,' I agree, fanning my face which I'm pretty sure is now bright salmon pink.

And so we go to find somewhere to get a couple of cheese toasties.

* * *

Over breakfast at the Sidewalk Cafe on the beachfront, Gary and I relax into a conversation and there's a sort of unspoken agreement that we don't mention how odd this all is, or that he has a fiancée, or that I am going home tonight. We just hang out. He tells me about a script he's read – something his friend Olive wrote about a broken family travelling across the world for a will reading. The way he talks about it is so, so passionate. He describes the character and his eyes shine with enthusiasm.

'He's an asshole. It's so funny. And the story is real

quirky. Kinda like Wes Anderson meets *The Full Monty*. My manager isn't keen though. She read the script and she thinks it would be a step backwards.'

'What does she want you to do?'

'A superhero movie…'

'Wow.'

'I know! I mean, it sounds cool, I guess, and I would be so lucky to do something like that, but… after this experience of being in a big movie it's…I don't know.'

'Fucking crazy?' I ask.

Gary snorts. 'Yes. Fucking crazy. I thought it would take years to get famous. That I'd have a ton of time to do whatever roles I wanted…'

'Why can't you?'

Gary fiddles with a napkin and I can see the vulnerability behind the movie star charisma. 'Because there's some kind of trajectory happening now. It's not the done thing to move backwards to smaller projects.'

'Fate loves the fearless,' I say, echoing my parents and feeling the truth in that statement more than ever right at this moment. 'I've spent so long hiding out, afraid of doing anything that might upset the cocoon I'd built around me. I realised recently that it was a colossal waste of time. There's magic to be found on the other side of the things that scare you.' I peek up at him. 'Surely even fleeting magic is better than none at all.'

Gary smiles. 'You're very wise, Nora.'

'That did sound super wise, didn't it?' I giggle, surprised at myself. 'I should write this shit down.' I mime grabbing my phone and typing out what I just said.

Gary laughs. 'There's magic to be found on the other side of the things that scare you… that would make a great bumper sticker for sure.'

'Do you think? Or maybe one of those wall decals people put above their beds. Could be lucrative.'

We smile at each other for a smidge longer than is

normal for two near-strangers, even if one of them has secretly been stalking the other for the last two weeks.

* * *

After paying the bill at the diner, we continue walking along the beach and Gary, concerned about the increasing redness on my face and arms, pops into a general store to grab a bottle of sun cream, which, in my rush to get out with him this morning, I forgot to put on. He sprays the white cream very liberally over my face and arms but refrains from attempting to rub it in, which I'm surprisingly grateful for. If he started rubbing me right now, I would lose every shred of this composure I've managed to uphold so far. I rub it all over my face and when it's done, we carry on walking.

'You don't want to check your face in the phone?' he asks.

'No,' I say. 'Should I? Shit, is it not rubbed in properly?'

'No, it's fine. It's just Tori always…' He trails off and clears his throat. He puts his sunglasses back on as the beach and boardwalk start to get busier.

'Oh!' I say as the famous Santa Monica Pier Ferris wheel comes into view. 'I've seen that in all the movies. It's so pretty! You must have been on it a million times, living here.'

'I've… weirdly never been on it. I meant to, but it's one of those corny tourist things and I just never got round to it… but I've heard the views are incredible.'

'We should go on it!' I say excitedly, walking more quickly now. 'Should we? Or am I being totally corny right now?'

Gary shakes his head. 'I'm in the mood for corny today. Let's go.'

* * *

The Pacific Park amusements on Santa Monica Pier are busier than I thought they would be considering it's still only morning, with people lining up to go on the rides. We have to queue for ten minutes to get on the Ferris wheel but the time flies by as we talk about everything and nothing. I tell Gary about my work at Virtual Assistants 4U. I tell him about the time when I was eighteen that I got separated from my friends on a fancy dress night and had to look for them, wandering the bars alone dressed as Jim Carrey in *The Mask*. Gary counters with a story of about the time he thought someone he'd just met was holding their hands out for a hug. He awkwardly gave them a massive hug only to realise, too late, that they had only wanted a high five. We properly laugh and it takes everything in my power not to just lean into him, nestle my head into his shoulder.

On the Ferris wheel, we start our slow ascent to the top, the aquamarine sea stretching out ahead of us, the crowds on the beach looking like colourful splotches on the sand.

'You mentioned at brunch the other day that you write songs and sing? Tell me more. What kind of music do you make? How did you get into it?' He takes his sunglasses off and looks at me, genuinely interested.

I smile. 'When I was about eight, my parents had sent me and my sister to bed early for arguing over some Barbie. I crept downstairs to spy on them because I was maybe a weird and creepy child. They were sitting on the sofa together watching this show and there was this woman on screen, holding a guitar and singing this gorgeous song about pain and love and hope. It was Joni Mitchell. I didn't really get what she was singing about then, but I knew, right there on the stairs, that I wanted to do what she was doing. I had never sung before or played an instrument, but seeing her there and hearing her felt like someone had lit my life up. I didn't know why I wanted it. I just knew that I did more than anything.'

Gary breaks into a warm grin. 'That's exactly how I feel about acting. I didn't have a singular moment like you did, but I did this summer camp when I was twelve and we did *Peter Pan* for the end-of-summer show. I was one of the Lost Boys and I just knew that the days when we were rehearsing and I got to pretend to be someone else were the best days of the whole camp experience.'

He gets it.

'I stopped writing songs for a couple of years. I actually just started again. Being in LA... jump-started the urge.'

'Why did you stop?' he asks.

I break eye contact and notice we're at the top of the Ferris wheel now. The view of the glittering ocean stretches out as far as I can see. I peer to the side and gasp at the mountain ranges in the distance. It's truly beautiful.

'Well... I stopped because I had a showcase gig in London for a record label. My parents got in a car crash on the way to the gig. They died. It... well, it broke me.' My voice cracks. I've never talked about this to anyone apart from Imogene. 'I thought it was my fault. I'm only just realising that it might not have been. But, yeah... It was fucking horrible. The feeling of missing them is just always, always there as well as the weird guilt.'

I look at Gary to see his eyes are glistening. 'I know the exact feeling you're talking about.'

'You do?' I frown.

'My mom passed away giving birth to me. It's taken me a lot of therapy to stop blaming myself.'

Joan Didion wrote something once about how grieving people have a certain look, something recognisable to those who have seen the look on their own face. I can see it in Gary's eyes and my heart twists with sadness for him. 'Wow. I'm so sorry you know how it feels.'

'It sucks, right?' He swallows hard and holds up his hand for a high five. 'Dead Parents Club!' he jokes before immediately flushing red, his eyes panicked. 'Sorry, that was a stupid joke. I'm really sorry. Brain fart.'

I chuckle softly. 'Yeah, that was a bit dark…' I say, before tentatively picking his hand up and slapping mine to it in a high five. 'Dead Parents Club.'

As we high-five, Gary grabs hold of my hand and wraps his around it, intertwining his fingers with mine and stroking his thumb across my thumb.

He doesn't let go for the rest of the ride.

CHAPTER FORTY-NINE

Nora

After three goes around on the Pacific Park Rollercoaster, a game of whack-a-mole that I win and a game of hoop throwing in which Gary destroys me, we start walking back towards the house, chatting the whole way, mostly about light things like the *Harcourt Royals* books and each other's favourite artists and how annoying it is when people in restaurants start their order with the words 'I'm going to do the...'

It's after lunchtime now and getting increasingly crowded. Gary is safely back in his sunglasses and baseball cap and I try not to think of the fact that I am the main reason he's wearing them. And the idea that he might discover that leaves me breathless with fear.

Back on Venice Beach boardwalk, the warm winds whip up a notch and I shield my eyes as much as I can to avoid another wind dirt incident. We pass street performers every ten metres or so. A young, tanned magician with long curly hair is stunning passers-by with incredible feats of fire-eating and card tricks. A group of hot guys dance in a troupe, jumping over one another and lifting each other into amazing acrobatic positions. Further down, an old man strums on an acoustic guitar and sings 'Mambo No. 5'. We stay to watch him and it's so catchy that we can't help but jig from side to side. The old man is good – I'm surprised there's not more of a crowd around him.

When he's finished the song, he sits down on the wooden chair next to his microphone stand and sips at a large bottle of water, holding it up with two hands.

Gary nudges his elbow into mine and nods towards the guitar and mic stand. 'Hey, will you sing me one of your songs?'

'No way,' I say immediately. 'Absolutely no way! I have terrible stage fright.'

'I thought you said you'd been singing again recently?'

'Only when I've been drunk,' I protest. 'I haven't performed sober in two years.'

Gary gives me a pointed look. 'You know, a wise stranger once told me that there is magic to be found on the other side of things that scare you.'

I tut. 'Sounds like something naff from a bumper sticker,' I scoff.

Gary lifts his sunnies onto his head and looks into my eyes. 'Come on. I have this feeling that you're really good... but you could also be really terrible. Either way, it would be great for me to know. To remember.'

To remember. Because I am going home tonight, and he is getting married and has no intention of not going through with it. And although neither of us have said it, I think we somehow both know that this is the only time we will spend together. This one magical day.

I screw up all of my courage and head towards the old man, asking him if I can sing a song. He rolls his eyes as if he's had many enthusiastic amateurs asking him this over the years and says, 'Sure, kid. Just go easy on the guitar. It's a—'

'Vintage 1957 Hofner Club 50,' I cut in. 'She's a cracker.'

The old man raises his eyebrow and nods in approval. I pick up the guitar, immediately feeling at home with the weight of it pressed against my stomach.

I glance up at Gary and his encouraging smile transforms the nervous bubbles in my chest into excitement. I want to show him what I can do. If all we're going to have left is memories, then I want him to remember me at my happiest – belting out the words and melodies I store in my heart.

I start to sing the song I sang at Jama's bar the other night when I got drunk with Brandon. The song that Gary doesn't know is about this trip to LA, about him. I close my eyes and all of the emotions I've felt over these last couple of weeks pour out in the croak of my voice, the ring of the guitar, the high notes and the chord changes.

When the song is finished, I revel in the joy of performing for a few more seconds before I open my eyes. When I do, I'm surprised to see a small crowd has gathered. A few people record me on their phones and others start asking me questions.

'What was that song, honey?' a woman calls across. 'You got a SoundCloud?'

'It sounded like an Adele song. Was it an Adele song?'

'What's your name? Will you be here tomorrow?'

'You got IT, kid.' The old man grins as I hand him back the guitar.

Red-faced, I head back over to Gary, who looks like he is the one who is about to throw up with nerves. His face is pale, his eyes wide and his mouth ajar.

'Are… are you okay?' I ask. 'You hated it! Argh.'

Gary shakes his head in astonishment. 'It was…' He narrows his eyes. 'Were you at Trash Karaoke bar a few nights ago? I walked past and heard a woman singing and—'

Oh my goodness.

'That was me!' I tell him, laughing in disbelief. 'I can't believe you heard me.'

'Nora,' he says in a low voice, his eyes darker than I've ever seen them. He takes a step towards me and...

'Yo, is that Gary Montgomery?' comes a voice from behind me. And then another. 'It is! It's Gary Montgomery! OMG! Gary!'

The crowd of people start to swarm around us and, without thinking, I grab Gary's hand and yell, 'Leg iiiittt!'

So we do.

* * *

We barely say anything the rest of the way back to Kennedy's. I didn't think there could be any more tension between us, but after holding hands on the Ferris Wheel and Gary hearing me sing, the mood has shifted. It's heavy and confused and electric.

Outside Kennedy's house, we face one another. This is it. This is when I say goodbye to Gary Montgomery. This was the best day of my life.

'Weird question but... are you wearing some of that pheromone perfume that sends guys crazy?' Gary asks.

'Ha!' I laugh out loud. 'Afraid not. I didn't even put deodorant on this morning.'

Real sexy, Nora.

'So...' I say.

'So...' Gary says. 'I guess this is goodbye.'

I swallow down the lump that has come to my throat. 'I had a really good day.'

'The best,' Gary murmurs. He looks at me for a long moment, his obsidian eyes unreadable.

The Santa Ana winds start to whip warmly around us, making my hair fly out behind me and rustling and shaking the leaves of the palm trees so they make a noise like maracas.

Gary looks up at the sky and then back at me. Tentatively, reticent almost, he places his hands on either side of my head, leans forward, stops halfway to look into my eyes and then…

He kisses me. His lips touch mine, and I swirl and melt and fizz and all those things they say in the books and the songs and the films.

I kiss him back, my hands running up into his hair, knocking off his baseball cap. He kisses me harder, his breath coming thick and fast. He groans slightly, pushing me against Kennedy's front door and pressing so close to me that it feels like we have melted into one another. He runs his hands across my waist and I feel how hard he is through his shorts. I have never felt so wanton and turned on in my life. I want every part of him. Right here. In broad daylight. On Kennedy's doorstep.

'Oh god,' he moans.

'I know,' I murmur.

And then, as if he's just been electrocuted, he jolts away from me, breathing rapidly and looking at me with a pained expression.

'I can't,' he says. 'I'm engaged.'

I look down at my feet and wonder how many times a heart can break. I thought it was once, but it really isn't.

I can't take it. I wipe a tear away from my eye and take a deep breath. I have to do the right thing. 'Goodbye, Gary,' I say, my hand on the door handle.

'Goodbye, Nora,' he says, his voice catching.

And then, at last, after everything, it's all over.

CHAPTER FIFTY

Nora

As soon as I open Kennedy's door, Winklepuff rushes over to me, yelping with delight. At the sound of the commotion, Kennedy hurries out of the kitchen, followed, to my surprise, by a pissed-off Imogene. Both of them are holding glasses of, judging from the orangey colour of it, organic peach wine. And going by the pinkness in their cheeks, they've already had at least a glass each.

'Thank god!' Imogene says. 'Where the hell have you been? You turned your phone off. I was worried!'

'I sent a text!'

Kennedy crosses her arms. 'She was really worried,' she echoes. 'She thought you had gone to see Gary, that you were gonna get yourself into trouble, that you weren't going to make your flight. You really shouldn't turn your phone off, Nora.'

Imogene narrows her eyes, noticing the expression on my face. 'What's wrong? Did you get in trouble? Are you okay?'

What just happened, the whole day I've just had, seems to hit me all at once and I dive for the sofa, fearful that the overwhelming emotion of it all is going to make me pass out.

Kennedy and Imogene rush over to me. 'Nora, what's wrong?'

'I…I saw Gary,' I whisper.

'Oh no!' Imogene says. 'Are you actively *trying* to get yourself arrested?'

'What did you do now?' Kennedy adds. 'I thought you had stopped with all that?'

I press my fingers to my still tingling lips. 'He… he kissed me,' I murmur. 'Gary Montgomery… kissed me.'

'Oh fuck.' Imogene downs the rest of her wine. 'She's fully lost it. It's finally happened: she's cracked. Don't worry, Nora. Oh, my poor sister. We'll get you home, sort all of this out, okay?'

'He really kissed me,' I repeat, a dreamy smile making its way across my face. 'He really really did.'

Kennedy crouches down to my level and takes my face in her hands. 'Have you taken something, Nora? Hmmm, her pupils are very dilated…'

Winklepuff starts barking and scampering frantically about again as Brandon emerges from his room and heads down the stairs. Oh great.

'I… um, I think she's telling the truth,' he says, his own face pulled back into a shocked expression. 'I saw it from my window, I think. He was kissing her. Gary fucking Montgomery was kissing… her.' He blinks as if he can't quite fathom it. 'The way he looked at her. She was… My god, was she right all along?'

'What?' Kennedy shrieks, standing up quickly.

'Was it some sort of lookalike?' Imogene asks sensibly, neat HD brows furrowed. 'Did you find him at an agency? I mean, it wouldn't be the *worst* way to get closure.'

My eyes meet hers and I sort of half-shrug, my ability to make sense fully absent.

Imogene stares at me for a moment, still frowning,

and then she takes a quick sharp breath and presses her hands to her cheeks, her eyes almost popping out of her head. 'Oh. My. God…' she whispers. 'Gary Montgomery kissed you.' Her voice gets louder and she starts sort of bouncing up and down on her heels. 'GARY MONTGOMERY KISSED YOU! OH MY GOODNESS! OH MY GOOOOOOOOOOOOOD!'

'Gary Montgomery kissed you?' Kennedy squeals, catching sight of Imogene and starting to fan at her face in a slightly panicked way. 'He kissed you?'

'WHAT IS HAPPENING?' Imogene looks around the room as if someone will pop out from behind a cream sofa and tell her that this is all an elaborate prank.

'WHAT EVEN IS HAPPENING?' Kennedy adds, dashing into the kitchen and returning with the half-full bottle of organic peach wine.

Imogene holds out her glass without taking her eyes off me and Kennedy fills it up, before taking a swig straight from the bottle.

'How?' Imogene says, sitting down on one side of me. 'Why? I mean HOW?'

'Does this mean you're going to stay?' Kennedy asks excitedly, sitting on the other side of me and taking another hit of peach wine. 'What about Tori? What about the stalking? Does he know? What did he say? WHAT DID HE SAY, NORA? Is his engagement off now?'

I shake my head in an attempt to clear it. 'He doesn't know that I came here for him. That it was me at the movie lot and at the handprint ceremony. He doesn't need to.'

'Hmmm, I'd say that was pretty important,' Brandon says, sitting down on a white wicker chair. Winklepuff jumps onto his knees and stares at me as if, he too, has many questions he needs answering. Or more likely is just wondering if all of this excitement somehow involves upcoming ham.

I look between each of them. 'It was weird. We didn't really talk about anything. But we talked about everything too. It was like… Fuck, it was so weird. It was like we both knew that something amazing was happening. He was just a guy and I was just a girl and we were supposed to meet. But…'

'But?' Kennedy urges, leaning forward off the sofa. 'But what?'

'But, I don't know… it's like we knew it was just this one day. He's engaged. I live in England. But mostly he's engaged. And *deliriously in love*,' I say, recalling what Aileen said at the Chinese Theatre.

'His tongue in your mouth doesn't sound like the actions of a man deliriously in love with someone else,' Imogene scoffs.

'You have to do something!' Kennedy says. 'You can't just leave it like that.'

'I agree,' Imogene says. 'He kissed you!'

I give them a bemused look. 'You're the ones who have been telling me to stay away! That the way I feel is just an infatuation, or a crush, or a manifestation of my grief, or that I'm losing it.'

'That was before he kissed your mouth,' Imogene replies, shaking her head as if she cannot believe she is saying these words out loud.

'I felt his boner too.' I sigh.

'His boner?' Kennedy breathes.

I nod. 'Yep. His honest to goodness boner.'

'Boners don't lie,' Imogene looks thoughtful. 'They don't know how.'

'But then he said he couldn't do this, that he was engaged and then he ran off. Down the beach. Away.'

'Did you tell him how you feel?' Brandon asks, his usual scorn replaced with bewilderment.

'No! How could I? I didn't want to freak him out. Or ruin what was the most perfect day I've ever had.'

Kennedy shakes her head slowly and starts walking around the living room at speed. 'You need to tell him how you feel. You have to. Face to face.'

Imogene stands up and joins Kennedy in her circular speed walk around the room. 'I agree. You cannot leave it like this. Our flight is at ten past eleven. It's not long, but it might be enough.'

'I can't!' I cry. 'It all feels different now I've met him, that I've kissed him. It's real. It's fucking real. I can't put him through that. I could ruin his life! Even if things did work out, how could we ever go public as a couple? The heart-throb and the crazy stalker? He'd never star in a movie again. He was probably just having a touch of cold feet. I mean, he said he'd been feeling overwhelmed lately. He might have just wanted to be distracted for a little while and I was there with my adoring smile and my massive tits.'

But even as I say this, I know it's not true. It was more than that. It was so much more.

'What are the pros and cons of you telling him how you feel before we leave?' Imogene says, her sensible side making an appearance, although she has now taken to grabbing the peach wine off Kennedy and swigging it straight from the bottle too.

'Cons,' I say. 'Possible ruination of multiple lives, humiliating Gary and Tori and myself for ever, breaking up an engaged couple, getting assassinated by John Alan…'

'And the pros?' Imogene asks softly.

'True fucking love,' I say plainly. 'That's all.'

Imogene grins. 'True fucking love.'

'True FUCKING love,' Kennedy choruses.

Brandon just looks between the three of us, his face still pale with amazement.

'I don't think I can actually do this to another woman,' I say, twisting my hands together in my lap.

'But he *kissed* you!' Imogene says. 'Would you want to marry someone who kissed another woman?'

'He felt awful about it. He literally ran away!' I point out.

'Even so,' Imogene replies, 'people in happy relationships don't kiss other women, even if they do feel bad about it. He clearly is not as deliriously happy as you thought. And if he's not, then it's pretty certain that *she's* not deliriously happy either...'

I bite my lip. Could that be true? Was Aileen lying when she said that Gary and Tori were deliriously happy? But then... why are they engaged?

'You'd be doing them both a favour,' Kennedy urges. 'Do you really want to go home without ever knowing? This is your chance! Your one chance!'

She's right. If I go home, I will always wonder what might have been and I don't want that. The entire reason I came here was to follow this crazy feeling. I was willing to go home if I met Gary and he had zero interest, if it turned out that I was nothing more than a freaky stalker. But then... today happened. That kiss happened.

I look up at the three of them. 'I need to know,' I say with a firm nod. 'I need to tell him how I feel and I need to know if he feels the same way.'

'Yes!' Kennedy cheers before her face immediately crumples into a worried frown. 'But how will you get to him? We don't know where he lives.' She takes another swig of wine. 'WE'RE RUNNING OUT OF TIME!'

'He said he lives fifteen minutes down the beach,' I tell her, standing up from the sofa, adrenaline starting to course its way through my body. 'I'm not sure exactly where.'

'SO CLOSE!' Kennedy gasps. 'We could just knock on all of the doors...'

I glance at the clock on the wall. 'But he's got his

engagement garden party. He said it was at twilight. What time is that?'

'It's mid-August and sunrise today was at 6.14 a.m.,' Kennedy says, looking out of the window, concentration gathering her eyebrows together. 'So that means twilight will start at 5.47 and end at 8.05 p.m. precisely.'

'She's a weather reporter,' Brandon tells Imogene, who is openly goggling at Kennedy's knowledge.

'5.47? That's in twenty minutes. I don't even know where his engagement garden party is!'

Imogene rolls her eyes. 'Engagement garden party. Is that a thing here?'

And as she says it, a memory pushes at the edges of my brain. I close my eyes and think hard. The fuzziness merges into a clear image of Billy Fever at the salsa club. He said he was performing at an engagement garden party today.

I tell this to Imogene and Kennedy.

'What are the chances?' Kennedy says. 'Could it be the same one?'

'At this point, I'd say it's pretty bloody likely.' Imogene laughs manically.

'Do you know how to get in touch with this Billy Fever?' Brandon asks.

I nod. 'He made absolutely sure I did,' I say, dashing into my sleeping area to route in my bag for the card Billy gave me. I hold the card aloft. 'Here's his number!' I announce.

Imogene hurries over and grabs both of my hands in hers. 'Fate loves the fearless, right?' she says, her eyes shining.

I nod, a lump in my throat.

'Let's do this!' Kennedy yells, now clearly more than a bit pissed. 'TRUE FUCKING LOVE. JOY AHOY!'

CHAPTER FIFTY-ONE

Gary

Hey.

So... I am a piece of shit. I've had two neat whiskies and I have to say that it has not helped a bit. This is clearly me having some kind of commitment freak out. Why did I even go to the beach this morning? Why did I kiss a complete stranger... and why do I miss her so much that my heart literally aches?

Fuck.

Tori asked why I was acting so oddly when I got home. I hadn't realized I was, but Seth and Olive agreed that I looked like I'd taken drugs or something, which, to be honest, it felt like I had. Seth pulled me aside and asked if I was alright and I couldn't even find the words to explain to him what had just happened.

Am I losing it?

I'm writing this as Tori is having her hair and nails done for the engagement garden party and she looks so happy and excited. She is kind and ambitious. She is beautiful and elegant. She loves Janet as much as I do. I'd still be waiting on tables and living in a leaky Panorama City basement if it wasn't for her. She needs someone who will be committed to her. Who won't break her heart. She's a good person. I hate that she's so obsessed with fame, celebrity and influence, but beneath that bluster she's a good person who doesn't deserve a man who just kissed another woman.

Should I tell her? I don't need to tell her, right? The fallout would be insane. It was just one weird, wonderful day and one kiss I'll never forget. It's jitters about getting engaged. Nothing more. It can't be anything more. It won't be anything more.

Tori taps something out on her phone, frowning. When she notices me watching, she puts down the phone, her face immediately transforming into a dazzling smile.

I promised I would never make her cry.

And I'm not a man who breaks his promises.

I need to focus on the woman in front of me. The one who supports me and sticks by me. The one who *actually* knows me. Who has known me for longer than one day, at least.

Fucking hell, Gary.

CHAPTER FIFTY-TWO

Nora

The phone rings for exactly seven rings before Billy Fever picks up. He sounds out of breath. I flip it on to speaker-phone so the others can listen in.

'Billy Fever here,' he says. I hear barking and what sounds like someone clattering through a kitchen.

'Hi Billy. Um, this is Nora Tucker. You might not remember, but—'

'Nora!' Billy shouts over the sound of barking. 'My dear fan! Sorry! My puppy Jesse Carmichael wants his dinner, but I cannot find the can opener. One moment.'

'Jesse Carmichael is the name of the keyboardist in Maroon Five!' Kennedy hisses, laughing. 'Amazing.'

'Shhh!'

'Okay, I am back! I am not working in the car tonight I'm afraid. I have a professional gig—'

'Yes!' I say. 'You told me at the salsa club. An engage-ment party?'

'An engagement *garden* party,' Billy corrects. 'It is a very big deal.'

'Yes. Uh, this might turn out to be a weird question but… um, is it a party for Gary Montgomery? And Tori Gould?'

The other end of the phone goes silent for a moment. 'I am afraid I am not allowed to divulge this information,' Billy says evenly. 'I can neither confirm nor deny.'

'That means it is,' Imogene gasps. 'It's Gary's party!'

Oh my goodness. If Gary Montgomery is Billy Fever's 'number one fan' surely that is another big flashing sign that this is the right thing?

'I did not say that,' Billy replies. 'I did not tell you that.'

'Listen, Billy,' I say nervously. 'I know this sounds bonkers, but… I'm in love with Gary Montgomery. And I'm supposed to be leaving Los Angeles in a few hours, but I need to tell him how I feel before I go. Would you tell me where the party is so I can find him?'

'Everybody is in love with Gary Montgomery right now!' Billy says. 'He is a hot ticket. I cannot tell you where the party is. You will make a scene and this is my professional gig! I am sorry. You are my beloved fan, but I will have to disappoint you.'

My shoulders sink.

'Help her, Billy Fever!' Kennedy yells down the phone. 'This is True Fucking Love!'

'Billy,' I say softly, 'you told me that I cannot let the fear stop me from finding out what I can do! You said fate loves the fearless. My mum and dad used to say that all the time.'

'Fate loves the fearless,' Billy echoes. 'My favourite Adam Levine quote.'

'Um, I'm pretty sure it's not an Adam Levine quote. James Russell Lowell said it.'

'I heard Adam Levine say it on VH1,' Billy declares, audibly prickling.

Imogene hisses at me to leave it alone.

'Okay,' I say. 'The point is that I am trying to be fearless. I love this man and I think he might have feelings for me too.'

'And why do you think that?'

'Because about thirty minutes ago, he kissed me.'

'WHAT?' Billy shouts down the phone. 'You are telling a lie?'

'Nope. It's true.'

'Wow… What about his fiancée Tori? She would be very angry. I once drove her in my car and she was very bad-tempered. She said no when I offered her my free performance. I imagine she would be very angry with you for attempting to steal Mr Montgomery.'

I sigh. 'I don't know what else to do, Billy. I mean, if he says no, I'll respect it and walk away, but… I need to hear him say no.'

To the surprise of us all – even Winklepuff who cocks his ear at the sound – Billy stars to sing down the phone.

'One more "No" and I'll believe you
I'll walk away and I will leave you be
And that's the last time you'll say no, say no to me
It won't take me long to find another lover, but I want you
I can't spend another minute getting over loving you…'

Brandon and Imogene look at each other, impressed with Billy's beautiful Adam Levine-esque timbre. Kennedy's eyes shine with tears.

'More beautiful words from Adam Levine,' Billy says with a wistful sigh. 'My number two fan is in love with my number one fan… It is very unusual. Okay. I will help you, Nora. However, my performance is at 6 p.m. when the party starts and you must promise to wait until I have finished singing. You cannot ruin my gig, okay? This is very important.'

'I promise,' I say as Imogene clasps her hands together in excitement.

'Okay,' Billy Fever says. 'Get a pen – here is the address…'

CHAPTER FIFTY-THREE

Nora

Due to the fact that Imogene and Kennedy are now more than a little drunk, it is, surprisingly, Brandon who comes to the rescue and offers to drive us in Kennedy's convertible because his truck only fits two people. Billy told us that the engagement party was being held in Pasadena at the Unmei Japanese Garden.

Because the unfortunate timing means that we – or, hopefully, just Imogene – will likely have to dash straight to the airport, I've packed up my case and we super speedily grabbed Imogene's stuff from her B&B. I'm wearing exactly what I've been wearing all day, my face full of old sun cream, my pits less than fragrant. I asked if I had time for a quick shower because we had to wait until Billy had performed anyway, but Kennedy fully shot me down and told me that we simply do not have time for me to 'soap my ass'. Which was an odd thing to say, but a fair point.

Kennedy, sitting in the front beside Brandon and with Winklepuff snuggled onto her lap, sets up a playlist and presses play. It's a playlist of wedding songs.

'Too much!' I shout over the music. 'We're going to possibly destroy an engagement. We have to have some humility. We are the villains here!'

Kennedy apologises and switches it over to The Beach Boys as we zoom off towards one of LA's many motorways, Brandon every so often shaking his head and muttering 'fuck' as if his whole worldview has been shaken to the core by what is happening right now.

The crawling traffic means it takes us almost ninety minutes to reach Pasadena. Eventually, we approach a gorgeous white stuccoed building with columns and lines of perfect trees down each side. We start to head down a driveway when Kennedy squeals, 'Turn around! Turn around, Bran!'

Brandon does as he is told and reverses quickly out of the driveway.

'What the hell!' Imogene cries as the pair of us knock into each other.

'What's wrong?' I ask.

'Didn't you see the security at the valet?' Kennedy turns back to look at us with wide eyes.

'Shit.' My heart sinks. 'Was it John Alan?'

Dammit. My head is so full today that it didn't occur to me that John Alan would be here to protect Gary from... me.

'I don't know,' Kennedy says.

I can't see him, but there is definitely security there.

'What should we do?' Brandon asks.

Kennedy purses her lips for a moment and then she makes a little 'oooh' noise. 'I have some blankets and clothes in the trunk,' she says. 'We'll cover you up with junk and smuggle you in! Like when Esme is trying to sneak Bastian into the Delacourt Mansion.'

I pull a face. 'I don't remember that bit.'

'I saw it on some, uh, fanfiction online.'

'Ooh! Send me the link.'

'Yeah. Okay. Pop the trunk, Brandon.'

Kennedy brings a couple of Winklepuff's travel blankets which smell like Winklepuff post-run and pre-bath, a random bit of tarpaulin, plus a beach towel, then, instructing me to sink down as far as I can into the seat, proceeds to dump everything on top of me. Imogene makes a little space so that I can breathe.

'This is great,' she says. 'It just looks like a big messy lump of junk.'

'Not the worst insult I've had,' I shout back, my voice muffled by the smelly blankets and crap.

I hear Kennedy get back into the passenger seat and instruct everyone, and especially Winklepuff, to 'act cool'.

The car starts moving forward, I'm assuming up the driveway, and my heart is thudding in my ears. We come to a stop.

'Hi, Kennedy Jane Cooper here for the Montgomery-Gould engagement garden party.'

'You're running very late,' I hear a gruff voice respond.

'OMG! Traffic was, like, a nightmare.' Imogene pipes up in a terrible valley girl American accent, clearly not following Kennedy's instructions to act cool.

'Invitation please?' the gruff voice says.

I hear a rustling and then Kennedy says in a voice much sweeter than her own. 'Oh, dang! I've forgotten it! What a fool I am.'

'I can't let you past without an invite. Strict orders.'

Well, that's not ideal.

'Come on, man,' Brandon tries.

'No. Sorry.'

And then comes another voice. A slightly nasal-sounding deep voice.

'Kennedy Cooper? Is that you?' the voice says. 'Holy shit, it *is* you!'

'Hi!' Kennedy says in a kind of strangled voice that

makes me think she has no clue who this man is who clearly knows her.

The man speaks again, seemingly thrilled.

'Joel, this is the chick who does the weather! You know! On KLCLA! "*Keep cool out there, folks.*" She's the one who says those *actual* words!'

'I don't watch the weather, Cleetus. I just check invitations at famous people's parties.'

'She's the best!' Cleetus exclaims. 'You're the best. Can I get your autograph?'

I try to hold a little laugh because, of all the famous people that must have been seen by these two guys today, it's Kennedy that causes one of them to be star-struck. I feel a little flicker of pride.

'Of course I'll give you my autograph!' Kennedy says. 'Hand me a pen.'

'She doesn't have an invitation,' the gruff voice repeats.

'She's on the TV almost *every* morning, Joel. Everyone in Hollywood knows everyone else in Hollywood. They're fine.'

'This is on your back.' Joel grumbles.

'I'll vouch for you, Kennedy,' Cleetus says, amidst the sound of a pen scratching onto a paper.

'Thank you, Cleetus,' Kennedy says sweetly. 'Here you go. I'm so grateful. Better hurry!'

'Have a great day!' Cleetus says brightly. 'And... keep cool out there.'

'No, you keep cool!' Imogene cries in her weird American accent, finishing with a little burp.

Before anyone can check the validity of a clearly tipsy Imogene, Brandon puts his foot on the pedal and we zoom off down the driveway towards destiny.

Thank you, Cleetus!

Ugh, I think I have a dog hair in my mouth.

* * *

While Brandon waits in the car in case we need to make a swift exit, Kennedy, Imogene, Winklepuff and I head into the white building where an usher directs us through the indoor lobby and back outside towards a little wooden bridge lit by lanterns. She tells us that the Gardens are at the end of the bridge.

I gasp as I hear Billy Fever finishing a rendition of 'Animals' to rapturous applause.

Halfway across the bridge, Kennedy stops and hands me the sunglasses that are sitting atop her head. 'John Alan may be in there, you'll have more time if you wear these.'

Imogene pulls the small silk scarf that is looped around the handle of her handbag and wraps it around my head, tucking my hair underneath. She nods approvingly. 'It suits you. Very Hollywood.'

I take a deep breath as we continue to walk down the bridge. We come to a small clearing of trees and beyond it is one of the most beautiful, most elegant parties I have ever seen. There are round tables filled with stunning people, many of them, oddly, with professional cameras. On a makeshift stage, framed by lanterns, Billy is taking down his microphone to make way for a cellist. Little fish ponds are dotted here and there and at the centre of the garden is a gorgeous fountain.

I look up at the sky, it is dusky and purple and like something from a film, like someone designed the moment with care and attention. And then I see him. Gary. Dressed in a dark suit, his arm around Tori, who looks perfect in a long pink dress, holding a glass of champagne. She looks up at him and he leans down to kiss her on the cheek.

I can't do it.

I cannot be the one to ruin this perfect moment. Their potentially perfect life together. They look absolutely perfect for each other. They *match*. And Gary is smiling. A really big smile. I don't want to be the one who takes that smile off his face.

'No,' I whisper to Imogene and Kennedy, my eyes blurring with tears behind the sunglasses. 'I can't do this to him. To her. It's not right.'

'We came all this way,' Kennedy says, rubbing my arm gently. 'You might never get a chance like this again!'

'He kissed you, Nora. Brandon said he looked at you like a man in love,' Imogene adds.

'But look!' I point to Gary and Tori, chatting away to guests, their arms around each other, Gary leaning down to ruffle the head of his dog Janet – who is wearing some sort of flowery garland on her head. 'This whole party is perfect. They are perfect! It's not my place to—'

Before I can finish my sentence, Winklepuff starts sniffing the air frantically and, with a little yelp of excitement, leaps down from Kennedy's arms and, oh my god, begins to sprint through the garden. Oh no. No, no, no.

'Fuck!' Kennedy swallows. 'I was holding him tightly.'

The murmurs of the crowd get louder as they notice this tiny random Yorkshire Terrier running around and barking before he darts over to Janet.

'Winklepuff!' Kennedy hisses, but he doesn't hear her.

Gary and Tori stare down at Winklepuff in surprise, as he tries to climb up towards Janet, my face goes all hot. Shit. He is going to try to get with Janet again, right here, in front of everyone! Oh my god.

'Ham!' I yell frantically, hurrying down through the trees and along the gravelled path towards Winklepuff. 'Ham!' Bending down to scoop him up before he mounts a keen-looking Janet for the second time, Kennedy's sunglasses half-slip off my face and are left dangling off one ear.

'Nora?' Gary says, peering at my face, shock and confusion clouding his features. 'What are you...? Why are you...?'

'I'm so sorry. I'm so sorry,' I say over and over again, holding a wriggling Winklepuff to my chest and using my free hand to tug this stupid scarf off my head.

'It's you!' Tori gasps as the realisation that she has met me before dawns. 'And that awful dog. Oh my god, I knew I recognised you from the article.'

'You two have met?' Gary's eyes widen as he looks between the two of us. 'What the hell is going on?' He swallows hard. 'Nora, what are you doing here?'

Article? What is Tori talking about? I look around me in panic, all the guests at the perfectly set tables staring at me. I open my mouth to say something, anything, to explain myself, but nothing comes out. From the little stage, Billy gives me a sad, sorry smile.

I feel someone take my hand. Looking up, I see that it's Imogene and she's giving me an encouraging smile. Kennedy arrives on the other side of me, gently taking Winklepuff from my arms.

'Nora?' Gary tries again.

I open my mouth, but before I can say a word, Tori takes her phone out of her dress pocket and taps furiously on the screen. She narrows her eyes at me before holding the phone aloft.

'How do you know her, Gary? How do you know your own stalker?'

The floor seems to wobble, a vice-like tightness grips my throat.

'What the hell are you talking about, Tori?' Gary says in a low, angry voice.

'Where is John Alan?' Tori asks, looking around the garden frantically. She raises her voice even louder. 'Somebody get him now. Where's Mom?' She waves the phone about. 'We need security!' Handing Gary her phone, Tori steps slightly behind him as if I'm someone to be *afraid* of. 'TMZ dropped this about an hour ago,' she tells Gary in a voice loud enough for everyone in the garden to hear. 'I was going to show you later. I didn't want to spoil the party for you and I *figured* you'd be safe here! Jesus.'

'What's happening?' I ask, my heart starting to thud in my ears so loudly that it feels like what I expect running a marathon must feel like. Which is to say, not great.

Kennedy, along with the rest of the attendees, quickly pull out their phones. Kennedy frowns and then gasps, her eyes growing wide. 'Oh no,' she whispers. 'No, no, no.'

'Nora?' Gary asks, his eyes looking up from Tori's phone and meeting mine in horror, his voice cracking gruffly as he says my name. 'Is this true? It's not true, right? This is just dumb gossip?'

'What? Is what true? What does it say?' I start to rummage around my bag for my phone, but my hands are shaking and all I pull out is a lip gloss and a packet of ham which, of course, makes Winklepuff start to whine in desperation.

Kennedy shushes Winklepuff and wordlessly shows me her phone, Imogene leaning over my shoulder to read what everyone else here seems to be reading right now.

'Of course it's true!' I hear Tori screech. 'She must have followed me to the beach! She set that dog on Janet! Oh my god. Where the fuck is security? Seth, go find John Alan right now.'

I look down at the phone screen and the thudding in my ears stops. My whole heart seems to stop. My legs turn to jelly and I have to grab onto Imogene's arm to keep from fully falling down. It's right there, being read by everyone here and no doubt thousands and thousands of people over the world. The worst possible words, at the worst possible time, in the worst possible situation.

***Stalker Who Attempted Gary Montgomery Attack
Revealed as Brit, Nora Tucker, 27***

CHAPTER FIFTY-FOUR

Nora

Right there on the website is a picture of me. An old one from the Virtual Assistants 4U website. It's a photo my dad took a few years ago. My eyes are shining, my mouth open in an unselfconscious laugh. I scan the article, bile rising in my throat as it details my trip to Los Angeles after seeing Gary Montgomery in *Justice of The Peace*. How I tried to infiltrate his film set and attack him at the Chinese Theatre. And then, as I scroll further down, there's another picture.

'Oh fuck,' I whisper.

It's a picture of the Creepy As Fuck Soulmate Procurement Wall. The specific details on the printouts are pixelated, but the pictures and screenshots of Tori's Instagram and the huge poster of Gary are very clear to see. Beneath the photo, the caption says, *Ms Tucker's plan of attack, found on the wall of her accommodation in Venice Beach.*

How did they know… How did they get the picture?

I spin round to look at Kennedy. Her cheeks are flaming. She's shaking her head and stuttering. She wouldn't… she wouldn't have done this to me? Would she? I think of her frantically typing at her laptop, her interest in everything that happened with Gary, her help setting up the Creepy As Fuck Soulmate Procurement Wall and the fact that she was looking for a big story for her anchor audition. Did... did she use *this* story? Did she use me? Is that how she got the job?

'It's not what you think,' Kennedy blurts out, her eyes filling with tears.

Oh my god. She did this.

'Nora,' Gary says again. 'What is this? You need to tell me what the fuck is going on.'

I turn back to him, flinching at his eyes, which are no longer soft and warm like they were earlier today, but are now narrowed and full of distrust.

'It... I... Wait, I can explain...' I can't seem to formulate a sentence at all, let alone one that explains this article. I open my mouth again to tell him that it's not what it looks like, but how can I? It's exactly what it looks like. I mean, not the bit about wanting to hurt Gary, but the rest of it... why I'm here and what I did... it's true. I take a step towards him. 'I...'

'Where is John Alan?' Tori cries out, clutching Gary's arm as if I'm about to peel off his skin and wear it like a cape.

At that moment, John Alan appears from out of a small bamboo shack, followed by Aileen Gould. When John Alan spots me, his face falls and he starts sprinting, almost tripping over some small potted shrubs as he does so. When he reaches our little crowd of disaster, he grasps hold of my arms, pulls them behind my back and clasps them together while using his other arm to pat his pockets.

'Does anyone have a pair of handcuffs?' he calls out to the crowd, who are all watching this moment, absolutely rapt. The dozens of photographers present are busy taking picture after picture. John Alan pulls on my arms and I can't help but yelp as he yanks them roughly.

'Stop!' Gary cries. 'Get off of her!'

Imogene steps up to John Alan, her face red with fury. 'She hasn't done anything wrong! If you don't take your hands off my sister right fucking now, I will hurt you.'

John Alan half-smiles because Imogene is even skinnier than Tori. Hardly much of a threat to someone who is half-man, half-barrel. He turns to Gary. 'This woman has been stalking you, Mr Montgomery. I cannot in good conscience let her get any closer to you. She's dangerous.'

'She is not dangerous,' Kennedy cries. 'She's in love!'

At this, Tori throws her head back and laughs manically. 'Wow, you are ruining *everything*!' she yells at me. 'This was supposed to be perfect! I planned it so that it would be perfect!'

Aileen hurries to Tori's side and rubs her arms comfortingly.

'Take her away, John,' Aileen says. 'And call the fuckin' cops.'

Everyone starts talking all at once and as the sounds of anger and upset and chaos surround me, I look only at Gary and he looks at me.

'STOP!' he yells eventually. 'Everyone just fucking stop. John, get off of her. Please, everyone, could you leave.'

No one moves. John Alan doesn't let me go.

'I meant it, John,' Gary says in a low, angry voice I've not heard before. 'Get the fuck off of her.'

John Alan immediately releases his grip.

I shake my arms and rub at my aching shoulders, panting with fear and adrenaline and wondering how the fuck I can get out of here as soon as possible. This is too much. It's all way too much.

John Alan takes up a squat position, his hands in a

karate chop pose as if he is ready to pounce on me again at any given moment.

'Are you all right?' Kennedy and Imogene ask, crowding around me, shielding me from John Alan.

Gary steps away from Tori and over to me. 'Are you hurt?' he asks, swallowing hard.

'No, not physically,' I say.

'Okay, everyone.' I hear Seth's voice vaguely from behind me. 'Party's over. Let's go!'

'Do I have to go?' Billy Fever calls out from where he's been watching everything unfold, still on the stage.

'You too, buster,' I hear Olive say.

Billy frowns and gives me a sympathetic wave as he trails out of the garden, along with the rest of the reluctant-to-leave crowd.

'You need to fucking tell me what this is, Nora,' Gary says, pointing at his phone as Seth and Olive begin to shepherd the party guests out of the doors. 'I swear to god, you need to explain what the fuck is going on *right now*.'

I swallow and take a moment to find my voice. He deserves to hear the truth. I need to tell it.

'I… It's true,' I choke out eventually. 'Sort of. I *was* at the set that day. And I was the person who fell into the cement at the Chinese Theatre. But… I wasn't trying to attack you, I swear. I love you.'

'Oh my gosh,' I hear Kennedy murmur from beside me.

'Oh shit,' Imogene echoes.

Gary just screws his face up and looks completely confused.

'I didn't want to cause you any hurt,' I continue, taking a step towards him.

He takes a step back, Tori, clutching onto his arm so that he, Tori and Aileen are all sort of hanging on to each other.

'I came to LA to find you. I saw you in *Justice of The*

Peace and I knew I had to meet you. To see if what I was feeling was genuine, if you might respond to me in the same way I did to you. And if you didn't, then I would have left you alone forever, I really would have. I was going to. But... I think you do feel the same way. Today... We...'

'You... you came to LA to find me?' Gary looks utterly horrified, his mouth open in disbelief. 'After seeing me in a fucking *movie?*'

I nod, tears springing to my eyes and blurring his face. I wipe them away furiously. 'I know it sounds creepy and crazy, but it was never meant in that way,' I tell him, willing him to believe me, to understand that my intentions were never bad. 'When you see the person you think you're meant to be with, what are you supposed to do? Nothing? I couldn't do nothing. I had to see if what I was feeling was real. And then I saw how happy you were with Tori and I was ready to leave it be, I swear I was. But then today when you kissed me...'

'You kissed her?' Tori shrieks, breaking away from Aileen and Gary and pushing Gary in the chest. 'You kissed another woman on the day of our engagement party? What the fuck!'

When she pushes him in the chest again, Gary grabs Tori's hand in his. 'Stop! I didn't want to hurt you. It was a mistake, clearly.'

'After everything I've done for you?' Tori cries, fully sobbing now.

Oh my god. I have caused this absolute shitshow. This hurt, this pain. I am a bad, bad person.

'I'm so sorry,' I say quietly to Tori, my voice shaking so much that it comes out as sohohohohohory. 'I'm so, so sorry.'

Tori ignores me, still staring heatedly at Gary, her hands on her hips. 'I got you a top-tier manager, I gave you a place to stay when you needed it, I've promoted you on my Instagram, helped you run lines. For god's sake, I got you a handprint ceremony at the Chinese Theatre! And you kiss another woman, a nobody, no less. A fat nobody! What the fuck?'

'Oi!' Imogene shouts at Tori. 'She's not a nobody. *You're* a fucking nobody.'

'It's okay,' I shush Imogene. 'She's got a right to be angry. I deserve it.'

Gary drops Tori's hands and takes a step back. 'You got me the handprint ceremony?' His brow furrows.

Tori rolls her eyes and throws her hands up in exasperation. 'Oh come *on*. You've been in one hit film, Gary. You think they were just gonna give that to you? They had someone drop out and I made a deal that if they gave you a ceremony, you'd promote the theatre heavily on the *Nightcar* press junket and do a couple of TV spots for them. Mom and I were going to tell you tomorrow!'

Gary looks across at Aileen and, seeing that none of this is new information to her, stares down at his feet. 'Oh,' he says, almost to himself. 'That makes more sense.' His eyes track across to me, blazing with a doubt and an anger I can feel deep in my core. 'You tricked me, Nora – you followed me, made me think... You tricked me into... feeling something. But you're actually unhinged. What kind of person does this?'

'I'm sorry,' I say because I don't know what else to say, how to make this right. 'It's a mess, I know. But when a person falls in love...'

'You're not in love with me.' Gary shakes his head quickly from side to side. 'You don't even fucking know me, Nora. You violated my privacy and my trust. You need serious help.'

I look down at my feet and take a deep breath. 'You're right. I do,' I say as Imogene squeezes my hand tightly. 'But what I felt was real. Today was real. And that kiss? That was *real*, Gary.'

Gary's eyes bore into mine. 'That kiss was nothing more than a mistake, Nora,' he says in a low, gruff voice. 'You need to leave now, before I let John Alan escort you out.'

'You're just gonna let her go?' Tori screeches. 'She's ruined a ton of sponsorships for us! She needs to be charged. You can't just let her go!'

Gary ignores her and continues to stare at me, his chest quickly rising up and down. I try to find any inkling of softness or warmth in his eyes. Anything at all that might alleviate the pain in my chest right now. But there is nothing. His eyes are as cold as stone.

And that's my cue to leave.

* * *

As we walk out of the gardens, Imogene has to help me because my legs seem to have turned to wet spaghetti. Kennedy grabs my arm on the other side, but I shake her off.

'I swear I didn't leak the story!' she cries. 'I have no clue how TMZ got a picture of the wall or of you. I have no clue how they know anything!'

I stop walking and turn to face her. I want to believe her, but it's too much of a coincidence. Her secretively tapping away on her laptop, spending all of this time with me when she is clearly much cooler than I am, the fact that she needed a juicier story for her audition, the fact that she actually looks *guilty*.

'Is this how you got the job?' I spit. 'I thought we were friends. I'm such an idiot. Jesus, Kennedy.'

'Of course not!' Kennedy cries, reaching out to grab my hands. I clasp my hands to my chest and take a step backwards. Kennedy shakes her head furiously. 'I would never. We *are* friends! I wouldn't ever do that to you.'

I examine her face. Wet eyes have made her mascara

run down her face. Her normally smiling mouth is stretched into a clownlike frown. She looks desolate.

'I promise you, Nora,' she says desperately. 'I didn't do it.'

I believe her. But who else? No one else knows the details that were in the article? Who else could have taken a picture of the Creepy As Fuck Soulmate Procurement Wall?

And then I spot Brandon leaning casually against the car, innocently tapping away on his phone. Him!

Hot rage bubbles up into my chest, fuelling a surge of energy that brings my legs back to life. I march over to him.

'It was you!' I yell, poking a finger at his big muscled chest. 'You just couldn't handle that fat, weird little me thought she could do better than you. How could you be so cruel?'

Brandon blinks, holding his hands up at his side. 'Um… what?'

'You absolute dick,' Imogene hisses. 'You really are a piece of work.'

'It wasn't Brandon!' Kennedy cries, running to her brother's side protectively. 'He wouldn't!'

'How else did TMZ get a picture from *inside the house*?' I yell back. 'It's obvious, Kennedy. I know he's your brother, but he's got serious issues.'

'Excuse me, what the hell is going on right now?' Brandon is looking around the car park as if someone is about to pop out with a camera and reveal that he is being punked.

Kennedy takes out her phone, pulls up the article and hands it to Brandon, who reads it. 'Holy shit,' he mutters, shaking his head. 'I didn't do that,' he says firmly.

'You fat-shamed me, you made me feel like I was nothing, selling a story about me to a gossip blog is a logical next step. Just admit it. There's no one else it could have been!'

Brandon clenches his jaw together. 'You're right. I have issues. I was a real dick to you and I'm not quite sure why. I think your optimism, your belief in love just... showed me that I have very little of my own.' He takes a deep breath and fold his arms across his chest. 'And I am really sorry for that. I clearly have some work to do on myself. And I will... but... Nora, I didn't do this.' His eyes search mine. 'And, for the record... I thought that what you did today was really brave. Telling Gary how you felt, no holds barred. I... I'm sorry I made you feel like you were nothing. That's not what I think about you at all. Far from it.'

He looks like he's telling the truth, but I am evidently a person not in their right mind. I don't know what to think any more.

'I need to go home,' I mutter quietly. 'I... just need to go back to where I belong.'

The four of us stand there for a moment, the silence deeply uncomfortable. The sky is dark and the winds start to whip fiercely around us. This is the second worst day of my life.

'I think you guys should head off,' Imogene says calmly, now fully sober. 'We'll get a car service.'

My eyes blur with tears as I watch Brandon take our luggage out of his trunk and plonk it on the pavement beside us. I take Winklepuff from Kennedy and clasp him to my chest, the soft warm heaviness of him making my chest ache. 'I will miss you, bud,' I whisper into his fur. 'You are a really really good dog. The best of dogs.'

Winklepuff sniffs me a little before frantically attempting to lick my tears away, the sweetness of the gesture making me cry more. I hand Winklepuff to Brandon, who puts him into the car.

I turn to Kennedy.

'Bye then,' I say with a sad shrug. 'Thanks for taking me in.'

Kennedy puts her hands either side of my face, her fingers are trembling just a little. 'I'm truly sorry, Nora. What a mess, huh.'

I sniff. 'I know. I'm sorry too. This whole chaos has happened because of me,' I tell her, stifling a sob. 'That's the truth of it. I caused all of this. I'm sorry.'

'That's not true!' Kennedy says desperately. 'I'm going to figure this out, I promise you I'll find out how TMZ got a hold of this.'

I nod and smile grimly as she hugs me goodbye, squeezing me tightly and making me promise to call her as soon as I get home.

All I can think about right now is how I've fucked everything up so badly. Poor Gary whose life I have absolutely upended. And Tori who really didn't deserve this. Kennedy who has done nothing but be kind to me. And Imogene who flew here to bring me home and has ended up embroiled in my shit. Messing things up is a pattern of mine. I cannot seem to help it.

'Come on,' Imogene says gently as Brandon revs the engine of his car, giving a brief sad wave as he and Kennedy pull out of the car park. I watch as Kennedy waves goodbye from inside the car, her face streaming with tears. I wave back, not quite believing that this is how it's ending.

'It's time to get back to Brigglesford.' Imogene rubs my arm. 'Everything will be all right once we get home.'

I wait to feel a sweep of relief at her comforting words, at the notion of being back in my house, in my warm safe cocoon where I can't mess things up anymore. But it doesn't come. The reality of my life before Gary and Kennedy and Winklepuff and Los Angeles somehow doesn't feel quite so appealing as it once did. I know better now. If anything good has come from this disaster of a trip, then surely it's that.

Our car turns up and after a tearful but mercifully quick drive to the airport, we're ensconced on the aircraft, ready to leave this whole mad escapade behind.

As the airplane takes off, I stare out of the window and the glittering lights beneath.

'Goodbye, LA,' I whisper, pressing my hand gently against the glass. 'Goodbye, Gary Montgomery.'

CHAPTER FIFTY-FIVE

Nora

'My name's Nora Tucker and you've been a brilliant audience!'

I slip the microphone back into the stand and smile at the small but reasonably enthusiastic crowd at the quirky arts café in Camden where I've just performed. Gathering up my belongings and pocketing the meagre payment from the owner, I begin to walk back in the direction of my hotel, enjoying the feel of the cold November air on my face, the fierce chilly wind whipping the hair up off my head.

I stop off at a café to grab a quick lunch of a cheese toastie with a cup of tea. As I sit down at a table by the window, a reminder flashes on my phone for my therapy session tomorrow. Because I'm in London for a few days rather than Sheffield, it will be a telephone appointment, but I've been seeing Dr Hark for three and a half months now and I've made so many strides in terms of understanding why I am the way I bloody am that missing a session, no matter where I am, is not something I'm willing to do. I don't want to go back to the apathetic, almost numb way I was feeling before. I'm *determined* not to.

Having to talk about my feelings with a total stranger was deeply uncomfortable at first and after Imogene and I got back from Los Angeles I was so sad and embarrassed and guilty and, well, heartbroken, that I took to my bed, barely able to watch one of my beloved movies, let alone even try to begin to fix the mess I'd gotten myself in.

After two weeks of gently cajoling to no avail, Imogene showed up and lost her shit, practically dragging me out of the bed and to the clinic. I knew that it was important that I go, but that didn't mean I wanted to! I spent the first three sessions barely able to formulate my knotty jumble of thoughts and feelings in my own head and definitely nowhere near being able to organise and articulate them out loud. But eventually, with the help of Dr Hark, everything spilled out and together we learned that, as usual, Imogene was almost completely right about what had been going on with me over the last two years. That my grief and guilt over Mum and Dad and my part in their death had forced me into a sort of stasis. That as long as I could absorb myself in books and movies and fantasies of 'The One' then I could essentially ignore the way I was really feeling. I thought that as long as I hid away and didn't acknowledge anything or anyone, then I could stop hurting, could prevent myself from causing any more trouble.

Dr Hark said it in a much more eloquent way, of course, and went about setting me tasks in a bid to face my issues and improve my seriously flagging mental health. She didn't assign me a task as crazy as Imogene's because she didn't, you know, want to get struck off the UK psychiatrists' medical register. But after finding out that I'd got a good head start in 'living out loud' in Los Angeles, she gave me three vital tasks.

The first task – to exercise. After coming to love my

time in the ocean with Kennedy in LA, I spent the rest of the summer at home wild swimming in the River Derwent at Chatsworth House, imagining that Colin Firth's Mr Darcy might appear at any moment to sexily peel me out of my costume and go to town on me.

Imogene came with me the first couple of times until she got a leech stuck on her arse cheek, which made me laugh so hard I cried. When the weather turned colder in October, I continued my regular morning swims at the tiny, somewhat shabby Brigglesford Leisure centre, where I have made a couple of new real-life friends in the form of Bony Liam, the skinny lifeguard who likes to talk to me about how I should be reading paranormal fantasy books, rather than *Harcourt Royals*, and Blanche, who sits with me after our swims to drink hot chocolate and tell me about when she was a Fleetwood Mac groupie back in her younger days and how Mick Fleetwood said she gave the best blow job in all of Europe. Blanche is seventy years old.

I'm still learning not to feel nervous in front of new people, but I'm also remembering the excitement of it too, the possibility. I've even reconnected online with a couple of musician friends from my gigging days and have planned to meet them for drinks next week when I return from London!

The second task? To write a new song each week. Dr Hark thought this would be a great way for me to learn how to express my emotions in a more measured way than my usual patterns of either bottling them all up for ages or letting them all out in one big uncontainable mess at other people's engagement parties, and such. And so I now have a selection of sixteen new complete songs. Most of them are about Mum and Dad, a few are about Gary and there's an upbeat comedy song called 'Joy Ahoy' that is silly and cheerful and hopeful, just like the woman who inspired it. Most of the songs are shit and indulgent, but there are maybe five that have some potential.

A few weeks after I started therapy, I felt strong enough to start calling some of the old pubs and clubs I used to sing at and asked if I could do a short unpaid set. The first few gigs were a nightmare. Without alcohol or Gary watching me like he did the day we kissed, I properly stumbled, playing wrong notes and staring at my feet for the whole performance. At one open-mic night at a live music venue on Brigglesford High Street, my voice shook so much that I sounded like a dying sheep, which one member of the audience didn't hesitate to shout to me across the room. I felt like giving up again that night, but something inside of me knew that if I did, I would never pick it back up, and the thought of that made my whole body flood with sadness, which, frankly is an emotion I've had quite enough of. So I held my head high, gathered up the courage I somehow discovered in LA and I marched on, booking more free spots and open mics until eventually my old spark seemed to return and the pub and club owners started offering me money to come back in a professional capacity. I'm making enough money now that hopefully I can stop working at Virtual Assistants 4U in the new year, and maybe even save enough to record a demo in a studio.

The third, and most important, task that Dr Hark assigned me was to leave my house every single day no matter what. After the two solid weeks I spent in bed after my mortifying return from LA, this one was a bit of a wrench. For a start, I didn't really have many places to go beyond swimming or the park with Imogene and Ariana. So I started volunteering a couple of afternoons a week at the dog rescue in Sheffield city centre. Before I met Winklepuff, I thought dogs were mostly annoying, but since that stinky-breathed little rat wormed his way into my heart I've been longing for the feel of soft fur on my face, for that easy company that comes with zero expectations outside of affection and meat. I love walking the dogs, sneaking them bits of ham and trying out my songs on them.

Bit by bit, the memories of all the bad, humiliating parts of my time in LA made way for the good memories. The excitement I felt at being in my body for the first time in so long, the warm, ticklish feeling of the sun on my skin, the pride I had felt at trying new things I had been scared of, of interesting new people and eating marijuana ice-cream. Gary... I realised pretty quickly that I wanted more of those types of feelings. Of course in Brigglesford the energy and excitement isn't as frantic and exciting as it was in Venice Beach. But it's not nothing.

Imogene and I have been hanging out a lot more, which has been so lovely. She's in a much better place now that she confronted Dan about how fed up she was with his lack of input into the family. He was horrified and, like me, had thought that Imogene was doing absolutely fine. Once he found out the truth, he started making a real effort to do more than his fair share around the house and with Ariana. I mean, I will always think that she's too good for him, but she loves him and, as I now undoubtedly know, you can't help who you love. At least he's stepping up at last.

On the way to the hotel, I pass the billboard I've been seeing everywhere over the past couple weeks. It's a poster for Gary's next movie, *Nightcar*. The one he was filming while I was there. It's being released early next year. The poster shows him sitting behind the wheel of a neon-lit car, staring intensely off into the distance. His face makes me catch my breath.

I smile sadly, my heart aching with a strength that hasn't diminished one bit since I got back home. I might have fixed some of the holes in my life, or at least started to, but the hole in my heart feels like it will be there until the day I croak.

The one thing Imogene didn't get right about me and my problems was her belief that Gary couldn't possibly be my soulmate. If I know one thing now, I know that I was right the whole time. He *is* my soulmate. Well, was.

I read online that Gary had split up with Tori Gould, who is now very publicly dating a fitness Youtuber with three million subscribers. He also fired Aileen and, after finishing his *Nightcar* shoot, just disappeared from any sort of public life. He was never on social media anyway, but there was nothing about him on any of the gossip blogs or in the newspapers. Someone on Reddit claimed they saw him in Texas with his dad and another woman. Someone else claimed they saw him on a silent retreat in Bali, but they couldn't ask if it was him because of the whole silent retreat thing.

I spent two months hoping that he would contact me, since he was no longer engaged. At the very least I wanted to properly explain myself, to apologise for upending his life the way I did. But he didn't call me. Of course he bloody didn't. And the more time went on, I realised that he never would. How could he? The disaster at his engagement garden party was widely reported and incredibly embarrassing for everyone involved. Being seen with me, his stalker, would ruin the amazing career he had started to build. We lived on different continents and the fact is that he would probably always be nervous around me. Wondering if I was secretly planning to cut his hair off while he was sleeping, or set up spy cameras in the bathroom so I could watch him pee or other weird shit that film star stalkers fantasise about. I got why he didn't call. Doesn't mean it didn't hurt. Doesn't mean it won't always hurt. But I'll always have the memory of that one perfect day I spent with him. I'll carry that day with me for as long as I'm breathing.

Reaching the hotel, I run up the stairs and dive into the lift, zooming up to my room on the fifth floor. As I open the door, I giggle to myself once more at the sight of the gorgeously glam ball gown hanging up on the wardrobe door. With its pale blue, slightly booby lace top and massive taffeta skirt embroidered with silver thread, it's like something out of a modern-day fairy tale or, say, a really cool romance novel.

I shower quickly, blow-drying my hair as best I can so it lies smooth and glossy over my shoulders. I open the large cardboard box Kennedy had couriered over to my hotel this morning and laugh excitedly at the sight of the shiny gold plastic crown, dotted with fake but dazzling jewels.

I grab the stack of books I'm intending to get signed and head back downstairs.

My god, I cannot *wait* to see Kennedy again.

CHAPTER FIFTY-SIX

Nora

Text from Kennedy: *I'll meet you at the hotel bar. Don't forget your crown! Crown Kissers in da house! Kennedy x*

I smile widely as I spot tons of people dressed as *Harcourt Royals* characters, meandering around the hotel lobby. Everyone nods at each other as if we're in on some amazing secret, which, I suppose, we are.

My heart flips with excitement at the thought of seeing Kennedy. We've been in pretty close touch since I got back. Within a week of me leaving, she had used her 'wildly impressive journalistic skills' to find out that Erin was the one who had spilled the story to TMZ. Apparently, she'd been moonlighting for a few gossip blogs as a way to make some extra money while trying to become a serious news anchor. Kennedy felt awful because after they'd slept together she'd had a couple of glasses of wine and tipsily told Erin all the details about my trip, swearing her to absolute secrecy. Later that night, while I was in bed with Brandon and Kennedy was fast asleep in her room,

Erin wandered into my sleeping area and saw the Creepy As Fuck Soulmate Procurement Wall. She snapped pictures, wrote it up and tried to sell the story to KLCLA in exchange for the junior anchor position. Because they had a big interview with Gary Montgomery set up for a few weeks' time, and were unimpressed with her lack of loyalty to Kennedy, they didn't want it. Right after she found out that Kennedy had gotten the anchor position, Erin went straight to the editor at TMZ and sold it to them. Kennedy told KLCLA that Erin had been moonlighting, which was strictly against the rules of the network. She was fired from KLCLA and is now working as a full-time gossip blogger, which, according to Kennedy's intel, she despises because it's not the highbrow news career she was so sure she deserved.

I've missed Kennedy so much, but with our regular FaceTime sessions and getting to see her news reports online have kept me ticking over. I saw Brandon a few times in the background of her videos, which was more than a little awkward, having to pretend to be interested in saying hi to him. According to Kennedy, he's still not having much luck with women or his screenplay. I hope he figures it out.

I wait at the bar as promised, peering happily at all the fellow book geeks and their over-the-top costumes, when I hear an unmistakeable screech of joy.

'Noooooorrrraaaa!'

I spin around to find Kennedy running towards me, Winklepuff in her arms, his tongue poking out. He spots me and starts to do his little yelps. I suspect that the only reason he is excited to see me is because I am the ham lady. I pull a piece out of my handbag and feed it to him before gathering them both into a hug.

'I missed you, buddy!' I laugh as Winklepuff gobbles the ham up and snorts with joy.

'Hey, what about me?' Kennedy laughs.

'I suppose I missed you too.' I shrug with a wide grin. I notice Kennedy's everyday green and white floral dress and bright white sneakers. 'Oi, you're not in costume!'

'Oh, yeah. I, uh, spilled coffee on it!"

'You don't drink coffee.'

'I meant chamomile tea!'

'Okay...'

'Oh look, everyone's going in,' Kennedy says excitedly, pointing towards a stream of *Harcourt Royals* fans making their way into the hotel conference room. There's a huge banner overhead that reads 'The Inaugural Crown Kissers Con'.

We follow in behind the crowd to find that the boring old hotel conference space has been transformed into a fancy palace ballroom. It's all decorated with heavy red curtains, gold ornate chairs and long tables covered with white tablecloths. There are hundreds of twinkling fairy lights strung across the ceiling and flickering candles on every table. It's magical! This is exactly what I imagined Princess Esme's ballroom to look like!

I clasp Kennedy's shoulder in glee.

She looks back at me, her eyes shining. 'Very cool,' she says, nodding approvingly. Cheesy 90's pop songs – Bastian's favourite musical genre – blast through the speakers as attendees wander around the room, their faces full of delight, looking at the giant cardboard posters of every *Harcourt Royals* book cover. On one side of the room, there's a long buffet table filled with cucumber sandwiches, cream scones and pots of tea.

'I cannot believe we're about to meet CJ West in real life!' I squeal.

Kennedy laughs and ruffles Winklepuff's head. 'It's pretty fucking insane.'

A small, nerdy-looking woman on the stage, dressed as Bastian's pet goldfish Frankie, taps a microphone and clears her throat, before asking if the music can be turned down.

'Good afternoon,' the woman says. 'And welcome to the first ever Crown Kissers Con!'

A cheer goes up around the room. I whoop and Kennedy whistles loudly.

'The members of the Crown Kissers forum and Facebook Fan Group pretty much forced CJ West into doing this today,' the woman continues. 'She's brought so much joy and laughter to all of us and we thought it was about time we got to say thank you in real life. It is my absolute pleasure to welcome her to London for this – the first of what I hope will be an annual *Harcourt Royals* fan event. And so, without any further ado, I welcome to the stage… CJ WEST!'

I clap and cheer and look around the room for the first sighting of the secretive author who has made every person in this room laugh and cry and swoon with her campy, kitschy stories. Kennedy plops Winklepuff down onto the floor, hands me his lead and starts walking across the room towards the woman with the microphone. Huh? Where the hell is she going?

'Kennedy!' I call out after her, but my voice is drowned out by the sound of applause. When she reaches the tiny woman, she takes the microphone from her and turns to face the crowd, her cheeks flushed with pleasure.

What the hell? I look around in confusion. Why is Kennedy… Oh SHIT. NO… no, it can't be!

Kennedy clears her throat. 'It's my true honour to be here today.'

The whole room bursts into cheers.

Holy shit. Kennedy, *my* Kennedy, is CJ West? How? Why didn't she tell me? How did I not know this? What the hell!

I burst into shocked laughter, a hand covering my

mouth, as Kennedy speaks to the room, her head held high, warm confidence in her voice.

'I wasn't going to come,' Kennedy tells the room. 'In fact, it was my plan to never *ever* let anyone know that I am the writer behind these books. The reason for that? Well, I've grown up with parents who expected me to be someone else. Who desperately wanted me to achieve the things that they had wanted for themselves. They wanted me to write serious news stories, to be the next Kate Couric, if you will. But all I ever wanted to do, ever since I was twelve years old and reading *Sweet Valley High* books beneath the covers in my room, was write love stories, stories full of fun and laughter and friendship and *joy*.'

She gives me a pointed look.

I shake my head in amazement. Kennedy? KENNEDY?

'I was lucky enough to get the most amazing job as a junior news anchor,' Kennedy continues. 'And I took it. I thought that once I did what my parents wanted for me that I'd feel satisfied somehow. That I wouldn't feel the need to keep scribbling about Esme and Bastian every spare chance I got. But being a news anchor isn't going to satisfy me. I know that now. The only thing that really satisfies me is writing these stories and sharing them with you guys.'

Another cheer goes around the room.

I look around at all these people staring at my friend Kennedy with adoration. Pride blooms in my chest.

'For a long time, I was way too scared to tell anyone about my secret identity as a romance author,' Kennedy says. 'I was afraid I'd lose my job at the news station, that my peers would scoff at me. I was terrified that I wouldn't be able to make it into a sustainable career. But then, this past summer, I was visited at my house in LA by a fellow Crown Kisser…'

Oh! That's me! She's talking about me!

'And, you know, she taught me something important. She taught me that sometimes you have to just fucking do what you want. What *you* think is right. No matter how many people laugh at you, no matter how hard it might be, no matter if it all goes seriously, *seriously* wrong. If you believe in it enough, then you *have* to try. Because, as she told me time and again, fate loves the fearless.'

My eyes well up. I press a hand to my chest. Kennedy. My best friend. My favourite author.

Kennedy sniffs a little, tears brimming in her eyes too.

'Yesterday I quit my job,' she reveals, putting her hands onto her hips in a sort of Wonder Woman stance. 'And today I'm officially coming out to the world as the author of the *Harcourt Royals* series, CJ West!'

The crowd goes crazy. I hear a woman to my left, who is, like me, dressed as Princess Esme, yell, 'Ohmigod, she's amaaaaaazing!' People are snapping pictures and whistling and cheering out loud. This is nuts!

I applaud with the rest of the room and before Kennedy has even fully gotten down from the stage, I pick up Winklepuff, run over to her in my big heavy ball gown and gather her into a hug.

'You shit!' I laugh. 'Why didn't you tell me? Oh my god. I wondered how you seemed to know so much more about the books than I did! I'm in shock!'

'I was going to!' Kennedy holds her hands up. 'I swear I was. But then you spilled to Erin about my goose and cat story on that night out and I was worried you'd somehow let it slip to someone. And, you know, I wasn't ready for it to get out.'

'Hmmm. Probably for the best.' I nod, thinking about how my behaviour in LA wasn't exactly the most reliable behaviour of all time. 'Wow. We have even more to chat about now! I have a shit-ton of questions.'

'And I am going to answer every one of them proudly.

I have so much to tell you! I meant what I said up there. You really did inspire me to go all in, Nora.'

Happiness and pride spread throughout my body, warming every muscle. 'I'm so, so glad.' I point over at the rapidly forming queue of people waiting at a table stacked with special edition *Harcourt Royals* books to be signed. 'Your fans await, Ms West. Hey,' I quip. 'Maybe one of them is your soulmate. Ooh maybe one them has a Creepy As Fuck Soulmate Procurement Wall at home with your face on it.'

'Here's hoping,' Kennedy giggles, giving me a quick tight hug and then straightening my crown before skipping off to her queue of adoring readers.

The 90's pop tunes kick back in with the Christina Aguilera's classic 'Genie in A Bottle'. Shaking my head in disbelief at this most brilliant turn of events, I look around for someone to talk to. The familiar nerves and desire to hide out flare, as I expect they always will do, but Dr Hark said the best thing for me to do was practise and throw myself into as many daunting situations as possible. To, as Kennedy says, go all in and exude confidence even if I don't fully feel it. So I lift my chin, take a deep steadying breath and, pulling Winklepuff's lead, approach a group of five or six *Harcourt Royals* fans chatting by one of the candlelit tables.

'Hallo there!' I say cheerfully. *Hallo there?* What am I? An Enid Blyton character?

'Um, hey girl!' one of the women, who is dressed as Leah Plumbow Cavendish the sexy nineteen-year-old Marchioness of Dothberry, responds with a little wave. There's another Princess Esme here, along with two Queen Evangelines, two guys dressed as Bastian's sexy but evil twin brother Raphael and an older woman dolled up as Courtney Bucket, the sexy power-suited manager of Dreamy Dix strip club where Bastian works. 'Your dress is amazing!'

'Thanks,' I smile, brushing my hands over the ridiculously puffy skirt. 'This skirt is so gigantic, though. I did not think through how I'm going to navigate the loo in it!'

The group laughs and one of the Queen Evangelines looks down at her own gigantic dress and scrunches up her face. 'It is ze same with me,' she says, in a French accent. 'If you help me, I'll help you.'

'I want in on this,' says the other Princess Esme. 'It's like wearing my wedding dress all over again. I'll definitely need help.'

'We can all help each other. Team Toilet Rescue,' I say, which makes a couple of them titter.

Check me out. Holding court with strangers, admittedly they are all very lovely book geeks like me, but still. I came over here on my own. I'm living in the world, having conversations, not hiding in my house behind a fairy tale, fantasising about a future I was never willing to go out and get. Dr Hark and Imogene would be proud of me. Hell, I'm proud of me!

When the group decide it's a good time to join the book-signing line, I lead a bored-looking Winklepuff over to the buffet table. 'Let me get a cup of tea,' I tell him. 'And then we'll sit down and you can have some more premium ham. It's Ocado Gold ham you, know. It's proper fancy stuff. Only the best for my best buddy.'

Winklepuff sits obediently at the word ham and I laugh, shaking my head at how much I missed this bloody dog.

Grabbing a golden paper plate from the table, I stack a couple of cucumber sandwiches and a French Fancy cake atop it. I ponder the rest of the food, not quite sure whether I should add a scone too. Hmmm.

'Fuck it,' I say to myself eventually, grabbing a big jam and cream topped scone and adding it to my plate. 'Life is too short, eh, Winklepuff?'

I'm enjoying a rather hefty mouthful of cake when

Winklepuff starts to yelp enthusiastically and then I hear the husky Texan-twanged voice I've thought about every single day and night for the last four months. The voice I didn't think I would ever hear in real life again.

'Nora.'

I breathe in sharply, every hair on my body standing on end.

My breath catches in my throat. I turn around slowly, my gob full of French Fancy, to see Gary dressed as Bastian from *Harcourt Royals* and looking absolutely, utterly ridiculous. He's wearing an obscenely clingy white T-shirt, the tightest leather pants I've ever seen and a low-slung baseball cap that says 'I Heart Sea Life!'. Outside of the costume he looks great, his skin tanned and clear, his face a little bit fuller than it was in Los Angeles, his eyes clear and shining. He is heart-stopping and now that he is in front of me, I realise that four months has done not one jot to diminish the way I feel about him.

I quickly chew and swallow the rest of the French Fancy before I choke on it. Then I look around furtively for any signs of John Alan in case Gary has rethought his decision not to press charges for my bonkers behaviour. No sign of John Alan. Phew.

Winklepuff starts to climb up Gary's leg.

'Oi! Heel!' I scold, but Gary picks the dog up and holds him adorably to his chest, which doesn't help the desirous pounding in my chest.

'I remember you,' Gary says with narrowed eyes. Winklepuff licks his cheek frantically, causing Gary to pull away at the smell of his breath. 'Oh no,' he cries, plopping Winklepuff back onto the floor and laughing, his eyes wide in horror at the stench.

'We have the same dentist,' I deadpan, which makes absolutely no sense. It's like I'm actively trying to get him to find me disgusting.

Gary raises an eyebrow and says nothing.

'Not really,' I say quickly. 'I actually have good breath, I think. I use a water flosser and extra-strength medicated mouthwash. My dentist says I have the gums of an eighteen-year-old so...'

Shut up, Nora. Shut up!

Gary starts to laugh out loud. I'm not quite sure why he's laughing, but the relief of him not looking disgusted or angry at me and the shock of him being here makes me join in. We stand there for a few seconds just laughing hysterically for no tangible reason.

What the fuck is Gary Montgomery – who I have tried and failed not to miss with every inch of my body for the last four months – doing in London, dressed as Bastian the marine biology-loving stripper?

'What are you doing here?' I eventually manage to get out, wiping the tears from my face and realising that my carefully applied mascara is now likely streaked across my cheeks Alice Cooper style.

Gary wipes the tears from his eyes too and lifts the baseball cap up from his face a little. 'I'm actually in the UK for a shoot. I'm doing my friend Olive's movie. It's called *Chuffed*.'

'The asshole brother character.'

Gary smiles widely. 'You remembered.'

'Of course I did,' I say.

Gary nods slowly, his eyes travelling over my face.

'I, um, didn't know whether you were acting anymore,' I tell him. 'You seemed to... disappear. I mean, not that I've been tracking your movements or anything...'

Gary half-grins, a glint of amusement in his eyes. 'I took some time out. Spent a while with my Pops in Texas, thought about what I was gonna do next. You know, things got... pretty overbearing in LA.'

'Oh really?' I say casually. 'I wonder why? It's not like you had a crazy stalker who maybe ruined your life.' I immediately regret my stupid quip, but Gary laughs out loud again and rubs his hand over his stubbled chin.

'You're not a stalker, Nora. And you didn't ruin my life,' he says seriously, taking a step closer to me. 'You just… shook it up a little.'

My heart quickens.

'That's a very generous interpretation.' I respond.

'I'm a very generous guy, I guess… Seriously, though, I reckon I needed a little shaking up.'

We stare into each other's eyes for a moment and I realise that his are no longer the cold and distrustful eyes that last looked at me in LA. They are warm and curious and slightly nervous.

He reaches into the record bag he's carrying and hands me a CD case. I take it from him and try not to jump on him as his fingers touch mine and a bolt of desire shoots straight to the parts of my body that bolts of desire tend to shoot to. I peek down at the CD.

Billy Fever Sings the Greatest Hits of The Iconic Adam Levine

On the front is a photograph of Billy Fever dressed in a shiny purple jumpsuit. His hands are clasped sensually around a microphone and he's looking directly into the camera with a sexy smoulder. I burst into laughter. 'My goodness,' is all I can say. 'My *goodness.*'

'I know,' Gary says. 'He emailed me to say that he was giving me the first copy, seeing as I'm his number one fan. I mean, who even makes CDs anymore. Don't get me wrong, I am very glad that Billy Fever does, but *wow.*'

'Wow,' I agree.

'That one's yours. He asked me to give it to you.'

'You spoke to him?'

'He emailed me after the garden party. Apologised for telling you the address. He told me you were his number two fan and he thought that maybe I should forgive you.'

'And, um, what did you say?' I ask, failing to keep my voice casual.

'I said that it was really fucking weird that out of all the Lyft drivers in LA, we both got him, that we were the only two of his passengers to ever sign up for his newsletter.' Gary points over to Kennedy, who is still signing *Harcourt Royals*. 'And then your friend got in touch with me a day after that.'

'Huh? What? You mean Kennedy? Kennedy got in touch with you?'

'Yep. CJ West herself. I don't know how she got my email address, but somehow she did and when I asked her how, she said she wouldn't reveal her sources.'

Kennedy's mad journalistic skills. I look over at her and shake my head in astonishment. She catches my eye and smiles widely as she notices who I'm talking to, giving me a double thumbs up.

'What… what did Kennedy say?' I ask.

Gary takes another step towards me and the nearness of him makes me weak. 'She explained to me what really happened. She told me your side of the story from start to finish. How everything in LA came about after you saw me at the movies. How your sister challenged you to come and meet me. She told me that you were never stalking me. That you were planning to try to meet me once to see if there was something there and if not, you would leave me alone. She told me that you dropped the knife that day on the lot and the reason you had a knife was because you planned to make me a grilled cheese.' The corner of his mouth lifts with mirth. 'She told me how you got pushed when you fell into the cement. That, of course, you weren't trying to attack me.' He lowers his voice. 'She told me how much you were struggling with this weird, crazy feeling for a total stranger, but that you felt you needed to take a chance in case you were right about… us.'

I nod and look at the floor, my cheeks heating up. 'She told you a lot then.'

Gary brushes a strand of hair away from my face and I have to try very hard not to literally swoon. 'Nora. You *were* right about us…'

I look up sharply. 'W-What?'

Gary smiles tenderly and shakes his head as if he can't quite believe what he's saying. 'I… I felt the same way. I felt it the first time I saw you being taken away from the lot by John Alan and, well, I only saw your back. I felt it when I saw your little face print in the concrete. I *knew* it when you bandaged my arm so shittily. And then that day at Santa Monica Pier… I just… I didn't know what to think. And I definitely didn't want to acknowledge that my life could change like that, so quickly and without warning. I thought maybe it was pre-marriage jitters? That I was overwhelmed by everything that was going on with my career. I wasn't as sure as you that love just *happened* like that. In an instant. And I wasn't brave enough to see if it could.'

'And now?' I ask tentatively, still not quite believing that any of this is happening.

'And now I've had time for my head to catch up to my heart.'

I get a flashback to the night I talked to Mum about finding soulmates. *It might not be obvious at first,* she had said, *and sometimes it takes a little while for your head to catch up with your heart.*

Gary touches his hand to my cheek, his thumb lightly brushing the corner of my lip. 'I know that you're not crazy, Nora. Just that a crazy, unlikely thing happened to you. And, you were fearless enough to follow through on an instinct. Not many people would do that.'

'No,' I agree. 'It's pretty bonkers behaviour.'

'It's pretty incredible. I reckon you're pretty incredible, Nora.'

'Oh,' I say, a wide grin spreading across my face. Wow. *Wow.*

Gary gently lifts the crown off my head and kisses it, which makes me burst into laughter.

'I think that makes me an official Crown Kisser,' he says seriously.

'I could see how much you enjoyed kissing that crown,' I reply.

'Best crown I ever kissed.'

Gary places the crown back on my head.

'So… I think… I'd like to kiss you now, Nora,' he says, his face now mere centimetres from mine, his eyes travelling hungrily from my eyes to my lips and back again.

'That would be cool,' I say, my voice cracking.

He pulls me firmly towards him, wrapping me in his strong, sturdy arms. His lips meet mine. I weave my hands into his hair, knocking off his baseball cap. He pulls my hips closer to his and presses against me. Then slowly, he eases away and smiles, touching his forehead against mine for a moment and whispering my name.

I am breathless.

I knew it.

I freaking *knew it.*

Gary Montgomery is my soulmate, the one, my true love. And it is everything. It is my whole heart. It is a big thunderbolt. Right through the belly.

To a soundtrack of corny 90's pop, the pair of us kiss and kiss and kiss like we're already running out of time.

Turns out my mum and dad were absolutely right. Fate *undeniably* loves the fearless.

You'll see…

THE END

. . .

Dear Reader,

Hello! Thank you so much for reading HE WILL BE MINE. I wanted to write something that was sweepingly romantic and escapist, while still keeping a firm hold on the bonkers scenarios, quirky characters and outlandish laughs that you have come to expect from my books. I hope I managed it and that this story took you away from your worries for a little while. I hope it made you smile and feel optimistic that life can and will be extraordinary again.

It always feels a bit weird to request reviews in these reader letters but I'm going to cringe and do it anyway because they really do make a massive difference to authors. If you enjoyed reading Nora's LA adventure, sharing a few short sentences on Amazon, Goodreads or Bookbub would mean the world.

Some other things to know: You can sign up for my newsletter to get access to a couple of free short stories and bonus material for my books. I also use the mailing list as the main way to let you know about new releases and what I'm up to. I send an email about once a month and I am never ever spammy.

Oh, I also have a reader group on Facebook! It's called Kirsty Greenwood's Literary Darlings. We do behind the scenes posts, giveaways and a monthly book club on there. It's a great group of friendly bookish women all nattering about love life and the pursuit of funny books. We'd love to have you join us on there!

Okay. I have more writing to do and you surely have other books waiting to be enjoyed.

Thanks again for reading HE WILL BE MINE.

I send love and good wishes your way.

Until next time,

Kirsty xx

ACKNOWLEDGMENTS

Books take me a long time to write. I'm working on getting quicker, I promise! They wouldn't exist at all if not for the awesome support I receive from the following people. Thank you to:

Caroline Hogg who edited the living crap out of this book and helped turn it into something I'm really proud of. You are the best.

Hannah Ferguson for the always lovely encouragement and support.

Jade Craddock for the excellent copyediting.

Tina Snider for awesome PA-ing.

Angie, Net and Edd for the proofs.

Grace Frösén for the beautiful cover lettering.

Cesca Major for being my sounding board, confidante, early reader and general delight of a friend.

Cressida Mclaughlin for being such an open-hearted, cool and hilarious friend to me.

Elizabeth Keach, Victoria Stone and Keris Stainton for your friendship and chats.

Holly Martin for the super patient and very clever advice.

The awesome Bookcampers – what an incredible group of talented women. I can't wait for our next meet up.

Kirsty Greenwood's Literary Darlings. We're still only just getting to know each other but you're already making my days brighter!

The brilliant readers, authors, bloggers, bookstagrammers and bookclubs who buy, share, shout about and review my books. I am so grateful! You are the best bunch of readers a woman could hope to have.

My beloved family: Mum, Dad, Net, Nic, Tony, Mary and Will. I love you all more than you will ever ever know and can't wait until we can hang out again safely.

Edd – Thank you doesn't begin to cover it.

ABOUT THE AUTHOR

Kirsty Greenwood is a top ten bestselling author of funny, fearless and fast-paced romantic comedies about extraordinary love.

When she's not writing books she composes musicals, cooks new recipes with varying success, walks the blustery hills where she lives, buys too much glittery eyeshadow, sings to her dog, kisses her husband and reads all of the books she can get her grabby hands on.

To sign up for new release updates, monthly giveaways and more from Kirsty, add your name to her newsletter. The signup link is on her website.

www.kirstygreenwood.com

ALSO BY KIRSTY GREENWOOD

**YOU CAN READ MORE KIRSTY GREENWOOD BOOKS
(and they're all available in Kindle Unlimited too).**

Yours Truly

Big Sexy Love

It Happened on Christmas Eve

Jessica Beam is A Hot Mess

To sign up for new release updates, monthly giveaways and a free short story from Kirsty, add your name to her newsletter! The link is on her website.

Made in the USA
Las Vegas, NV
20 February 2021

18274820R00207